Praise for

WITHOUT
Compromise

"As Donald Trump rose to power, no journalist busted him earlier or better than the late investigative reporter Wayne Barrett, whose indispensable work is gathered in *Without Compromise*. Barrett's pieces provide an x-ray into Trump's soul, and into the civic corruption that fueled his rise. These stories are essential reading, alive with fresh insights and information illuminating today's politics, and remind us that rigorous journalism is still democracy's best defense."

—Jane Mayer, author of *Dark Money*

"An instantly classic collection by one of the greatest reporters New York ever produced, and one of the greatest of his era. Few could combine righteous fury with dogged attention to detail like Barrett. This collection is a treasure and (somewhat maddeningly) a reminder that the fools, crooks, and wannabe strongmen that have our republic dangling over a precipice have been this way for a long, long time."

—Chris Hayes, host of *All In with Chris Hayes* and author of *A Colony in a Nation*

"These pages bring Wayne Barrett back to life in all his investigative glory, his moral clarity, his righteous rage. Barrett was prescient, not just about Donald Trump and Rudy Giuliani, but also about how, time and time again, individuals and institutions would fail to rein in the greed of those who feed off the public trough and to address the racism that undergirds both public policy and private behavior. Wayne Barrett's life and work continue to inspire, especially at a time when truth and facts are under siege. He had a mantra: 'The job of our profession is discovery, not dissertation.' Journalists are paid to tell the truth, he said, and that he did, no matter who, no matter what."

—Sheila Coronel, dean of academic affairs and director Stabile Center for Investigative Journalism, Columbia Journalism School

WITHOUT
Compromise

WITHOUT
Compromise

The Brave Journalism That First Exposed
Donald Trump, Rudy Giuliani, and the
American Epidemic of Corruption

Wayne Barrett

Edited by Eileen Markey

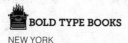 BOLD TYPE BOOKS

NEW YORK

Bold Type Books
116 East 16th Street, 8th Floor, New York, NY 10003
www.boldtypebooks.org
@BoldTypeBooks

Printed in the United States of America

First Edition: September 2020

Published by Bold Type Books, an imprint of Perseus Books, LLC, a subsidiary of Hachette Book Group, Inc. Bold Type Books is a co-publishing venture of the Type Media Center and Perseus Books.

The Hachette Speakers Bureau provides a wide range of authors for speaking events. To find out more, go to www.hachettespeakersbureau.com or call (866) 376-6591.

The publisher is not responsible for websites (or their content) that are not owned by the publisher.

Reprints courtesy of the estate of Wayne Barrett with thanks to Village Voice Media.

Print book interior design by Six Red Marbles, Inc.

Library of Congress Cataloging-in-Publication Data
Names: Barrett, Wayne, 1945–2017, author. | Markey, Eileen, editor.
Title: Without compromise: the brave journalism that first exposed Donald Trump, Rudy Giuliani, and the American epidemic of corruption / Wayne Barrett; edited by Eileen Markey.
Description: First edition. | New York: Bold Type Books, 2020. | Includes bibliographical references and index.
Identifiers: LCCN 2020019695 | ISBN 9781645036531 (paperback) | ISBN 9781541756809 (ebook)
Subjects: LCSH: Barrett, Wayne, 1945-2017. | Journalists—New York (State)—New York—Biography. | New York (N.Y.)—Politics and government—20th century. | Village voice (Greenwich Village, New York, N.Y.)
Classification: LCC PN4874.B327 A5 | DDC 973.933—dc23
LC record available at https://lccn.loc.gov/2020019695

ISBNs: 978-1-64503-653-1 (hardcover), 978-1-5417-5680-9 (e-book)

LSC-C

10 9 8 7 6 5 4 3 2 1

Dedicated to the memory of
Wayne Barrett,
truth teller, mentor, detective for the people.

It turns out that the powerful know perfectly well who their victims are + why there should be victims + that they have no intention of changing anything. This recognition is momentous no doubt the spiritual low point of the emergent revolutionary's edu... He had entertained certain hopes about the powerful: they can tell justice from injustice, they support the 1st, they are open to change... he is now instructed that these hopes are whimsical! At the heart of ...

lies the new certainty that there will be no change which he does not produce by himself ...

Barrett copied by hand an excerpt from *Containment and Change*, by Carl Oglesby, and saved the quote among his papers for 40 years. (Courtesy of the Briscoe Center for American History at the University of Texas at Austin)

The actors are pretty small and venal. Their ideas are small, never transcending profit. In it, however, are the men elected to lead us and those who buy them. And in it, unhappily, are the processes and decisions that shape our city and our lives.

> —Wayne Barrett article on Donald Trump
> published January 22, 1979

Get the list of looters. Particularly those who've pled.

> —Wayne Barrett notes on article about
> Sam Wright, 1978

Contents

Contents

PART VI Armed with a Notebook

We Deserve Better

Eileen Markey

WAYNE BARRETT didn't report a word on the Trump administration. He died the night before the 45th president took office. But as the many scandals of the Trump presidency began to unfold, Barrett's foundational reporting on the New York City real estate developer was cited almost ritually, Barrett inevitably identified as "legendary investigative reporter Wayne Barrett." His family, friends, and colleagues thought readers should have access to some of that reporting. This book is the result.

Barrett wrote in the *Village Voice* nearly every week for the better part of four decades, a steady accretion of knowledge silting up into hundreds of thousands of column inches. Collected here are just a few of those articles, accompanied by reflections from journalists who shared and continue his work. I've tried to select pieces that in their totality illustrate something of his craft and tell stories worth remembering at this long distance. The articles republished here have, in a few cases, been very lightly edited to facilitate publication in book format. Some pieces have been edited for space. Portions that have been elided are marked with ***. Where an insertion has been made to enhance clarity, the added words are in {}. Inevitably, most of what Barrett wrote, indeed entire mayoral administrations, are left out. The pieces included reveal the antecedents that shaped our present and the methods of a dogged reporter whose stock in trade was never conjecture or polemic but a relentless deluge of fact. Wayne Barrett believed in facts.

He did not, I'm fairly certain, believe in ghosts. His mind was clear and rational. But pulling together this volume plunged me into a New York crowded with ghosts of a different city, of a country we sold, of a robust journalism stacked now in microfilm drawers. I took on this project at the request of Fran Barrett, Wayne's wife, because I wanted to make sure we didn't forget. I wanted to save something, the way you grab a photo from a burning building so you can remember what you had. It's not only about the past; memory is about the future, too, and what might yet be possible.

My research began with a visit to the vestigial offices of the *Village Voice*. The *Voice*, like so many American newspapers, died a few years ago. But a remnant remains, two men in an office that once housed a crowd of unruly journalists, working like medieval monks to preserve the knowledge the *Voice* created. I walked up the wooden staircase (the elevator was out) to the seventh floor. Jazz was blasting. On the fire door was taped a page from the paper, circa 1985: a Jules Feiffer cartoon about a distracted media and Donald Trump, and a letter to the editor by a crooked Bronx pol complaining about Wayne Barrett.

To prepare this book, I was consumed with digging, first in the card catalogue that stands in a glass-doored alcove of the nearly empty *Voice* office and holds more cryptic secrets than the Sphinx, then in bound volumes of the paper, and finally in the special collections at the Briscoe Center for American History at the University of Texas at Austin, where the pages that once filled the narrow office on the second floor of Barrett's Brooklyn rowhouse and sprawled into his basement now reside, neatly sorted. I amused myself with thoughts of Barrett, in his terrible tank top and dad jeans, blinking in the shadowless Texas sun, folder under his arm, loping walk, taller than you thought, laser-focused and eager. It would be more fitting for the records to be in some corner of Brooklyn where people still talk out of the corner of their mouths or in a ratty municipal archive. But no. In Texas there are 294 boxes of New York's history. They are what Wayne Barrett knew (at least what he wrote down. A library died with him).

Like a hundred other people between the early 1980s and 2016, I was a Wayne Barrett intern. He taught us all to dig. He taught us that the facts were knowable, could be acquired. That they were written down and filed somewhere. That facts steadfastly accumulated could reveal what was hidden and be agents of justice. That to be a journalist was to be an honorable person, a detective for the people (not their enemy). He was a notoriously tough boss, but also generous, sweet to his charges: buying us dinner, listening to our worries, coaching us, taking delight in our successes, offering visits to his beach house, checking in, connecting us to jobs, opening doors forever. So, I went to Texas not knowing what I was looking for, just that I wanted to understand why this old print reporter mattered so very much to so many of us and how that was connected to what's become of our country and our profession.

I sifted through the boxes, chasing his ghost, hoping to find the right clue. I wanted to understand what drove him, what made him so maniacal. Somewhere in here would be the answer to why he worked the way he did.

Mostly what I found were printouts of Nexis searches. Lawsuits and depositions and grand jury reports no one was supposed to see. Audits and voter registration cards, presentencing reports and Donald Trump's real estate license. The vulnerability study for Rudy Giuliani's 1993 mayoral campaign. Manila folders and yellow legal pads with lists scribbled on them.

This is how Barrett worked: a task list that begat like a Hebrew Testament genealogy, and findings. The findings would eventually coalesce into a fact pattern. And then you had a story.

The files revealed that while his method was famously document-driven, it relied significantly on the physical touch. He didn't get what he learned from email queries to publicists; he got it from relationships built over years, source and confessor, a gruff voice on the phone and the man on your doorstep. He was willing to dig and notate payrolls and knock on doors of strangers and treat financial disclosure reports as beach reading to ferret out the truth. Almost none of it was online. He got it because he asked. And asked. And asked.

What I found in those boxes in the stony silence of the Briscoe Center library was the story of New York's looting, a prelude to the nation's. To read Barrett's long ribbon of work is to realize that year by year he documented the post-fiscal-crisis takeover of the city, our transformation from citizens to distracted serfs. In folder after folder was written the grubby story of NYC at the end of the century, in the years New York went from a working city and a creative powerhouse to a time-share for billionaires. The crooks, the hacks, the pols that fill the early years of Barrett's copy, they are picaresque nearly. You realize the guys who talked out of the side of their mouths at county dinners were just the front men. The ones who walked away with the bag money were the men in fine suits, gone home to abodes far above the city. Now they run for office and convince some of us they can save us.

Barrett began working as a reporter in 1970s New York. It's an era emblazoned in public consciousness by images of gutted, burnt-out buildings, piles of refuse and disastrous-looking subway cars—shorthand for crime and ruin. But when the image of crime in 1970s New York is daguerreotyped into our memory, it should be this one: a group of white men in suits gathered around a fine conference table, divvying up the spoils and congratulating themselves on their good work. They laid the groundwork for the impossible city we now live in, determining that the gravest threat NYC faced was that too few millionaires felt comfortable in its environs. They repurposed the mechanisms built to relieve poverty and direct aid into neighborhoods starved by segregation instead into stimulus for the already rich. It was an organized looting.

With New York again facing acute financial uncertainty in the COVID-induced recession, and profiteers circling, ready to smash and grab, the lessons of Barrett's work are urgently relevant.

In the restructured city, Donald Trump slimed up from the Queens sewer. The terrible truth held in those boxes in Texas is this: Donald Trump has 1,000 fathers, most of them respectable people. Most of them, it being New York, Democrats. Hugh Carey and Richard Ravitch. Mario Cuomo and Andrew. Ed Koch. The City Planning Commission and the Department of Taxation. Of course, Roy Cohn and Roger Stone. John Zuccotti (yes, fittingly, the Occupy Wall Street park is named for him). They were aware by 1979 of Donald Trump's court-documented racism and corruption. It didn't dissuade them from cutting him deals. There is nothing unusual or unique about Donald Trump. He's the logical outgrowth of our abandonment of the public good, a monster of our own making. The old clubhouse machine transmogrified into the global money set. Barrett didn't rant about this. But he did rage about it, painstakingly acquiring facts and marshaling them into column inches.

Barrett could document these crimes because he was securely employed. He was union-represented at a publication that each week fell with a thump on the mayor's doorstep. And if he didn't nab the offending party this week, he'd be back next week. As knowledge became a delta, he could stand on it and see, pull memory to inform the next story, link one scam to its cousin. He could report this way because his focus was local, particular and specific details built stories, one after the other.

The city and country were better when there were more reporters working this way. Barrett didn't have to attract followers or cite metrics or consider shareability or even what the reader wanted. The reader wants food photos. But also, somehow, democracy.

The relationship between real journalism and healthy democracy is fairly straightforward. As America's and New York's news industry atrophied, poisoned by the same caprice that looted the city, readers distracted into digital entertainments that make oxygen for manipulation and propaganda, we became the type of country that could elect Donald Trump.

There is something about living under this president and in this distracted milieu only as big as our phones that has made us feel that the country is rotten and we must be too. That we got what we deserved.

Barrett thought differently.

On my last day in the archive I was deep in Barrett's past, transported into his 1970s life in Brownsville, Brooklyn—he wrote poetry!—when I found the photos, notes, and draft for his first *Village Voice* feature. It was about a venal Brooklyn pol who eventually went to prison for turning the local school district into his personal bursary. Barrett and Fran had struggled beside black radicals to maintain local control of that district, to make it one that took the education of its children seriously. Sam Wright turned it into something grubby. Barrett's ur–task list stretched in a dozen directions, toward lease records and bills for office furniture and the arrest reports for people who broke into stores during the blackout of 1977.

Brownsville in the late 1970s was devastatingly poor, stripped bare by redlining and racism, the fiscal crisis and hopelessness. People were working together in a dozen ways to try to make it better, and here was some politician thinking he could line his own pockets. This last box held the notes of a young man whose outrage was fresh.

What he learned in Brownsville fed a fierce clarity that would keep Barrett focused for 40 years. While he eventually moved out of the neighborhood, he never really left. Or at least it didn't leave him. Most reporters with enough knowledge of inside politics to chronicle the tawdry business come to accept it as a game. They trade their outrage for cynicism. But Barrett, who knew where the bodies were buried and was fierce and difficult and prone to roaring, never shed his outrage—or his hope. He believed we deserved better. He thought we were entitled to honest leadership beholden to the common good. In our governance, in our journalism. In our expectation that it can be better. This is the photo I wanted to save from the burning building.

There in the last box, in Barrett's tight, surprisingly loopy script, was a task particular to the Sam Wright story, but it read like a motto: "Get the list of looters. Particularly those who've pled."

The card catalogue in the office of the *Village Voice* tells the story of New York City, its politics, its scam artists, and its choices. (Photo courtesy of Eileen Markey)

Preface

Joe Conason

B Y THE END OF HIS LIFE, on the day before President Donald Trump's 2017 inauguration, Wayne Barrett was already a legendary figure in American journalism. His tenacious investigative reporting on New York City politics and corruption had made him the scourge of City Hall, the bane of several mayors, and an essential member of New York's pugnacious press corps. He had published a revealing biography of Rudy Giuliani as well as an eye-opening book on that mayor's failures and omissions leading up to the 9/11 terrorist attacks. Barrett had been covering Donald Trump since the real estate scion turned reality-TV personality first began lining up public subsidies for private gain in the 1970s. He had published a scathing book about the man in 1990, during one of Trump's periodic financial collapses.

The rise of his old nemesis to the American presidency lent historical drama and even a touch of glamour to a life spent in relentless toil. The unscrupulous businessman and the conscientious journalist who chronicled his corruption had lived on opposite sides of a profound moral chasm. In the years following his death, Wayne would continue to haunt Trump, his byline invoked by a legion of reporters as they pursued the 45th president down trails Wayne had blazed.

Wayne's lifelong project was to muster journalistic truth on behalf of the downtrodden and against their oppressors. Pursuing that goal, he developed a method that produced some of the most rigorous, purposeful, and dogged investigative reporting ever written. It is a method worth revisiting now, when crucial facts often fail to penetrate public consciousness—even amid a deadly pandemic—and cable pundits seem to outnumber working reporters.

He didn't deign to hide his point of view. His writing was propulsive, emphatic, even damning, and always candid. As a champion scholastic debater, he knew that rhetoric can inspire, but he also learned that facts matter more. His approach to reporting was exhaustive, requiring the assistance of literally hundreds of former interns—who eventually went on to distinguished careers after months of checking off Wayne's impossibly long lists of interviews, document searches, archive visits, data crunches, and stakeouts. He never stopped believing in the evidence-based inquiry that spurred America's founders and undergirds every functioning democracy.

Wayne first achieved notoriety for his investigative profiles of celebrated figures in politics and business. Among the earliest Barrett targets was Donald Trump, who contrived his initial venture into Manhattan real estate with enormous state subsidies via connections with the shadiest elements in Brooklyn and Queens clubhouse politics. Indeed, Wayne scorched nearly every important politician of either party who crossed his path, from Ed Koch and Rudy Giuliani to Mario and Andrew Cuomo.

While he enjoyed dueling with politicians, however, Wayne brought equal passion to probing the faceless forces that immiserated the city's most impoverished communities. He had a deft touch with the personal interview and, despite his ferocious reputation, could charm almost any source into talking too much. But he was just as keen to spend hours poring over public budgets, city records, and all the eye-glazing data points that reveal how brutally society treats the most vulnerable—as in his classic series documenting Koch's "war on the poor," or his pioneering dissection of the original "poverty pimp," Bronx political operative Ramon Velez.

He was born on July 11, 1945, and raised in Lynchburg, Virginia, where he attended Catholic schools with his two brothers and two sisters. His father was a nuclear physicist and his mother was a librarian. He became editor of his high school's newspaper and led its debate team to second place in a national championship, a performance that earned a full scholarship to Saint Joseph's University in Philadelphia. (Some might observe that Wayne was very much the product of a Jesuit education.) There he met a Philly girl named Frances Marie McGettigan, whom he married in 1969. By then, he had graduated from Columbia Journalism School (where he later taught and mentored students) and moved on to teach school in Brooklyn's Brownsville community.

Like many bright young people who grew up in the 1960s, Wayne underwent a radical transformation even before he arrived in Brownsville. Going off to college as a Goldwater conservative who despised student leftists, he emerged as a long-haired Vietnam War protester and supporter of black-liberation movements—although unlike his hippie peers, he never smoked a joint and, for that matter, scarcely ever drank alcohol. If his teaching job began as a means to escape the draft, it quickly turned into a lifelong commitment to that very poor, highly segregated, and heavily African American neighborhood.

It was in Brownsville that Wayne came to understand investigative reporting as his instrument to confront inequity, injustice, and corruption. With a group of local activists, he founded a small newspaper called the *People's Voice*, aiming its mimeographed fusillades at the predatory landlords, failing schools, uncaring bureaucracies—and crooked politicians.

Within a few years, Wayne's exposés of local corruption drew the attention of Jack Newfield, the *Village Voice*'s premier political columnist and investigative chief. Jack brought Wayne into the *Voice*, where he published hundreds of articles over the next four decades, frequently in partnership with other reporters (including me). We both joined the paper as staff writers in 1978, just after Ed Koch was sworn in for his first term as mayor.

Our mission at the countercultural Manhattan weekly was not so different from what Wayne and his fellow activists had tried to do in Brownsville, except it took place on a much broader stage, with substantial resources, top editors, and thousands of paying readers. We exposed the power relationships in a city where real estate kingpins like Trump routinely greased elected officials— and exercised an unwholesome influence over policy and budget decisions.

Although the *Voice*'s circulation was smaller than those of the city's major dailies, the passionate engagement of savvy readers endowed us with clout. The dailies paid us the compliment of routinely lifting our stories, with or without credit. And in that era, before the internet and social media, newspaper stories mattered—even in an "alternative" weekly.

From a warren of cramped, rather nondescript offices and cubicles below 14th Street in Manhattan, we scoped the political landscape of city and state, holding elected officials accountable for their deviations from political integrity and public interest. Working at a "writer's paper," as the *Voice* was known, meant that we set our own course, pursuing stories that reflected the electoral calendar, the urgent issues of the moment, and the enduring priorities of our politics.

Every year, for instance, we shamed the city's worst landlords with a list that named names and catalogued atrocities. We spent months as a team in 1980 to produce an exhaustive three-part series on Republican corruption and mob influence in Nassau County—our bouquet to its favorite son, US Senate candidate Alfonse D'Amato. (He won that election, but Wayne finally took him out with a devastating story on his absentee voting record almost two decades later.)

We pursued this vocation with a certain ferocity, nobody more so than Wayne. As he explained on the occasion of the *Voice*'s 50th anniversary, in 2005, "we thought a deadline meant we had to kill somebody." He was only half joking. Every public figure in New York had good reason to fear and respect him.

Wayne expected the same fierce determination from everyone who worked with him, whether colleagues or interns. Scratching out scores of tasks on a yellow legal pad, he could get quite testy if someone failed to match his formidable work ethic. A caring friend with a wonderful sense of humor, he was also known to torment his editors and didn't always tolerate disagreement well, to put it politely. When we were producing a two-page news spread together every week, he would occasionally stop speaking to me over some unforgiveable offense—and for a couple of days I could only communicate with him via messages left with Fran.

Of course he could be lighthearted and funny, too; he loved to banter and gossip, and over the years he attracted a wide circle of friends that was even larger than his impressive list of enemies. But he was tough because he took the work seriously, and he kept working until his last day. He never stopped believing that investigative reporting could reveal wrongdoing, provoke outrage, spur reform, and change people's lives for the better. And after four years of a lying president who has done so much to damage people's lives—the lives of the vulnerable most of all—that faith seems more essential than ever.

With his innate consciousness of mission, Wayne defied the cynicism that too often infects modern journalism. Even as he grew into a highly sophisticated analyst of elections, media, finance, and government, he nurtured an idealism about democracy and the role of the press that could sound almost naïve. The tragedy is that we lost him just when we were about to need him most.

As a devout believer in the church's social-justice doctrine, he naturally lived in a state of perpetual indignation. The prayer card at his funeral, held in a Brownsville church where he remained a parishioner, displayed a Jeff Danziger cartoon of Wayne preparing to pepper the Almighty with tough questions. Even in the afterlife, he would surely hold the most powerful to account.

What follows in this book is a collection of that indefatigable sleuth's most compelling and salient adventures. What stands out in every single one is his drive for justice, which he charged us all to carry on.

Joe Conason is editor at large of Type Media Center, editor in chief of the *Daily Memo*, and the author of four books, including *It Can Happen Here: Authoritarian Peril in the Age of Bush* and *Big Lies: The Right-Wing Propaganda Machine and How It Distorts the Truth*. From 1978 until 1990 he worked at the *Village Voice*, alongside his friend Wayne Barrett.

PART I

Trump: Moral Larceny

Deal by Deal

Kim Phillips-Fein

WAYNE BARRETT told the story of the rise of contemporary New York, and reading his work today is a remarkable experience: the world he describes is at once familiar and strange. The publication for which he wrote his most famous work, the *Village Voice*, has stopped its print existence—the thick, tabloid-shaped, inky pages containing Barrett's long investigative pieces no longer there to be picked up—but despite this, his voice continues to resonate. His cast of characters peoples our media landscape even now, yet when he wrote, the future was still uncertain; it still appeared that things could go a different way.

Barrett chronicled the transformation of New York City after the fiscal crisis of the 1970s, the move toward a social policy that prioritized the needs of business and real estate development—even if this was sometimes justified in terms of raising revenues to fund programs to help poor and working-class New Yorkers. He always saw this as a bipartisan historical shift, not simply a move by economic elites and certainly not something carried out by the right alone. Perhaps his most prescient piece is his brilliant 1979 two-part exposé of Donald Trump and the Trump Organization, chronicling the emergence of Trump as a power broker in New York City. Unlike so much coverage of Trump then and now,

3

though, Barrett cut past the glitz and the lifestyle bravado to the deals that made his emergence possible. He interviewed Trump multiple times in the writing of the series, and captured perfectly Trump's calculated efforts to sway the story through threats and bribes alike—the extent to which, as Barrett put it, for Trump "every relationship is a transaction." But the point, for Barrett, was never Trump's outrageousness; it was the outrageousness of the political system that raised him up. "Donald Trump," he concluded, "is a user of other users. The politician and his money-changer feed on each other."

All throughout the 1980s and into the 2000s, Barrett's writing told the story of the way that New York City's government sought to pursue the rich and powerful, to woo corporations at public expense and through the slow evisceration of the city's social-welfare traditions. He spared no one in this account. Writing about Democratic governor Hugh Carey's budget in 1982, he denounced it as "a Democratic ratification of the Reagan war on the poor." Carey's "elegant" rhetoric aside, it did no more than "unflinchingly" pass along "the worst of Washington's new poverty program," spending hundreds of millions on new prisons while cutting funds for day care and senior services. He eviscerated the city's lavish gifts to American Express to build a new office headquarters as part of the World Financial Center in lower Manhattan. Equally notable was his reporting on the Industrial and Commercial Incentive Board, charged with dispensing tax exemptions to "politically generous developers" all over the city. As the city's own internal report put it in an early draft (not released to the public but obtained by Barrett), "There is little evidence that the program has mainly served applicants who needed the incentive in order to locate in NYC." Unsentimental, careful, meticulous, and jargon-free, Barrett's journalism reminds us that the city we live in now was carefully constructed, deal by deal and piece by piece—that it has a history, and that the future may be more open than we think.

Kim Phillips-Fein is the author of *Fear City: New York's Fiscal Crisis and the Rise of Austerity Politics* (Metropolitan Books, 2017). She is a professor at the Gallatin School of Individualized Study and in the History Department of the College of Arts and Sciences at New York University.

1

Like Father, Like Son: Anatomy of a Young Power Broker

January 15, 1979

In January 1979 the *Village Voice* published a two-part series on the brash young real estate developer Donald Trump. Barrett reported these pieces from court documents in Philadelphia and New York, campaign-contribution filings, interviews with people who did business with Trump, and fifteen hours of interviews with Trump himself. Barrett spent two months researching the story. —Ed.

D ONALD TRUMP. A 32-year-old self-proclaimed real estate colossus price tagged at $200 million. The brash, streetwise son of Brooklyn's largest apartment builder transplanted from his father's boxlike office at the Avenue Z tip of the borough to a Fifth Avenue penthouse bounded on both sides by his own stunning Manhattan ventures. The *New York Times* puffs him as the city's "number-one real-estate promoter of the mid-seventies...the William Zeckendorf of hard times."

But the most accurate description of Trump's real estate genius was contained in a deposition from a four-year-old Philadelphia bankruptcy-court file. When a Penn Central Transportation Company* representative was asked why he'd contacted Trump alone out of lists of developers interested in building publicly aided housing on the bankrupt company's West Side {of Manhattan} railyards, the witness replied: "The estate was putting its property in the hands of a developer. It was uppermost in our minds that…the developer…be very high in his political position. Trump is doing what, in our judgment, if anyone can do, he can do."

Trump's problem is not so much what he's done, but how he's done it. I decided at the start that I wanted to profile him by describing his deals—not his lifestyle or his personality. After getting to know him, I realized that his deals are his life. He once told me: "I won't make a deal just to make a profit. It has to have flair." Another Manhattan developer said it differently: "Trump won't do a deal unless there's something extra—a kind of moral larceny—in it. He's not satisfied with a profit. *He has to take something more*. Otherwise, there's no thrill."

In this, the first of a two-part series, I'll examine the character and history of Trump's Brooklyn base. In the second, I'll trace the details that led to his extraordinary acquisitions of the three Manhattan properties—and the government negotiations that are turning them into personal windfalls. Each history—the Brooklyn empire, the Manhattan purchases, and the government contracts—is a tale of overreaching and abuse of power. Like his father, Donald Trump has pushed each deal to the limit, taking

---

* The Penn Central Transportation Company (PCTC) bankruptcy was, at the time, the biggest bankruptcy in American history. PCTC was a merger between two railroad companies—the Pennsylvania and New York Central—in 1968; two years later PCTC declared bankruptcy after the federal government turned down a request that it guarantee a $200 million emergency loan. —Ed.

from it whatever he can get, turning political connections into private profits at public expense.

The Connections

Abe Beame,* whose municipal largesse to the Brooklyn {Democratic Party} organization that spawned him was cut short by the city's fiscal collapse, has left the Trump penetration of Manhattan as the only tangible sign of his administration's Brooklyn base.

Beame had known Trump's family for 30 years. They'd eaten the same clubhouse dinners at the same annual dances given by the borough's regulars. Like Beame—and most other pols who came up through the local machines—Fred Trump owed his biggest breaks to the county's party organization. In the beginning, Donald Trump used Beame's closest political associates—publicist Howard Rubinstein; lobbyist, lawyer, and fund-raiser Abraham "Bunny" Lindenbaum; and Bunny's son Sandy, now part of a large Manhattan law firm—as the major political brokers on his Manhattan projects.

But the Trumps were too shrewd to rely only on the power of the Beame brokers. There were contributions, too. Beame's recollections of the Trump firm's donations were hazy, but the former mayor did say: "I don't know if he [Trump] gave and when he gave, but he's a friend of mine. I know he tried to help every time."

What does seem clear is that Donald's success in acquiring and developing the Commodore,† the convention-center site, and, to a lesser degree, the 60th Street yards, was, in part, due to Beame's

---

* Abe Beame, mayor of New York City from 1974 to 1977. —Ed.
† The Trump-built Grand Hyatt on East 42nd Street now stands where the Commodore Hotel once stood. —Ed.

support. "It was the Brooklyn crowd at work," said one top city official.

Hugh Carey,* another product of Brooklyn politics, has virtually turned a state agency—the Urban Development Corporation—into a temporary Trump subsidiary. UDC is developing Trump's hotel, convention center, and some new projects, including a multimillion-dollar renovation of Grand Central Terminal. But as Carey has done for Trump, so Trump has done for the governor—to the tune of nearly $125,000 in campaign contributions from the family and their companies: $35,000 in 1974, $66,500 in 1978, plus a $23,000 share of a loan totaling $300,000, a group venture with an inner circle of other Carey financiers, including lawyer Bill Shea, MTA {Metropolitan Transportation Authority} chairman Harold Fisher, realtor Sylvan Lawrence, and ILA {International Longshoremen's Association} leader Anthony Scotto. The only individual to have exceeded Trump's election-year generosity was the governor's oil-rich brother.

In case the donations weren't enough, Trump retained chief Carey fund-raiser Louise M. Sunshine as his "director of special projects" and registered her as his Albany lobbyist for the convention-center plan. Additionally, Sunshine accompanies Trump to meetings at various government agencies throughout the state. When asked what she does on such trips, one official remarked: "She just hangs around...gets a document if it's needed... calls the governor...." During the three years she's worked for Trump, Sunshine has directed Carey's campaign finances—first, paying off the governor's substantial 1974 debt and then serving as his executive director of finance for the 1978 campaign. She

---

* Governor of New York, 1975 to 1982. —Ed.

was rewarded with a $17,000-a-year, one-meeting-a-month job as vice-chairman of the State Thruway Authority and a position with the Job Development Authority. Although the latter post carries no salary, it does provide up to $5,000 in expenses—and $34 million worth of industrial loans to administer.

The developer sees his companies' political contributions as part of the cost of doing government business—for tax purposes, most of the money is supplied as corporate contributions. For Trump, the donations are the glue that holds together the public/private relationships.

Although Trump says he joined the 1974 Carey campaign early because "I knew he was a winner," he hedged his bets pretty carefully. Ken Auletta, then campaign manager for Carey's primary opponent, Howard Samuels, recalls: "I got a call from Trump. He said he wanted me—as a Samuels staff person—to know that he'd contributed $10,000 to Samuels. Just so I'd know who he was if he ever called. I usually kept far away from the finance end of it, but I checked this donation—and he'd made it."

Besides the $125,000 donated to Carey, Trump-owned firms have recently contributed an additional $34,000 to city and state candidates in positions to affect his Manhattan projects—$10,500 to {Ed} Koch, after Beame lost; $5,500 to Beame; $4,000 to Mario Cuomo; $10,000 to State Senator Manfred Ohrenstein's personal or Democratic senate campaign committees; $2,000 to City Comptroller Harrison Goldin; $2,000 to City Council President Carol Bellamy; and $200 to City Planning Commissioner Robert Wagner Jr.

After Manhattan councilman Henry Stern led the opposition to his Commodore tax-abatement scheme, Trump called and offered Stern a contribution. "I declined," said the councilman. Few others have.

Finally, Trump has retained Roy Cohn as advisor on each of his major deals, on a host of legal actions, and as a conduit to the upper reaches of power—public and private. In recent years, Cohn and Sunshine have replaced the Lindenbaums and Rubinstein as young Trump's primary resources and agents. The Manhattan hard sell has supplanted the friendly, shrewd, understated style of the old Brooklyn days.

*** *This elided section includes a long accounting of Fred Trump's business practices around the development of Trump Village, a state-supported housing development in Brooklyn, including a 1966 report from the New York State Investigations Commission that "prompted the commission chairman, Jacob Grumet, to publicly assail {Fred} Trump, Lindenbaum, et al., as 'grasping and greedy individuals' and ask housing finance officials: 'Is there any way of preventing a man who does business in that way from getting another contract with the state?'" Fred Trump continued to do business with the state. His son began to shift the company away from building. —Ed.****

"We stopped building and started acquiring then," explains Donald Trump. Trump the builder became Trump the management firm. It is clear that while the company's properties are surely vast, they are exceeded by those of other landlords. The assessed value of the Trump holdings has varied considerably. Today, Donald hints at a figure well in excess of the $200 million estimate he offered the *Times* in 1976. He says the firm has acquired highly profitable land in Las Vegas and southern California. But *Business Week* quoted an independent valuation of $100 million. And the financial institutions backing Donald's Hyatt deal—with Fred as guarantor of the loans—took 18 months to decide that the Trumps were an acceptable risk (indeed, Fred Trump started Trump Village* as a private job in 1960, and though he'd been in the business 20 years, he couldn't get private financing).

In his interviews with me, Donald Trump repeatedly suggested that the firm was an awesome force in the industry. He also claimed that his convention center and hotel would be the largest in the country. They will not be. Real estate entrepreneurs do their own advertising, and Trump has a way of doubling or shaving every number when it suits him. In interviews, Donald Trump has laid claim to 22,000 units in Brooklyn, Staten Island, Queens, Virginia, Washington, D.C., and New Jersey. But his testimony in federal court put the total figure around 12,000 units actually owned and managed. Whatever the size or exact dollar value, however, there is no question about the racial, economic, and sexual character of the Trump holdings. Tenants are mostly white. People receiving welfare do not live in Trump-owned apartments. Households with substantial *male* incomes do.

The Race Case

Under the federal Fair Housing Act, the US Justice Department's Civil Rights Division brought a landmark complaint against the Trump organization in 1973. The suit charged that the Trumps refused to rent to blacks. After a year and a half of furious legal and rhetorical combat, the Trumps, in 1975, agreed to a consent decree described by the head of the housing division as "one of the most far-reaching ever negotiated." It required Trump to advertise

---

* Trump Village consists of seven high-rise residential buildings built between 1963 and 1964 in Coney Island, Brooklyn. It features nearly 4,000 units. —Ed.

vacancies in minority papers, promote minorities to professional jobs, and list vacancies on a preferential basis with the Open Housing Center of the Urban League.

Last March the Justice Department complained that Trump was in contempt of the consent decree and filed pending motions in Brooklyn federal court to compel compliance. The new complaint charges that "racially discriminatory conduct by Trump agents has occurred with such frequency that it has created a substantial impediment to the full enjoyment of equal opportunity."

The evidence for the original charge against Trump was largely obtained through Urban League testers—white and black—who sought apartments in various Trump-owned complexes. Whites got them; blacks didn't. The case was also based on a series of individual complaints to Eleanor Holmes Norton, then chairperson of the city's Human Rights Commission. Norton resolved a half dozen individual cases by compelling Trump to admit black complainants. She asked the federal government to look for a pattern. But perhaps the most compelling evidence came from Trump employees and former employees.

According to court records, four superintendents or rental agents confirmed that applications sent to the central office for acceptance or rejection were coded by race. Three doormen were told to discourage blacks who came seeking apartments when the manager was out, either by claiming no vacancies or hiking up the rents. A super said he was instructed to send black applicants to the central office but to accept white applications on site. Another rental agent said that Fred Trump had instructed him not to rent to blacks. Further, the agent said Trump wanted "to decrease the number of black tenants" already in the development "by encouraging them to locate housing elsewhere."

Donald Trump charged in the press that the suit was part of a "nationwide drive to force owners of moderate and luxury apartments to rent to welfare recipients."

"We are not going to be forced by anyone to put people... in our buildings to the detriment of tenants who have, for many years, lived in these buildings, raised families in them, and who plan to continue to live there. That would be reverse discrimination," he said. "The government is not going to experiment with our buildings to the detriment of ourselves and the thousands who live in them now."

Trump's attorney, Roy Cohn, filed an equally shrill affidavit with the court, charging that the government sought "the capitulation of the defendants and the substitution of the Welfare Department for the management corporation!"

In March 1974, Donald Trump testified as president of many of the Trump housing companies. He assumed a color-blind posture throughout much of the questioning, claiming he "had no idea of the racial composition" of his tenants or employees (he lapsed when he described "an all-black job in Washington," and conceded that the company owned projects that were 100 percent white).

He was, he continued, "unfamiliar" with the Fair Housing Act of 1969, and said that the company had made no changes in its rental policies since the law's passage. He claimed that the only test of tenant eligibility was that the tenant's rent should not exceed 25 percent of his income. He testified twice that "we don't generally include the wife's income; we like to see it for the male in the family." Then he changed his testimony the next day, to try to include some assessment of the wife's income.

Cohn explained the Trump policy of only advertising apartment vacancies in the *Times*: "We think the *Times* is geared to minorities. It supported a Puerto Rican for mayor against a Jew. . . ."

In October 1974, Cohn filed a motion to dismiss the case and charged—in an ironic reversal of his earlier McCarthy days—that federal agents were engaging in "gestapo-like tactics" against his client. Cohn's affidavit described the agents as "stormtroopers." In court he said the Trumps were being subjected to "undercover agents going in and out of their buildings, lying as to who they are and where they are from . . . trying to trap somebody into saying or doing something."

The judge found Cohn's charges "utterly without foundation" and said, "This is the first time anyone's charged FBI agents in a civil matter with . . . gestapo-type conduct." Cohn, who fundraises for the J. Edgar Hoover Foundation, suddenly switched: "I have never brought a charge against the FBI in my life. I have personal reasons why I haven't and I never would. My relationship is much too close."

The disastrous failure of the dismissal motion—which may have been prompted more by what the agents were finding than by how they were looking—was the last Trump offensive in the case. A few months later, the firm settled the decree. Trump's press statement at the settlement was an unreconstructed version of the release the company sent out when the case began. It said the agreement satisfied the firm because it did not contain "any requirements that would compel the Trump organization to accept persons on welfare as tenants." I asked Donald Trump why he'd stopped advertising vacancies in the *Amsterdam News* when the two-year court mandate had expired. "It's a neighborhood paper for Harlem," he said.

I've interviewed a couple of dozen people about Trump—in and out of government. Many had vague awareness of the charges against him, but no one seemed to think that the Trump race record should affect what the company gets from the city or state. In fact, no one had bothered to ask the US Attorney's Office in Brooklyn, which is handling the case for the Justice Department, just what the facts are. Trump has proposed housing on the West Side—perhaps the most integrated neighborhood in the city. He's justified the city's largesse in the Commodore deal partially by pointing to the long-term jobs it will generate. Trump's 1974 deposition in this case was 100 pages of uncontained contempt for the whole issue. Cohn said it for him: "This is a spit in the ocean." I got the sense when I interviewed him that Trump has mellowed into a low-keyed indifference to the suit and the issue. It has nothing to do with profits or what he calls commercial "creativity." It is not part of his real world. Neither is it for the people in government who keep making deals with him.

Early in the reporting of this story, I was at the state's Urban Development Corporation, reading records on Trump's Commodore deal in a conference room. No one knew I was there but some UDC officials, and I hadn't intended to talk to Trump until I'd learned what I could about him from documents. The phone in the office where I was working rang, and the secretary said it was for me. It was Trump, buoyant over his surprise call: "I hear you've been going around town, asking a lot of negative questions about me. When are you going to talk to me?" he asked. "I'm circling," I said.

I met him three times after the call—twice in his Manhattan apartment and once, at my insistence, in his Avenue Z office, still the base of the Trump organization but not where Trump likes to entertain reporters.

"Donald is embarrassed by his Brooklyn roots," one of his business associates told me. "He uses Manhattan as his business address to put distance between himself and Avenue Z." When I asked Bunny Lindenbaum what he thought of Donald's—and his own son's—preoccupation with Manhattan, his voice rose:

"They want to do their work in Manhattan. I was born in Brooklyn, I always practiced in Brooklyn. I still live in Brooklyn. I still have my offices in Brooklyn. They can't take Brooklyn out of me."

Wealth is supposed to convey an enviable status. I rode with Trump through Manhattan in his double-car-length silver chauffeured Cadillac with its "DJT" plates while he talked about how hard New York is on a developer, how communities fight him, how other cities want him. Through 30 blocks of slow Manhattan traffic, not a single New Yorker peered into the back of the carpeted limo.

The West Side groups who'd challenged him on his grandiose housing plans for the 60th Street yard had placed demands on his wealth and were not impressed with the symbols of it that he rushed to accumulate. Why lurch through Manhattan streets in an expensive advertisement of one's wealth if no one even notices?

Until the last couple of weeks—when he became uneasy about what I'd been doing—Trump would call me for progress reports on my story: "Tell me," he'd say, "you finding out what we've been doing is good for the city? What do people say about me? Do they say I'm loyal? Do they say I work hard?" But at the last interview, before I began my questions, he went through a prepared speech about his reputation: "I really value my reputation and I don't hesitate to sue. I've sued twice for libel. Roy Cohn's been my attorney both times. I've won once and the other case is pending. It's cost me $100,000, but it's worth it. I've broken one writer. You and I've been friends and all, but if your story damages my reputation, I want you to know I'll sue." Then, back to the smile—"But everything'll be all right. We're going to get together after the story."

He'd been working gentler versions of this carrot-and-stick approach since the first interview. When I arrived at his apartment the first time, he opened with: "The *Voice*? That's owned by Murdoch, right? Don Kummerfeld is running Murdoch's operations, right? You know the former deputy mayor? He's a good friend of mine." At our very first meeting, he'd even begun talking about someone he'd threatened with a slander suit over a harmless comment.

When he found out I lived in the battered Brownsville section of Brooklyn, he called to say: "I could get you an apartment, you know. That must be an awfully tough neighborhood." I told him I'd lived there for ten years and worked as a community organizer, so he shifted to another form of identification. "So we do the same thing," he said. "We're both rebuilding neighborhoods." And again: "We're going to have to really get to know each other after this article."

Trump was testing me, to see what would work—convinced that either fear or the suggestion that I could have some undefined future relationship with his wealth or his influence could help shape the story. He only had to figure out what I wanted. Every relationship is a transaction.

He told me that he'd had to move from a prior Manhattan apartment because a reporter had printed his address. The rich are supposed to insist on privacy, right? But the *Times* had photographed him in the living room of one prior address, and he'd used the other at the top of his business letterhead. The next time I saw him he said he'd moved because he'd lived across from Gucci and that was no place to raise his new son. Now he lives across from Central Park.

His tendency to view things to his own advantage was made clear to me when I asked him about campaign contributions. He told me he had not contributed to Beame's 1977 campaign. To do so, he said, would have been a conflict because of the Commodore and convention-center deals. But I found $5,000 in Trump-company contributions to the Beame deficit filed at the Board of Elections in 1978.

He angrily denied that he'd ever given a dime to Ohrenstein individually or to his campaign for Senate majority and threatened to sue anyone who said he did. The Trump organization was among the largest contributors to Ohrenstein individually one year and helped bankroll his campaign for Senate majority. Does he lapse into his fiercest denial when he just doesn't know? When I confronted him on the Beame and Ohrenstein contributions, he said the donations must have come from his father.

Similarly, in his deposition in the federal discrimination case, Trump refused to acknowledge responsibility for accepting or rejecting individual tenants. Those statements were a material part of his testimony since they went to the heart of the case—Trump's ability to control the discriminatory practices of his companies.

Shortly after he'd given his deposition, he was interviewed by a field investigator for the secretary of state. The interview had nothing to do with the federal case; the investigator was trying to determine if Trump met the experience requirement for a real estate broker's license. The report states: "Mr. Trump further stated that he supervises and controls the renting of all apartments owned by the Trump organization.... During my interview with applicant he showed me hundreds of files.... Each contained numerous leases both for commercial and residential tenants... and rental records, all of which contained applicant's signature and handwriting." Trump's lawyer, Mathew Tosti, also claimed in a letter to the secretary of state that Trump had "negotiated numerous leases for apartments."

Yet he'd testified in federal court:

Government: "Do you *ever* have anything to do with rental decisions in individual cases?"

Trump: "No, I really don't."

Donald Trump is a user of other users. The politician and his money changer feed on each other. The money changer trades private dollars for access to public ones. Trump, Sunshine, Lindenbaum, and their counterparts Carey and Beame are classic expressions of this relationship.

2

Donald Trump Cuts the Cards: The Deals of a Young Power Broker

January 22, 1979

THIS IS THE PROFILE of a power broker at work. It is also the deal-by-deal account of how a $400 million convention-center site was acquired and selected. Next to Westway,* the convention center has been New York's single largest development issue of this decade. At center stage is Donald Trump, the young man who managed the land deals, profiting by his relationship with a mayor and a governor. He has left a trail of tradeoffs behind him that is—in a city where political brokers learn to cover their tracks—exceptionally clear.

It is a November day in Philadelphia, 1974. On sale in a federal bankruptcy court are the largest undeveloped tracts of land left in Manhattan—the West Side rail yards, stretching along the waterfront from 30th to 39th Streets and 59th to 72nd Streets. One of these properties—the 30th Street parcel—has since become the designated site for the city's convention center. The other is being

---

* Westway was a plan to build, under landfill along Hudson River, a sunken six-lane highway on the lower West Side of Manhattan. Met with years of opposition from neighborhood and environmental advocates, the plan was abandoned in 1981. —Ed.

promoted as a 5,000-unit housing project surrounded by parks and a shopping area.

The seller is the bankrupt Penn Central Transportation Company (PCTC), which is attempting to reorganize itself by turning its real estate portfolio into capital. The buyer is Donald Trump, then 28 years old, the son of Brooklyn's largest apartment builder.

Trump proposes to build up to 30,000 units of partially subsidized housing on the sites. He seeks an exclusive option on the property and offers PCTC the promise that he will obtain the required zoning changes and taxpayer subsidies to guarantee a minimum land-purchase price of $62 million—the least he expects to obtain in government mortgage funds. Trump's firm advances no cash.

But, of course, without City Hall's cooperation, this remarkable proposal would have remained just that. Trump's father, Fred, had known Abe Beame, then the mayor, for some 30 years—and had been a campaign contributor for 20; the firm is tied to the same Brooklyn Democratic machine which spawned Beame's political career. Trump's attorney Bunny Lindenbaum, seated beside him in the courtroom that morning, is Beame's oldest and closest friend. PCTC representatives began negotiating with Trump two weeks after Beame became mayor. Trump's option is scheduled to end when Beame's term is up. There can be no misunderstanding: Trump, in that Philadelphia courtroom, was executing a political option.

Edward Eichler, who had represented the railroad in its negotiations with Trump, explained what had led to the acceptance of Trump's proposal. In a 150-page deposition he said the railroad had had lists of real estate brokers, developers, and attorneys who were interested in the sites. But PCTC chose not to contact any of them.

The basis for that judgment—at least in part—could have been a meeting Trump had arranged some months prior to submitting his proposal. Present were Abe Beame, Trump and his father, and Eichler. According to Donald Trump: "I called the mayor because Penn Central wanted to know whether or not the city was interested in developing the land. The mayor said his administration would be...." Eichler told me that Beame had indicated "he'd known the family and that it was a good organization."

Further, Eichler said, PCTC was looking for the developer "who seemed best positioned in the New York market to get rezoning and government financing." He emphasized that zoning is a "highly political activity in the city of New York," and that there had not been a "rezoning of this magnitude on a piece of property this politically sensitive in the recent history of the city."

"There are going to be opponents from the neighborhood," Eichler continued, "who have already...stated that they are going to oppose anything but very low densities. They are going to oppose very high buildings and view-blocking...and the real swing in value is...to a high density."

Trump was selected to transcend these petty community interests. After all, records on file with the board of standards and appeals show that over a 10-year period, clients of his attorney, Lindenbaum, have received more zoning variances than clients of any other attorney in the city. With Beame as the new mayor, Lindenbaum's batting average was improving.

But there were two other significant actors in the courtroom drama unfolding that morning. One was Herman Getzoff, a Manhattan real estate broker who had previously worked with PCTC and had opposed the Trump transaction for months. The other was David Berger, senior partner of Berger and Montague, a Philadelphia law firm representing the stockholders and unsecured creditors of the Penn Central Transportation Company. Berger's clients, whose stock had lost its value with the PCTC collapse, had the strongest interest in maximizing profits from the sale of the railroad's properties. So Berger, too, was opposing the Trump deal.

Earlier, Herman Getzoff had brought in other potential buyers. Through friends, he'd learned of the Eichler/Trump negotiations—which had been conducted in secret—and, in July, he'd submitted to Eichler a formal offer from the Starrett Brothers and Eken Co., another major New York builder. According to Getzoff, Starrett had offered a $150 million purchase price for the railroad's land, as opposed to Trump's offer of $62 million plus a share of the potential development profits. Though Getzoff had made daily efforts to reach Eichler after the bid's submission, he never did. And toward the end of July, a week after the Starrett bid had been submitted, Eichler went to court and put forth Trump's bid as the recommended proposal of the trustees. He had not met with Starrett, though he wrote an internal memo conceding that Starrett's 30th Street offer "would generate more money than the Trump deal." But he stuck with Trump because "the rezoning will only be the result of an especially powerful political effort, which Trump is much more likely to pull off...." Then he wrote Starrett a letter, suggesting it apply for "other parcels."

On August 7, Trump and Starrett's chairman, Robert Olnick, met. The same day, Olnick withdrew the Starrett offer. According to Trump: "Starrett and Trump are partners in Starrett City, of which we own 25 percent, and they own 5 percent. Frankly, if we hadn't put in the $7 million equity, the project wouldn't have been built. We have a big relationship with Starrett." Olnick never responded to a half dozen calls from me.

Getzoff then obtained a second bidder, HRH Construction Company, another housing developer. Richard Ravitch, HRH president, wrote to the court: "We've been interested in developing the yards over a period of almost a decade.... However, we were not advised that the trustees were considering selling the yards until after a petition was filed with the bankruptcy court...."

The HRH offer, like Starrett's and Trump's, was dependent on obtaining a government-guaranteed mortgage to finance both the land purchase and the housing construction. The difference between Trump's proposal and the HRH/Starrett offers was that neither Starrett nor HRH sought a percentage of the land profits. Trump required 15 percent, which meant that in fact PCTC would only get 85 percent of the sale price. Another difference was that neither Starrett nor HRH demanded that PCTC foot the bill for $750,000 worth of risk capital investment to be used to develop the project. Trump did.

What Trump offered the railroad that Starrett and HRH did not was an option for the company to pay for and obtain an equity interest in the projects eventually built. According to HRH, the primary value of such an interest in a Mitchell-Lama housing project was in a highly speculative tax-loss sale. The return to PCTC on such an interest depended on the unpredictable state of the tax laws four to 10 years later.

The final, and most important, difference between the Trump and HRH offers was that Trump's attempt to share in the land profits appeared to violate the then applicable Mitchell-Lama guidelines barring a developer from profiting on land he does not own when he submits the site to government agencies for approval.

The consequence of Trump's ill-conceived sharing plan was that, if the project were approved at all, the government agencies would have to purchase the land at its minimum price in order to eliminate potentially illegal Trump profits. The HRH offer contained a minimum that doubled Trump's.

Getzoff's early ally in opposing the Trump transaction was David Berger, attorney for the PCTC stockholders. An associate in Berger's firm at the time, Edward Rubenstone, took the deposition from Eichler, stating on the record that "no honest attempt was made" by Eichler to "determine what other persons were willing to pay for these properties."

Rubenstone also grilled the appraiser selected by Eichler in a 235-page deposition that revealed that:

- The Philadelphia appraiser had never estimated a New York residential or industrial property. His appraisal assigned no value to the existing structures on the two sites, which had been previously assessed by the city at $6 million. In arriving at his value for the 30th Street yards (as zoned), the appraiser compared the parcels exclusively with land sales in Queens, Brooklyn, and the Bronx.

- The resultant appraisal pegged the 30th Street yards at $4 per square foot—or $8 million—as currently zoned, with the value increasing to $27 million if rezoned for residential use. These depressed values were compared by Rubenstone and Getzoff to two nearby PCTC sales—at $26 and $32 per square foot. The land under Manhattan Plaza, located in between the two yards on the West Side, had gone for as high as $82 per square foot after rezoning. Even the land for Trump's own Starrett City project in Brooklyn had sold for $11 per square foot.

- Most important, the appraiser conceded that he had applied a 50 percent discount on the land to cover the time and costs a developer would incur over the years it would take to complete such a large project. The appraiser did not anticipate that under the Trump deal a major portion of these costs was to be assumed by PCTC. He figured them as the buyer's burden and discounted for them. HRH had indicated a willingness to pay the undiscounted price of $124 million for the 30th Street and 60th Street properties.

Rubenstone told me: "I thought we had the deal broken. The appraiser's deposition was pretty devastating in terms of the fair-market value of the property."

The same day Rubenstone took the appraisal deposition, he called Getzoff and asked him to come to Philadelphia to testify at the hearing as a witness for the stockholders. Getzoff was to testify about the Starrett bid and withdrawal as well as the terms of the forthcoming HRH offer.

When Getzoff arrived in Philadelphia on November 11, he learned that Berger, Eichler, and Trump (Rubenstone had been taken off the case a few days before the hearing) had been meeting for several days and Berger no longer wanted him to appear as a witness. In fact, Berger said, he would now speak on behalf of the Trump deal, which had been amended to increase PCTC's share of the land price as well as the size of its option in the development project. Trump had also amended the contract to provide that if he were not allowed to share in the land profits—as the guidelines indicated he would not—then he could walk away from the deal. The only loser would be PCTC, which would then forfeit the $750,000 it would have advanced to cover the developer's preliminary expenses.

Getzoff was stunned. But even more indicative of Berger's new attitude was his approach to Getzoff and a housing consultant who had accompanied him to Philadelphia that morning. Getzoff wrote a memorandum to himself immediately after these events. It reads: "Mr. Berger took us aside and suggested that 'instead of fighting,' wouldn't I 'withdraw the HRH proposal so the whole matter could be settled at the hearing.' Mr. Berger stated that he was 'sure that if we played ball, he could work out a very satisfactory brokerage commission' for us … We [Getzoff and his consultant] informed Mr. Berger that 'we don't play that kind of game.' "

Getzoff also recalled that later that day Trump approached him with a similar question: "This arrogant young man patted me on the back in a most patronizing manner and asked me if I might be his broker. I assured him that I was not in the need of having a patron builder. He said that it's rare that you people—meaning brokers—are honest."

"I don't think I said that. If I did, fine," Trump said to me.

I also talked with Edward Rubenstone, now a member of another Philadelphia law firm, who confirmed Getzoff's account of his conversation with Berger: "I do recall being a little distressed at what happened there." Asked if he could explain the Berger shift, he replied: "To tell you the truth, I really can't…. The negotiations were really taken over by Berger. What happened was that at some point it was decided that we were not going to continue to oppose the sale to Trump. And there was really no substantial explanation given. I thought I had 'em nailed. I wasn't in a position to argue or make a stink. I thought we had a pretty solid case and suddenly it was decided not to pursue it. That troubles me."

One immediate consequence of the Berger switch was that Getzoff would no longer be able to present the HRH case as a witness for a party to the action. Indeed, PCTC attorneys tried to prevent him from detailing the offer in court at all by arguing that he had no legal standing. But Judge John Fullam wanted to hear it, complaining that, "I am not at all satisfied…that there has been necessarily adequate consideration given to the competing offers…." Fullam reserved decision and ended the hearing.

The debate continued. Ravitch wrote Fullam in January 1975, enclosing a 20-page comparison of the Trump and HRH bids and requesting that he reopen the hearing. Instead, the judge issued an order that March, confirming the Trump deal. His basic reason: "No party to the reorganization proceeding has expressed objections to the present proposal." Berger's switch had been decisive.

Fullam said that it is "the function of the trustees to make business judgments" and that he "should interfere with the trustees' proposed actions only if they are legally impermissible." The Eichler firm's (and thus, the trustees') support of the transaction had also been decisive.

Fullam concluded that the HRH had not "placed itself in a position of litigating." Ravitch had expressly refused to file a motion to reopen the case. His attorney later explained: "He did not want to litigate. He was content to make the bid and not go beyond the bid."

This curious reluctance might have been prompted by the relationship both Ravitch and Trump enjoyed with the new governor, Hugh Carey. Trump had been Carey's largest postprimary contributor in 1974, having donated a total of $35,000. Both he and Ravitch had just been named by Carey as the only developers on the statewide housing task force. Ravitch had also just been asked by Carey to take over the fiscally troubled state Urban Development Corporation. A public court fight between Ravitch and Trump over two prime Manhattan housing sites would have been unseemly and time consuming. Ravitch told me that his failure to press his bid legally had nothing to do with his and Trump's relation with Carey. He said that his appointment at UDC had left him "with no time to pursue new business ventures." In the end, Trump got his land, investing nothing but his time and effort, and squeezing every ounce of potential profit out of the deal.

The Berger Connection

On January 19, 1977, Fred and Donald Trump filed a $100 million antitrust suit in Brooklyn federal court against nine major oil companies for fixing the price of heating oil. The suit was not a class action; only those landlords listed as plaintiffs will benefit from a favorable settlement. It seeks damages, to be divided between Trump and the law firm that had originated the case in 1974 and is listed on all court records as attorney for the Trumps: David Berger of Philadelphia. It should be remembered that in 1974 David Berger was also the attorney representing the PCTC stockholders.

The suit began in July 1974 with a single plaintiff—the Lefrak organization. Richard Lefrak says that "Berger felt that more than one plaintiff should be involved." Berger's reason for having additional clients was not just to raise the total amount of damages from which Berger takes one-third. Each plaintiff landlord also paid an advance to Berger, a former Philadelphia corporation counsel and unsuccessful candidate for DA. Berger was experienced in oil-company conspiracy cases, having won a $29 million settlement in a gas-price-fixing case in New Jersey in 1973. "Berger is running the case," Lefrak said. "He's the bandleader."

The record of the heating-oil case revolves around the issue—raised by the oil companies—that in 1974 and early '75 Berger actively engaged in the recruitment of potential plaintiffs for it, a violation of the legal canons and grounds for disqualifying Berger from the suit. As evidence of this allegation, the oil companies introduced blank law-firm retainer forms on Berger letterhead, describing the terms of the agreement between Berger and the plaintiffs. The forms were being widely distributed to co-ops and apartment owners by a New York real estate firm.

Berger denied that he'd had any knowledge of the real estate firm's activities, though an associate in his law firm stated in court in January 1975: "We are going to have to have a substantial number of additional plaintiffs, some of whom fall into the commercial relationship as Lefrak, others who may be cooperatives and the like."

The judge dismissed the issue, commenting that "the distribution of the law-firm retainer forms...was regrettable, since one not privy to the intricate chain of events could misinterpret the distribution as involving improper solicitation."

Eight plaintiffs joined Lefrak, bringing the damages sought to almost $1 billion. Berger's advance fees were based upon the number of apartment units each plaintiff brought into the case. Trump's number of apartments was among the largest.

I asked Trump how he'd gotten involved in the suit, and first he described himself as one of the "original instigators" of the case. "Though I was involved in the case from its inception," he said, "I didn't file as a plaintiff until later."

When I raised the subject again, noting Berger's roles in the PCTC case at the same time, Trump began to emphasize that his suit had occurred two years after the PCTC sale. He also contended that it was another attorney, Eugene Morris of Demov and Morris, who contacted him about the case, not David Berger. But Richard Lefrak, who'd started the suit with Berger in 1974, recalled that "Trump was involved in the beginning. He joined the case within 90 days of the filing of the complaint." Lefrak said that Trump had attended meetings at the office of realtor George Mehlman "three or four years ago." Mehlman confirmed Trump's attendance at an early meeting: "He went along right away. This was in 1974, and may have been prior to the filing of the case. Berger came up and attended the meeting, too." Lefrak said, however, that Trump "may not have filed his complaint until 1977," because there were different categories of complaints, and the case was broken into separate parts...."

Last month Trump made a deposition in this case. While he would not pinpoint just when he began his involvement with it, he said it was "a very substantial number of months" before the January 1977 filing. Whenever the oil-company attorney attempted to question him about how he'd entered the case, Berger's associate instructed Trump not to answer. At one point he said, "There will be no questions about the nature of why the Trump organization is or is not a plaintiff in this lawsuit...."

In my brief interview with Berger, he was just as evasive. He began by contending that he hadn't represented Trump on the case; that Demov and Morris did. I countered by pointing out that Demov and Morris's name didn't appear in any case records until November 1978. He replied that he couldn't explain that. I pointed out that his name had, again and again. In fact, Berger had been present at Trump's deposition.

What seems clear is that Trump's association with this case—one of Berger's most important and potentially profitable legal actions—dates back to the same time frame of his sudden switch on the PCTC transaction.

The Palmieri Connection

In September 1973, prior to the Trump negotiations in the sale of the PCTC railyards, a small Los Angeles–based investment and management firm, Victor Palmieri and Co., had been retained by the PCTC trustees as an outside contractor "to develop, sell or lease" PCTC properties. Edward Eichler was then Palmieri's vice president. The company's profits were, in part, pegged to a percentage of sales negotiated. Palmieri and Co. would negotiate a sale, propose it to the trustees, and, with their approval, petition the court for acceptance. That is how Trump obtained not only the 30th and 60th Street yards but the Commodore Hotel, which he is now transforming into a government-aided $80 million Hyatt Hotel. All of Trump's historic Manhattan ventures, and the extraordinary terms he negotiated for these purchases, are rooted in his relationship with Palmieri.

Victor Palmieri, 49, is the founder of VPCO, a company that has made a fortune out of the collapse of Penn Central Transportation Company. In addition to the fees he has received managing PCTC real estate, he's already made in excess of $21 million in incentive fees alone—on top of salaries, expenses, and a flat annual fee—for handling the assets of other PCTC subsidiaries. In a profile last year, the *Wall Street Journal* cited Palmieri critics who claimed that he'd gotten his lucrative court assignments "due to his influence with the important people he knows." The *Journal* said he is described by these critics as "an active Democratic Party member." Other critics have gone even further. They say that Palmieri's contracts create a momentum to dump properties simply to accumulate fees.

There is no question that Palmieri's political connections are national in scope. In 1967, he was named deputy executive director of the Kerner Commission on Civil Disorder by President Lyndon Johnson. In that position, he made contact with a host of national political figures—including commission member John Lindsay. His aide at the commission, John Koskinen, wound up working for Lindsay and for Connecticut senator Abraham Ribicoff, before rejoining Palmieri as a principal of VPCO in 1973. Palmieri was active in John Tunney's 1970 Senate campaign in California and, through Tunney, is said to have entered the Kennedy political circle.

Last year Palmieri was selected by the scandal-ridden Teamsters' Central States Pension Fund to manage its $600 million worth of real estate west of the Mississippi River. The selection was made by the Teamsters themselves, though approved by the Department of Labor.

Palmieri and Trump were drawn together. It is clear from the Eichler affidavit in the PCTC case that the Palmieri strategy is to identify political entrepreneurs not merely to develop sites, but to develop relationships. Palmieri and Trump operated in the same way—Palmieri was a national broker in search of a local broker and ally. One sign of the relationship was that in 1976 Trump located an office for himself next door to Palmieri's. Recently a note on the door indicated that packages for Trump could be delivered to Palmieri's office. The business relationship between Trump and Palmieri soon extended beyond the PCTC properties. In July 1975, Palmieri was named by a Connecticut federal judge to manage Levitt and Sons, Inc., a home-building company that International Telephone and Telegraph was being forced to divest as part of a government antitrust action.

The judge told me he'd picked Palmieri in part on the reference of another federal judge who'd known Koskinen when both had worked for Ribicoff. A bonus was built into the contract with Palmieri. The quicker they sold Levitt, the larger Palmieri's take. But that was no simple task: for four years there'd been no takers.

In early 1977, Palmieri suddenly had an interested potential buyer, Starrett Housing Company. The leadership and name of Starrett had changed since the 1974 bid on the PCTC sites: Olnick was gone, but Donald Trump was still a principal equity owner of Starrett City and had just selected Starrett to build his Hyatt Hotel (Starrett's largest domestic contract that year). Starrett studied

Levitt and its potential market for what it described in its annual report as "many months." In February 1978, Starrett purchased the company for $30 million. Although Trump admitted to being the broker for the deal, he refused to say what his commission was.

Neither Palmieri nor the judge was too clear on just what Palmieri's profit on the sale was either—though the judge was certain that part of the healthy fee was due to his speedy disposition of the company.

As part of the acquisition package arranged by Trump, Starrett gave a five-year employment contract to Levitt's top executive, who had been installed by Palmieri. Levitt's president—now operating on a lucrative Starrett contract—is none other than Trump's old friend Edward Eichler, who'd handled the PCTC deal with Trump.

Birth of a Convention Center

Even before Trump's deal on the 30th Street yards had been confirmed by the court, he had dropped any pretense of developing it as a housing site: "I envisioned it as a convention center prior to the final court decision," he said. Despite the clear terms of his agreement with PCTC, which called for housing on 30th Street and foreclosed a role for him in any government purchase, he began to promote the site.

The problem was that Abe Beame and City Planning Commissioner John Zuccotti, both of whom had aided Trump in the acquisition of the yards, were committed to another convention-center site, on the waterfront at 44th Street. Even Bunny Lindenbaum, his son Sandy, and publicist Howard Rubenstein—the brokers closest to Beame—were under retainer to the 44th Street convention center corporation formed by the state legislature.

In 1974 some Clinton* opponents of 44th Street had actually advocated the 34th Street site as a possible alternative. However, after the Board of Estimate voted to fund a rehabilitation plan for Clinton around the 44th Street site, neighborhood groups became persuaded that the only way the city would deliver on its promised rehabilitation was to accept the convention center.

But, just as community opponents were becoming resigned to the center, its political supporters were pulling back. Tom Galvin, then executive vice president of the Convention Center Corporation, said he quit in May 1975, because: "With Beame as mayor, I could see the death knell of the project coming." Though the city continued to pour money into the site, paying $1,500 a month for Rubenstein and $36,000 to the Lindenbaum firm—ultimately wasting up to $17 million on it—the project was going nowhere.

Neither Beame nor Trump can recall when they first discussed the 30th Street yards as a convention-center site. But Trump told me that when he conceived the idea, his "initial approach was to Beame directly." Since he had been spending money on the site, Beame, clearly, had not discouraged him, although Trump remembers the mayor as "skeptical."

A Palmieri affidavit filed in Philadelphia dates the beginning of Trump's negotiations with the city as October 1975, around the same time as Beame, citing fiscal problems, announced that the city would pull out of the 44th Street convention-center project.

A few weeks after the Beame announcement, Trump retained Howard Rubenstein, quickly ending three years of Rubenstein's promotional efforts on behalf of the 44th Street site. The same week Trump brought in Sandy Lindenbaum, who had handled

---

* A neighborhood on the West Side of Manhattan, also known as Hell's Kitchen. —Ed.

zoning on 44th Street. Bunny Lindenbaum, who also left the 44th Street project, told me he began working with Trump "more in the role of an informal family adviser than as a lawyer."

Trump's proposal of a privately financed state-guaranteed center was, on the face of it, dubious. If attainable at all, it was as applicable to 44th Street as it was to 34th. He now concedes that this proposal—made primarily to counterbalance a sudden Battery Park City proposal—was not serious. "I never wanted to be the developer of the convention center," he said. "I wanted the site to be chosen.... There was no way a profit could be made as a developer." But Battery Park City emerged with its own financing. Tom Galvin recalls that the Port Authority had been quietly trying to strike a deal with Beame, offering to finance the center. The Port Authority's willingness to take the expected operating losses on the center could have been counterbalanced by the city's willingness to waive other Port Authority payments. Beame balked. He and the Port Authority did announce, however, that the authority would do a $100,000 feasibility study of the Battery Park City site for the city.

The Sun Shines on 34th Street

For this new enemy—which Trump characterized as the "Rockefeller interests"—Trump needed new, up-front allies. Trump says that "in the middle of 1975" he had begun discussing his convention-center idea with Carey fund-raiser Louise Sunshine at a dinner to pay off the governor's campaign debts. Sunshine, who was the finance director of Carey's 1974 and 1978 campaigns, was the right person to talk to. In addition to her role with Carey, she was treasurer of the state Democratic Party and national Democratic committeewoman from New York. She had been a fund-raiser for former assemblyman

Albert Blumenthal and had important political relationships on the West Side, where Trump needed allies to counter 44th Street. One significant contact was with State Senator Manfred Ohrenstein, who, as minority leader, had named her to the Advisory Council to the Democrats of the New York State Senate.

"I told her I was looking for someone to take the burden of the convention center off my back," Trump told me, "and asked who she'd suggest I hire. She called me the next day and said she'd driven to the site herself. She said it was the greatest site for the convention center. She worked on it a long time without pay. Finally she came on staff."

Rubenstein issued a press release announcing Sunshine's position in February 1976, at the peak of the enthusiasm for Battery Park. She registered as a Trump lobbyist with the secretary of state. In November, Trump filed the obligatory, end-of-session corporate statements, detailing $13,058 worth of salary and expenses associated with Sunshine's lobbying efforts.

[Sunshine failed to file her presession lobbyist statements in 1977 until she was reminded by the secretary of state's office at the end of the session. She didn't file at all in 1978, nor did Trump file his corporate report. Since Trump refers to her continuing efforts on behalf of the convention-center site, it appears that she is currently an unlicensed lobbyist, having failed to file her 1979 presession statement. The last record of Sunshine's lobbying activity is Trump's report of her $25,000 salary in August 1977. Failure to file annually constitutes a class "A" misdemeanor for both employer and lobbyist under the existing disclosure laws.]

In her 1976 filing, Sunshine had stated that she "intended to appear before the legislative committees and the governor upon all measures affecting the proposed 34th Street convention-center site." While she lobbied, she would retain her positions as an advisor to Senate Democrats and as fund-raiser to the governor. Carey has since appointed Sunshine to the Thruway Authority and the Job Development Authority.

Her alliance with Trump was widely perceived as the tangible sign of Carey's commitment to Trump's site. That is how Trump intended it, to counter any movement toward Battery Park.

Because she worked simultaneously for Trump and Carey, Sunshine's functions as Carey appointee, lobbyist, and fund-raiser had blended together. The largest individual Carey campaign contributor (exceeded only by the governor's brother) was none other than Donald Trump's companies—$125,000 since 1974.

Howard Rubenstein says that Sunshine made the great bulk of the contacts that produced lists of 34th Street supporters. Not surprisingly, those lists read like a Carey campaign financial statement. Many of the new corporate and real estate boosters were quickly shifting allegiance from the 44th Street site, which had become the site championed by the Clinton groups and Community Planning Board 4, whose area included both the 44th and 34th Street sites.

Trump eventually forced the Port Authority to add his site to its study. By the time the Port Authority reported in June, the political impetus and financial feasibility of the Battery Park City idea had already receded. The report gave the Port Authority's evenhanded blessing to either site. It also put to rest Trump's ruse of private financing and concluded that a bond-issuing authority would have to develop the center.

Trump started manufacturing reports. In November 1976, a group of graduate students at the New School for Social Research did a class study of the available sites and favored 34th Street. Then–City Councilman Robert Wagner Jr., who taught at the school, served as an adviser on the study, which was never released. He and the school agree: "The study did not, in any way, represent Wagner's views." But Trump wound up with a copy and started touting it as the Wagner report. Wagner says that he later told Trump and Sunshine to stop using it. Nonetheless, Trump described it to me as "a professionally done report" and said: "Bob Wagner Jr. came out with a very strong statement that 34th Street was the best site."

Then Trump parlayed Sunshine's relationship with Manfred Ohrenstein into a stunning blow against the 44th Street site. In 1973– '74, Ohrenstein had refused community pleas that he support 34th Street. But, by 1976, after the special zoning district had been created and Clinton had been promised rehabilitation, there was a near-unanimous community consensus around 44th Street. Beame's decision to forego building the center was seen as merely a temporary setback.

Suddenly, according to neighborhood activists, Ohrenstein released a report favoring 34th Street. "He consulted no one in the neighborhood," said one. In 1976, Trump began contributing to Ohrenstein's personal and Senate-majority campaign committees. He's given $10,000 since.

But the Ohrenstein—and implicit Carey—support did not move the defenses now formed around 44th Street, headed by Deputy Mayor John Zuccotti. Around the time of Ohrenstein's report, Zuccotti had formed the State/City Working Committee and stacked it with proponents of 44th Street. Beame told me: "I didn't name anybody to the thing. Zuccotti sparked that. I had no objection." The working committee had a staff component and a quasi board of high-level officials. The staff favored 34th Street, with various caveats. The board leaned toward 44th, with some advocates of the Battery. So, in April 1977, the committee disbanded without reaching any public conclusion. Zuccotti later left the city, and Beame moved into his mayoral primary campaign, promising that after the election, he'd finally settle this thing.

Beame had, in effect, killed the 44th Street site in 1975. He'd killed Battery Park City in 1976, when he'd turned a cold ear to those Port Authority officials who had wanted to finance and operate a center, but only at the Battery.

Indeed, court records suggest that Beame had quietly acquiesced to the 34th Street site as early as April 1976, when Palmieri and Co. had asked Judge Fullam to change 34th Street from a housing-use site to a convention-center site. The new terms anticipated approximately a $17 million increase in the cost of the land to the city and built into the agreement a Trump fee of up to $2 million. (Not surprisingly, David Berger, who was only months away from formally representing Trump in the oil-company case, raised no objection to the new deal—even though Trump's fee would come out of whatever amount the city or state would pay Berger's clients, the PCTC stockholders.)

Since the PCTC appraisal had valued the convention-center portion of the site (roughly half of the 30th Street property) at $4 million, the city could have probably acquired it by condemnation for that amount and avoided the payment of any fees to Trump.

Under the amendment, Trump was cut into a condemnation sale and guaranteed a flat fee of $500,000. He was also given a third sales price if he could drive the city's price past a minimum of $13.5 million. Trump is now seeking $21 million for land the city or state might have got for roughly $4 million three and a half years ago. Ironically, Palmieri and Co. had described the site as a "wasting asset," declining in value, in order to get court approval of the original sale in 1975.

These amendments—plus the affidavit stating that Beame had "abandoned" 44th Street and indicating that the Port Authority was the only obstacle to the 34th Street site—were formally served on the city. The court awaited any comments or objections. Finally, Judge Fullam approved the amendments in late

May 1976. By an act of omission, the city had permitted approval of the terms that had made Trump's search for convention-center support so potentially profitable to begin with.

Shortly after his primary defeat, Beame appointed another committee. Richard Ravitch—who'd lost the site to Trump in Philadelphia and whose firm had subsequently been retained by Trump to cost out his convention center—chaired it. Ravitch's report, while favoring 34th Street, concluded that the differences among the three sites were marginal.

Ravitch reported and Beame endorsed the site right before he left office. Last April, Koch, Carey, Ohrenstein, and Trump confirmed Beame's selection and jointly announced agreement on 34th Street. Since then, Ohrenstein has been introducing legislation and the Republicans have been blocking it. After last month's special legislative session, Carey and Majority Leader Warren Anderson indicated that they'd agreed on a plan of state funding.

But word out of Albany is that State Senator John Marchi, angered by what he regards as the Ohrenstein-organized and Trump-financed electoral challenge he just went through in November (a product of Ohrenstein's drive to elect a Democratic majority in the Senate) says he will block any convention center built on Trump-owned land. No one is quite sure how serious Marchi is. But in Trump's world, there is something fitting about Marchi's strange reasoning. It is a kind of ultimate quid pro quo in a transaction plagued, in every detail for half a decade, by quid pro quos. There is bound to be at least one deal too many in this chronology.

There is nothing terrible about Trump's convention-center site. It is, I am sure, as good as the others. In hours of interviews Trump almost sold me on it, and he's clearly prevailed with some government officials—like City Planning Commissioner Robert Wagner—despite, rather than because of, his brand of political intrigue. My quarrel is that $400 million of state funds could salvage entire neighborhoods; that New York City already is the top convention city in America and has an exhibition hall that is turning a profit for the city; and that Trump's site will never pass any fair environmental test, precisely because it sees Midtown as the city and will concentrate thousands of people—with their cars and their sewage—right where the city can't cope with them. Trump's answer to this kind of pro neighborhood argument was contained in a *New York Times* piece about him two years ago: "I think the city will get better," he said. "I'm not talking about the South Bronx. I don't know anything about the South Bronx."

What he doesn't understand is that the South Bronx *is* this city. Its problems were created by someone else's deals. And the problems remain, at least partially because of deals that ignore them. Deals like his own.

There is one final twist to this story. State laws provide that no one can get a broker's commission on a transaction unless he was a licensed broker throughout the negotiations of the deal. Trump and the City Planning Commission have described Trump's services on 34th Street as those of "a broker." The problem is that young Donald Trump didn't become a licensed broker until after his contract with PCTC had been completely negotiated and approved by Judge Fullam. But brokerage licenses are merely pesky requirements of the law.

In this two-part history we've been looking into a world where only the greed is magnified. The actors are pretty small and venal. Their ideas are small, never transcending profit. In it, however, are the men elected to lead us and those who buy them. And in it, unhappily, are the processes and decisions that shape our city and our lives.

State of New York,
Department of State. } ss.:

I Hereby Certify That I have made diligent and complete search of the records of the Department of State, Division of Licensing Services relating to _____ Article 12A of the Real Property Law _____ , as amended,
(Statute)
with respect to Real Estate Brokers and Salespersons _____
(License Category)
which records are in the custody and under the control of the Secretary of State, and find the following:

Licensee's Name ____ Trump, Donald J. ____
Residence Address ____
Present Status ____ Individual Broker ____ License # 046960 ____
Business/Employer's Name ____ Donald J. Trump ____
Business Address ____ 600 Ave Z, Brooklyn, NY 11223 ____
Qualified for Licensure By* Examination, Reciprocity or Attorney Status ____
Disciplinary Action ____ None ____

REAL ESTATE LICENSEES	COSMETOLOGY/BARBER LICENSEES
Broker From at least	Dates of Licensure
*11/01/83-07/31/91	
Salesperson *	School Attended
Education Completed Continuing	NYS Approved Hrs. Completed
Education Complied With	Graduation Date
Title Of Office n/a	Examination Dates:
	Practical
	Written

* Indicates records prior to 1983 which are unavailable due to our scheduled rate of destruction.

Witness my hand and the Official Seal of the Department of State, at the City of Albany, this 24th day of October , one thousand nine hundred and ninety .

Donald Trump negotiated the Penn Central Transportation Company deal before he had a broker's license. When Barrett was writing *Trump: The Deals and the Downfall*, he asked the New York Department of State for Trump's broker's license. This document shows that he had a license at least as far back as 1983. Earlier records were destroyed as part of routine paperwork destruction. (Courtesy of the Briscoe Center for American History at the University of Texas at Austin)

3

The Seduction of Mario Cuomo

January 14, 1992

Barrett maintained a profound and complex relationship with former New York governor Mario Cuomo. Liberal Democrats raised with the same stark Cold War Catholic moralities meant to protect them from cesspool characters like Trump, they spoke the same language. This didn't soften Barrett's criticism of the governor when Cuomo failed to meet the ethical standards the reporter thought they shared. It may have sharpened it. Governor Andrew Cuomo, Mario's son, began his eulogy at Barrett's funeral with a booming sentence: "The first time I heard my father curse, he was on the phone with Wayne Barrett." —Ed.

THE MOST DISTURBING MYSTERY surrounding the saga of Donald's brief career as a football phenom was the questions it raised about his curious, yet unmistakably compelling, influence at the highest levels of the Cuomo administration. Vincent Tese* was no renegade commissioner; in fact, no one in Mario Cuomo's government was in closer touch with him. And the Urban Development Corporation's (UDC's) supine performance for Trump had its equivalents in other state agencies on matters wholly unrelated to the stadium,† especially at the State Transportation Department, which championed Trump's agenda in planning improvements on the West Side Highway, adjacent to Donald's 60th Street yards.

Donald had long had a special knack for ingratiating himself with public officials, but Mario Cuomo was not just another inviting political target. Donald's penetration of the Cuomo inner circle was a textbook case in seduction, and his compromising relationship with the administration would last even into the months of Trump's collapse in 1990.‡ Other than Tese's golf dates with Donald in Florida and New York, there was little of a personal touch to the mutually beneficial Cuomo/Trump arrangement. It was all business.

What made Cuomo such an unusual government target for Trump was that when he defeated Ed Koch for governor in 1982, he ran against virtually every monied interest in New York politics, most of whom, like Donald, rallied to Koch because of his 30- to 40-point lead in the early polls. And almost from the moment he became governor, there was an extraordinary undercurrent about the dignified and brilliant Cuomo that marked him as a man who might be president. His speech at the 1984 Democratic

---

* Chief of the Urban Development Corporation and later director of economic development under Governor Mario Cuomo. —Ed.

† Donald Trump won permission from New York State and New York City in 1985 to build a football stadium in Queens, near the present-day Citi Field. It never came to pass. —Ed.

‡ Donald Trump's Taj Mahal, an Atlantic City casino, declared bankruptcy in 1991, the first of six Trump business bankruptcies between 1991 and 2009. —Ed.

Convention transformed this onetime unarticulated presidential murmur into so persistent a question it became, both at home and occasionally across the country, a Democratic preoccupation. This national fascination helped Cuomo become, through the eighties and into the nineties, the master of New York politics, isolated from the pack by his deliberate hermetic style, a recluse in Albany whose intelligence and rhetorical passion were seen only in glimpses.

Part of Cuomo's above-the-fray appeal was his religion. It wasn't just that he was a Catholic; his predecessor, Hugh Carey, was Catholic enough to have twelve children, yet no one ever thought of him as a man to whom morality was a mission. Cuomo publicly wrestled with the Lord, weighing the heaviest questions of life and death as if it was the responsibility of a leader to help the people to understanding. He talked soaringly about values. He invoked Saint Thomas More as his guardian, a man who died for a principle. This spiritual quality, combined with the hometown presidential hopes that seemed to last forever, insulated him from inspection and criticism like no other public figure in the state.

From the beginning of the Cuomo reign, the insiders who bankrolled and benefited from the government game were studying the new Albany team, looking for weaknesses, waiting for messages, hunting for opportunities. They read every signal, interpreted every nuance, and none did it better than Donald. Figuring Cuomo out was a riddle for Donald, finding a path to him was a necessity.

Trump knew he had a bit of history going for him. In 1958, Mario Cuomo had joined his first law firm—Brooklyn's Comer, Weisbrod, Froeb and Charles. Senior partner Richard Charles, who became Cuomo's mentor at the small firm, had already been representing Fred Trump for decades, and Cuomo was assigned as a young associate to help with the Trump work. Fabian Palamino, then a young associate with Cuomo who became his counsel as governor, remembers their travels out to Fred Trump's headquarters on Avenue Z for business lunches at which Trump dished out the cheese sandwiches himself.

When Cuomo became Hugh Carey's running mate in 1978 and was elected lieutenant governor, {Donald} Trump contributed $4,000 to his minuscule campaign committee. While Trump had backed Koch in the 1982 race, he'd called Cuomo's old friend and finance chairman, Bill Stern, on October 11, 1982, and made a $3,500 donation for the general election.

Trump did not contribute again to the Cuomo committee until November 13, 1984, a month after the stadium project was approved and a month before he submitted his own plan. Several Trump business entities combined that day to give the Friends of Mario Cuomo $15,000—making Trump one of the top donors at Cuomo's annual fund-raiser. Cuomo had personally approved Trump's invitation that August to serve on the campaign committee's board of advisers. The board was formed as "a permanent finance committee" of thirty to fifty prestigious individuals, from every major region and industry in the state, to raise a minimum of $30,000 each at Cuomo's dinner.

But the contributions were merely door openers. Donald was looking for the right insider who could get him beyond access. All he had to do, it turned out, was look at the top of the governor's fund-raising apparatus, just as he had in 1975 when he recruited Carey's finance chief, Louise Sunshine, as a lobbyist.

Bill Stern had long since stepped down as the head of the Friends committee, which he'd formed way back in 1978 to help pay off the costs of Cuomo's losing mayoral campaign the year before. Stern, who stopped fund-raising for Cuomo when he became head of UDC, was replaced at the campaign committee in 1983 by Lucille Falcone, a 30-year-old lawyer so unknown in the circles that fund political campaigns that she was seen as merely an appendage of the governor's office. Falcone had surfaced publicly in early 1983, when she was hired by Stern at UDC, a job she quickly resigned when news stories described her as the girlfriend of Cuomo's 25-year-old son, Andrew. She then scurried back to her law firm and took over the Friends committee. It was Falcone who recommended that Trump be named to the board of advisers in a letter to Cuomo.

Falcone was the only person to have worked at both of Mario Cuomo's law firms. She was a young associate at the Charles firm in Brooklyn, recruited from law school in 1976 by Cuomo's close friend, Pete Dwyer, the treasurer of his 1977 mayoral campaign. In early 1981, she was asked to join a new firm that had just been formed at Cuomo's request by Jerry Weiss, who had been Cuomo's special counsel as lieutenant governor. Cuomo encouraged Weiss to put the firm together so he would have something to fall back on if he lost the gubernatorial campaign.

The small firm that the 38-year-old Weiss assembled was intimately connected with Cuomo from the beginning—law student Andrew worked summers there, the campaign finance committee met there, and the firm's biggest client became the campaign's most generous donor.

Shortly after Cuomo won his astonishing victory, the firm was recast with two new partners as Weiss, Blutrich, Falcone and Miller and began to prosper quietly, though every one of its partners was only "30-something." Andrew joined the Cuomo administration as a one-dollar-a-year special assistant and soon became the second most powerful state official, but Cuomo insiders openly anticipated that he would soon wind up at the family firm, and he never denied it. He'd begun dating Falcone in 1982 and worked closely with her on the annual dinner dances in 1983 and 1984. Though she frequently worked round the clock on the committee's activities, the struggling new firm was generously understanding about her unpaid efforts.

A few days after Trump's December 1984 meeting with Cuomo about the stadium, Bill Stern got a surprising call from Donald about Lucille Falcone's little law firm.

"Bill, I saw Lucille Falcone at this fund-raising meeting and I got the feeling I should retain her law firm," Donald told him. "What do you think?"

It was an awkward moment for Stern, who had been bickering with Andrew and Mario Cuomo for months, complaining, among other things, about what he saw as the increasingly disturbing signs of the Weiss firm's attempts to influence state agencies. He had informed them about Weiss's call to him raising questions about the propriety of a UDC bid process on an upstate job where Weiss represented a client who'd lost the contract to another builder by more than a million dollars. Stern had also told the Cuomos about Falcone's call to him claiming that he was excluding big-time developer Bill Zeckendorf from UDC's gigantic 42nd Street development project. Zeckendorf had retained the Weiss firm in 1984, the developer later conceded, on the recommendation "of somebody who knew their way around the Democratic side of state politics" because "we thought they could help us politically."

Stern also recounted to the Cuomos the insight of another 42nd Street developer, frustrated at the small slice of the project he was getting. "I know a way I can get a bigger cut," the developer told Stern. "Hire Jerry Weiss's law firm."

As Stern saw it, Trump was hardly alone in picking up the Cuomo signal. "I don't recommend law firms," Stern told Trump.

"But Lucille Falcone is a good person and a fine lawyer." It was the best compromise Stern could work out in his head, but it still troubled him. He had already had one bitter scene with Mario Cuomo about the firm, back in November, with Stern demanding that Cuomo distance himself from it and Cuomo responding: "You're holier than everyone else, Bill. You judge souls; I don't." Stern had been shocked at the personal attacks Cuomo had heaped on him that day—related and unrelated to the law firm controversy. He decided to get out of the administration, but he wanted to get out cleanly, without a war with Cuomo.

Forty-five minutes after Stern's conversation with Trump, Andrew Cuomo called him. He said that he'd heard Trump had called about the firm and asked Stern what he'd said. When Stern told Andrew that he had praised Lucille's legal ability, the young Cuomo said, "Lucille told me you said that." Andrew thanked him, and said: "I respect you very much."

Unbeknownst to Stern, a storm was stirring inside the firm. Not only would Andrew soon become a partner; he would replace Weiss himself. Stern first learned about Weiss's departure from the governor himself, who in late December casually mentioned to him: "Jerry's leaving. Did you know he made $800,000 this year?" When Weiss left, the State Investigations Commission was examining some of his activities on behalf of upstate developer Shelly Goldstein. The allegation was that Weiss had used his influence to dramatically reduce the value of a state lease in a building that Goldstein was trying to buy. The state official who ordered the lease reduction—which was theoretically done to force the owner to sell to Goldstein—was Andrew Cuomo. After Andrew joined the firm in May of 1985, Goldstein would become his principal client and partner in real estate and banking ventures. (The investigation closed without any findings against Weiss or Andrew.)

Shortly before 25-year-old Andrew became the young firm's youngest partner, Trump quietly retained it. His relationship with the firm would last for almost two years, though it did not surface publicly until August of 1986. The legal work it did for Trump remains unclear, apart from Andrew Cuomo's concession that it represented Trump in lease negotiations involving possible commercial tenants in the stores planned for his West Side yards project. When Trump's retention of the firm did hit the newspapers in 1986, Trump's response was: "They are now representing us in a very significant transaction."

Though Andrew insisted in later interviews that the firm did not interact with state officials on behalf of clients, Falcone did just that for Trump on another project. She arranged and attended a July 21, 1985, lunch at the World Trade Center with Trump and Sandy Frucher, the president of the state's Battery Park City Authority. During the lunch, Trump expressed an interest in being designated for a choice hotel site on the Battery Park site, just off Wall Street. Frucher urged him to bid when a request for proposals was announced, but Trump was looking for an inside track. When Frucher didn't offer it, Trump didn't bid.

Donald was not the only one with an interest in Trump projects to retain the Cuomo firm. Abe Hirschfeld, Trump's limited partner on the West Side and an increasingly close ally, also hired the firm in November 1985 to represent him in a disputed real estate closing. Hirschfeld publicly said in a later interview that he thought hiring the firm was a way "to get in the good graces with the governor." While Andrew Cuomo and his partners have attempted to lowball Trump's business with the firm—never offering a total for him or Hirschfeld—the fact is that the unwanted publicity about the long-secret retainer killed the relationship before the "significant transaction" Trump cited could close, obviously limiting the Cuomo firm's fees.

The retention of the Falcone firm was hardly Trump's only Cuomo move. In November 1985, Donald hired Albany lobbyist and former transportation commissioner Bill Hennessy, who'd just resigned as chairman of the state Democratic Party. When Cuomo installed Hennessy as head of the party, the *Times* saw it as an indication of the governor's "intent on staying deeply involved in organization politics, since Hennessy has never held a party post and thus has nothing to fall back on other than Cuomo's support." For Trump, the main job of the Hennessy firm, to which he paid a $2,000-a-month retainer plus a $500 per diem rate, was to lobby some of the very transportation officials Hennessy had appointed for favorable rulings on an array of West Side yard issues.

As potent as the Falcone and Hennessy combination was, Donald did not stop there. In the spring of 1986, Trump hired UDC's in-house counsel, Susan Heilbron, who had worked extensively on the stadium project for the agency. The two first discussed the job while they sat together in December 1985 during the final stadium designation talks. Well known at the top levels of the Cuomo administration, Heilbron helped engineer the selection of her best friend as Tese's new counsel, Joanne Gentile, an attorney who had worked under Trump attorney Harvey Myerson at Finley Kumble.

Trump also tried, over a period of six months in 1986 and 1987, to lure Sandy Frucher into his lair. Frucher, one of the governor's half dozen top advisers, eventually declined, after countless courting sessions.

On Falcone's recommendation, Sive, Paget, and Riesel, the 10-member environmental law firm Trump retained for the lucrative West Side yards approval process, hired Richard Gordon, the executive director of the Friends of Mario Cuomo. Gordon, who had worked with the Cuomos since the 1982 campaign, remained director of the campaign committee, even though his law firm had a multiplicity of matters before state agencies.

Trump's most unusual reach, however, was for a very special driver and bodyguard, Joe Anastasi. A state trooper assigned to UDC, Anastasi had been Mario Cuomo's personal bodyguard for years, starting when Cuomo was lieutenant governor, and had accompanied him throughout the 1982 gubernatorial campaign, starting most mornings in Cuomo's kitchen in Queens over a cup of coffee. After Cuomo became governor, Anastasi was on his security detail in New York City until, in late 1984, Bill Stern told Cuomo that his agency needed an investigator to do background checks on state contractors and Cuomo suggested Anastasi. Anastasi worked at UDC for three years, but was seldom seen there, reportedly because he was "in the field" at UDC construction sites.

In 1986, Anastasi began accompanying Trump on various trips across the country. He told friends he was setting up his own security business and that the Trump work on his résumé would help him attract business. Top Cuomo officials, including the governor himself, learned of Anastasi's Trump duty and viewed it as a conflict with his UDC post. He was told to end it, and he soon resigned from state service.

In addition to surrounding himself with everyone from the governor's son to his bodyguard, Donald tried to score political points with Cuomo on several fronts. He let it be known to the Cuomos that he'd been recruited by state GOP boss George Clark to run against the governor in 1986, and he went public in 1987 with a highly questionable account of a meeting he had with national GOP kingmakers, including Roger Stone, the

GOP consultant Trump had hired as a lobbyist. They had supposedly tried to convince him to oppose Cuomo in the next election, which would not occur until 1990. In both instances, of course, he'd said no. He also cooled down his irate partner, Abe Hirschfeld, who ran for lieutenant governor in the 1986 primary but was knocked off the ballot by Cuomo. Hirschfeld was considering backing Cuomo's GOP opponent and assailing Cuomo publicly, but Trump convinced him not to.

More important, though, than any of these local political gestures was Trump's willingness to talk openly and favorably about Cuomo's possible presidential candidacy. From the governor's perspective, the public praise of a Republican icon like Trump had a national impact, enhancing Cuomo's plausibility as a probusiness candidate. Of course to Donald, his calculating praise of Cuomo had nothing to do with the governor's public performance. Trump had not even bothered to vote in either of Cuomo's gubernatorial elections, nor when Cuomo ran for mayor in 1977.

The final thread connecting Trump and Cuomo was Tese himself. Tese's business connection was not with Donald directly, but with Donald's lawyer. Neither Harvey Myerson nor Tese disclosed—to the NFL or to the federal court in the antitrust case—that Tese was a private client of Myerson's firm. In fact, Myerson had the nerve to object, in a sidebar conversation with the judge, about a small retainer one of the NFL firms had with UDC, charging that it "raises a potential or actual concern for impropriety." But he misled the court about his own UDC work—claiming it was "unrelated" to the stadium when he had a contract to handle the stadium bond issue for the agency—and failed to report at all his deeper, private ties to his witness, Tese.

More surprising was that Myerson's firm decided to waive payment on $122,000 in fees due from the Tese companies in

1986—the same year Tese testified—and wrote off another $157,000 the next year. The bankruptcy trustee in the Finley Kumble case ultimately labeled these forgiven fees—as well as waivers granted other favored clients—a "fraudulent transfer" of the firm's rightful earnings. Indeed Myerson was personally involved in some of his firm's legal work for Tese.

The bankruptcy trustee eventually brought a lawsuit to recover these fees plus interest, and lawyers for Tese's companies responded by contending that Myerson's firm had agreed to the write-offs because it had overbilled the companies. The trustee's suit wound up going nowhere—with the Tese firms assailing Myerson's "inflated, overstated and padded" billings and the trustee insisting that compliance with discovery demands could not be made without violating the lawyer/client privilege. But what appeared to be beyond dispute in this two-year litigation was that in the midst or aftermath of Tese's United States Football League testimony, the Myerson firm was slashing the fees it once claimed Tese's companies owed it.

*** *This elided portion contains detailed reporting on contracts and billing between Tese's company, Myerson's law firm, and the UDC. —Ed.****

The casual ethical judgments implicit in this disturbing intertwine occurred against the backdrop of all the other Trump ties to the Cuomo inner circle. In fact, the Myerson firm itself—at least at the point in 1986 when Tese testified—was part of the Cuomo circle; Bill Hennessy was its Albany lobbyist as well, and Andrew Cuomo would personally spend several weeks during this period at the firm's office, negotiating a major real estate deal with Myerson's closest friend in the firm. Through Myerson, and all his other levers of compromise, Donald had managed to insinuate himself, almost imperceptibly, within the Cuomo government, and the benefits of this relationship would extend far beyond the doomed stadium.

On the West Side, for example, Donald's grand Television City design required the approval of several state agencies and, from late 1985 through 1987, Donald was methodically lobbying for special favors, especially at the Department of Transportation. Trump wanted changes in DOT's planned rehabilitation of the elevated West Side Highway, which ran over the 60th Street site along the waterfront. When the site was owned by another developer a couple of years earlier, DOT decided that a partially built and never-used southbound ramp off the highway at 72nd Street—the tip of the Trump site—had to be removed entirely for safety reasons. Donald wanted it retained and converted into a permanent ramp running right into the retail mall he planned to build underneath his office and residential tower complex. Not only did DOT back the new plan, but the agency was also willing to let Donald pay for only part of it, while the other developer had been required to finance the entire cost of removing the old structure. The ramp—which state memos freely conceded "was needed" for Trump's project "but would otherwise not be needed"—was designed to deliver customers to the very stores whose leases Andrew Cuomo's law firm was trying to negotiate. When the plan was presented to the federal highway officials who were funding the rehabilitation project, they warned DOT that the ramp was so clearly designed to benefit the Television City project that the traffic and other impacts of both TV City and the highway improvement would have to pass environmental review standards to be built. That warning killed federal funding for the ramp.

DOT also approved a new connection from a northbound ramp off the highway directly onto the boulevard that Donald planned to run through the heart of Television City. The state's anticipated widening of the West Side Highway was likewise designed to meet Trump concerns, with the new roadway extended exclusively on the western, waterfront side, rather than on the east, where Donald wanted to construct his project as close to the highway as he could. This decision meant that the widened road would hang out over 1.4 acres of the already small park that Donald had promised along the water, reducing the opening to the sky by fourteen percent. Trump's planned southbound ramp would have also cut into the planned park, narrowing it to a mere thirty feet in width—barely the size of a sidewalk—in some places. And while the state had removed that ramp from its federal rehabilitation agenda because of the objections raised in Washington, it quietly encouraged Donald to construct the ramp on his own before the rehabilitation formally started. DOT so closely tracked Trump's desires for the site that internal memos acknowledged the agency's acquiescence but observed that this high level of cooperation was being extended "as discreetly as possible."

Trump's success with DOT was largely a result of the lobbying of Hennessy. In fact, John Shafer, the assistant commissioner at DOT who helped steer much of the Trump plan through the agency, was so close to Hennessy that when Cuomo named Hennessy to chair the Thruway Authority in 1987, Hennessy made Shafer the authority's executive director. Lucille Falcone was also involved with the West Side planning, occasionally attending the weekly meetings Donald chaired of his West Side working group. While there was no indication that either she or Andrew played any personal role with DOT, there are memos indicating that the governor's top staff at the capitol was monitoring very carefully the department's handling of the roadway issues.

The Grand Hyatt, the Midtown hotel that UDC had helped Donald build in the '70s, also got its own special state service in the Cuomo years. The benefactor again was Vincent Tese, whose agency was still the Hyatt's landowner and was required to collect the hotel's annual property tax payments and pass them on to the city. When Trump suddenly slashed his payment by 80 percent in 1987, UDC just accepted it without raising any questions, though it had a right to audit the Hyatt's books under the terms of the lease. Several months later, the city asked UDC to allow its auditor general, Karen Burstein, to audit the hotel's paltry $667,000 payment, and UDC went along. The city audit revealed that Trump had shortchanged the city by $2.8 million.

In meetings between city and UDC officials, however, Tese and his counsel vigorously resisted the audit's findings and its release. Though UDC was merely acting as a pass-through collection agent for the city, Tese formally notified the city that he had hired an independent accounting firm "to review the audit." His counsel adopted Trump's position that the public release of the audit "would breach the mandate of confidentiality" in the lease. The tensions between Tese and the city were so great that Koch, Burstein, and other top staff didn't tell UDC until the last minute that they were going to announce the audit findings at a City Hall press conference. Tese responded by criticizing the audit in public statements to the newspapers, his spokesman saying that they wanted an outside accountant to determine that the city's charges were the result of sound accounting practices, not of "a special political agenda."

Tese even refused to serve a demand notice on the hotel for payment as requested by the city, forcing the city to threaten legal action against UDC. The city, which calculated that Trump had already saved $60 million in taxes since the Hyatt opened, was adamant, and Burstein demanded to know "whose side" UDC was on at one heated meeting. Tese finally had to give in, agreeing to seek payment from Trump.

In the middle of the audit dispute, Lucille Falcone hosted the annual Cuomo fund-raiser at the Sheraton. Trump bought the most expensive ringside table, and Tony Gliedman, the former Koch housing commissioner who had become Donald's main emissary on the audit issue, spent the night mingling with a crowd that included the governor, Tese, and Andrew. Trump was Cuomo's biggest 1989 corporate giver, donating $25,000.

A few nights after the fund-raiser, Donald went to a second, private Cuomo affair—Andrew Cuomo's birthday party at a Midtown pub. The party was cohosted by one of Andrew's closest friends, Dan Klores, the fast-talking aide to public relations czar Howard Rubenstein, who had handled the Trump account for years. But Donald barely spoke to Klores at the party, instead huddling with Andrew for a half hour. Andrew would later claim that it was the first time he'd ever met Trump—his way of minimizing the client relationship that had a transparently troubling side to it. It was just one more rhetorical Cuomo ploy—hiding a compromising business arrangement behind the supposed detachment of personal distance.

By Donald's decade, this sort of political intrigue had become the essence of what it meant to be a real estate mogul in New York—a specialized form of social engineering. Without a flair for ensnaring the public officials whose discretion could make or break development schemes, the New York entrepreneur was dead in the water. It was the only way to bring grand projects to life, the inevitable route to publicly allocated wealth. The Cuomo episode just demonstrated what a master Donald had become at it. Tempting, captivating, inveigling, and baiting those with public power were the tricks of his trade, and for the moment, Donald, preserving miraculously his air of innocence, was its unchallenged, brash new champion.

PART II

Crooks, Scams, Pols, and Setups

Most articles Barrett wrote weren't about Donald Trump or Rudy Giuliani. They were about garden-variety corruption by crooks whose names most people have forgotten. Barrett's reporting made use of campaign finance reports and the financial disclosure forms city officials are required to file—and underscored their necessity. But Barrett didn't just read the names of big donors; he dissected this paperwork—and bank records and mortgage documents—with the zeal of a coroner searching for poison. The dot-matrix computer printouts that formed stacks in his office told the story of who was getting rich and who called the shots, who owned the city and what shape it would take for generations hence. —Ed.

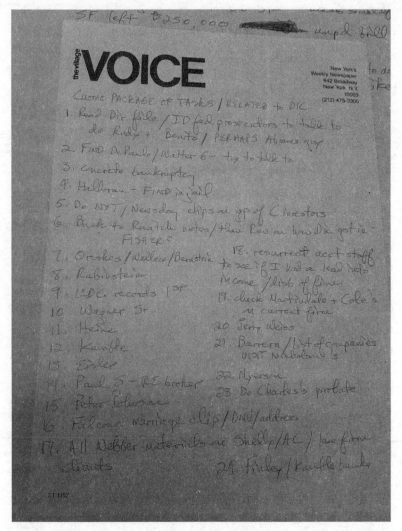

Barrett organized even the most complex investigations with a series of task lists, pursuing every avenue of inquiry until a fact pattern emerged. (Photo by Eileen Markey)

The Barrett Book
Errol Louis

I T DID NOT SURPRISE me to learn that my friend and mentor, Wayne Barrett, had enrolled in seminary as a young man, with plans to become a priest. Although he quickly scrapped the idea of entering the priesthood—thank God—Wayne would have done fine in the ministry. In the decidedly secular world of political journalism, he never lost the urge to search out evil, probe men's souls, and speak bitter truths like the prophets of old.

In the pages and paragraphs of Wayne's column, as in scripture, sinners were offered a choice: repent, or be damned.

Wayne wasn't just old school; he openly and unashamedly invoked ancient notions of right and wrong, truth and falsehood. His investigations were municipal morality tales, with the words, deeds, and motivations of bad actors laid out in dense, unforgiving detail. It wasn't enough to name a wayward judge or party hack. Wayne would give you their lineage: what club they came out of, what elections they won or lost, and who their mentors, allies, and financial backers were.

Wayne was, in the preinternet age, actively solving a major challenge of modern journalism: how to supply enough background, history, and context to convert a flood of far-flung facts into a coherent story that guides the reader to what is meaningful and important.

For most of the years Wayne covered New York City, an enterprising journalist who knew where to go could purchase a small, bound copy of something called the *Green Book* that listed the name, title, and salary of nearly every employee in NYC government. All the major newsrooms had at least one copy on hand, along with the New York State version of the same thing, known as the *Red Book*.

But without context and history, those compendiums were a useless jumble of names. The books, alone, would not tell you whose political clubhouse Commissioner X was affiliated with, or which real estate donations had turned Councilman Y into a wholly owned subsidiary of unscrupulous developers, or which party leaders had supported the appointment of a judge or Board of Elections official. You couldn't make sense of the 300,000-member city workforce without a guide. Wayne printed the scorecard.

So next to the *Green Book* and the *Red Book*, for many of us, was a "Barrett Book," the lengthy *Voice* investigations by Barrett and his partner, Jack Newfield, that poked under the hood of power in New York and showed the often-tangled wires connecting cash, political clubs, legislation, and agency actions.

As a wide-eyed college student hundreds of miles from New York, I waited for every issue of the *Voice* and pored over the tales Wayne and Jack told of scammers and scoundrels, henchmen and heroes. I clipped and saved and reread the columns. I thought Wayne's crusades were the wildest, grandest epic I'd ever heard of, and I literally could not wait to get involved.

Many years later, as a host of *Inside City Hall*, a nightly television show about New York City government, I was especially thrilled to have Wayne bring his near-encyclopedic knowledge of local political history to our weekly Reporters Roundtable. He knew where all the bodies were buried (and in more than a few cases had personally helped put the politician being discussed in the grave).

Years of government reform and the digital revolution have made more information than ever publicly available. We have plenty of information but not enough wisdom. What's missing is a modern Barrett Book to guide us through the daily data dumps to the essential truths about who's who and who did what, as a new generation of heroes and villains continues the eternal fight for the soul of a great city.

Errol Louis is the host of *Inside City Hall*, a nightly politics show on NY1. He is a columnist at the New York *Daily News* and previously directed the Urban Reporting program at the Craig Newmark Graduate School of Journalism at the City University of New York.

4

Runnin' Scared*
(The Time Meade Esposito, the Poster Boy for Political Bossism, Claimed Not to Be a Political Boss)

August 6, 1979

"After years of watching election cases in Brooklyn courts, I learned that the critical moment in political cases is when the judge is assigned," Wayne Barrett wrote in this masterful—and funny—piece on the shameless machinations of the Brooklyn political boss Meade Esposito. Among the most powerful men in the state of New York, Esposito leveraged his unelected political power into control of the judiciary and lucrative insurance contracts. Barrett and his partners at the *Village Voice* attacked Esposito, who was on the payroll of multiple mafia families, for years. "I've been very successful in business," Esposito once said. "I owe it all to politics." This piece includes many of Barrett's trademark practices: he's clearly having a great time of himself, he draws out the cat's

---

* Runnin' Scared was the name of the *Voice*'s city politics column in the 1970s and early '80s.

cradle of political influence and favors, he greatly an-
noys a powerful man, he gets himself to an archive to
do digging no one else had thought to do. —Ed.

S TATE SUPREME COURT JUDGE Alvin Klein's
recent dismissal of a legal motion to unseat
Brooklyn Democratic boss Meade Esposito was in part the result
of a series of compromises and a lack of prosecutorial zeal by State
Attorney General Robert Abrams.

Abrams, who inherited the complaint against Esposito from
former Attorney General Louis Lefkowitz, cooperated with Esposito's attorney in the selection of Judge Klein to hear the case,
allowed Esposito to miss two default deadlines, failed to use important evidence he had gathered against Esposito, and did not
even seek out other available and obvious evidence. Last week
Abrams, who was supported by Esposito for attorney general in
1978, refused to answer specific questions about the case directly,
despite repeated requests by the *Voice*. Instead, Abrams's press
aides selectively responded to some of the questions and issued a
general denial, calling "any insinuation that the Esposito matter"
wasn't handled thoroughly and professionally "reckless and totally
inaccurate."

The County Leader's New Clothes

Klein's decision itself represents a cynical attempt to isolate the
law from the real world, surrounding Esposito with legal fanta-
sies so bold as to nullify the last century of machine politics in
this city. The essence of Klein's ruling was that Esposito, who has

become a caricature of the county party boss, is in fact no boss at
all and thus cannot be penalized for breaking state laws that limit
the commercial activity of a county leader.

The complaint alleged that Esposito violated a 25-year-old statute that requires public and party officials to forfeit their office if
they do any business with a racetrack. Esposito was charged with
sharing in the insurance and mortgage fees for the Parr Meadows
racetrack in Suffolk County. (He was paid as a partner in two
firms that represented the track.) Two weeks ago, Klein decided
that Esposito couldn't be required to give up the office of Brooklyn
county leader on the novel ground that there is no such title in the
Brooklyn party. A few hours after Klein's decision was released,
Abrams announced his intention to appeal. But indications are that
Abrams contributed to the awkward result he is now challenging.

Klein based his decision on the fact that Esposito, like every
other county leader in every borough for decades, holds the title
of "chairman of the executive committee" of the Brooklyn organization. A strict reading of the rules of the organization, claimed
Klein, reveals no reference to the term "county leader." The language of the statute used against Esposito covers "county leaders"
and a host of other titles, but does not specifically list the title
"chairman of the executive committee." So, concluded Klein, the
law does not apply to Esposito. "He is not the county leader,"
wrote Klein, "since no such position exists."

Klein granted Esposito's motion for summary dismissal of the
case, meaning that the question of whether or not Esposito is a
county leader is so beyond doubt that it is not a "triable fact."
Though Esposito's attorney, James LaRossa, submitted an affidavit
denying that Esposito was a county leader, Esposito himself was
not even asked by Klein to do so. If Klein had asked, it would've
blown the whole house of cards. Esposito wouldn't have denied

he was county leader in a sworn statement because that would've invited a perjury prosecution.

Unless the appeal prevails and a trial before a jury is eventually ordered, Esposito may never have to admit in court that he is in fact the cigar-chomping, jowled, potbellied, gravel-voiced party boss he's been playing these 10 years. If the facts stand as Klein left them, Brooklyn will have but a shadow leader, masquerading at Foffe's Restaurant and on Court Street as a kind of historic replica of the old machine tradition. Klein has abolished the position in order to allow Meade to continue to hold it. But, after Klein's decision, all Esposito will legally hold is an obscure and bureaucratic title having something to do with an executive committee. Brooklyn, the grand old county of organization politics, will have no official leader.

When I visited Klein and his law clerk, Steve Zarkin, I asked them why Esposito hired one of the most expensive criminal lawyers in town to defend a position he didn't hold. Since the worst that could have happened to him under this statute was the forfeiture of the title "county leader"—not the loss of the executive committee chairmanship—why fight to keep a title that Klein insists doesn't exist? Seemed to me, I said, that his willingness to pay to defend the title proved he had it. Klein looked bewildered. Zarkin laughed. "To tell you the truth," said Zarkin, "we never thought of that." Apparently neither did Bob Abrams. But then again, it might not be much of a legal argument. It makes too much sense. And Klein was bent on redefining the universe, turning his courtroom into an abstraction uncomplicated by the nuisance of real life.

There was a kind of "Free Meade" hysteria beneath the surface of both the decision and my interviews with Klein, Zarkin, and others about this case. The statute used against Esposito is viewed as ancient, and the violation as technical and ill-matched to such a grand loss of power. As a result of this thinking, there were few limits on the willingness by Klein and others to invent frivolous dodges that sidestepped the obvious. But the statute is a sound and tested conflict-of-interest prohibition, and the clear intent of the 1954 legislature that adopted it was to bar political leaders able to influence racing legislation from acquiring an interest in those same racetracks.

Picking the Judge

After years of watching election cases in Brooklyn courts, I learned that the critical moment in political cases is when the judge is assigned. I recall one case where countervailing political pressures twice succeeded in changing the judge assigned and, with each switch, the preordained winner also changed. Two powerful, regular Brooklyn organizations were battling over the assignment and, once the judge was finally in place, the leaders who lost the assignment battle never even appeared for the hearing. Everyone knew how the county had decided the case would go.

In his last month in office, prodded by insistent revelations in *Newsday* concerning Esposito's interests in the racetrack, Lefkowitz brought the case against Esposito in Manhattan Supreme Court. The technical grounds he used to bypass Brooklyn courts was that the attorney general's office is in Manhattan. Lefkowitz's choice of venue was an implicit indictment of the Brooklyn judiciary. But the chances of finding an independent judge in Manhattan to handle so extraordinary a political case were only slightly better than in Brooklyn.

The Manhattan judicial district includes the Bronx, and Alvin Klein became a judge after a lifetime of politics in the Bronx regular Democratic organization. For 14 years he was personal secretary to the legendary Bronx county leader and congressman, Charles Buckley. In 1963 Buckley decided to reward Klein with a civil court judgeship. But Buckley's antagonist, then mayor Robert Wagner Sr., balked momentarily, in part because the bar association had rejected Klein as unqualified. So county leader Buckley called a meeting of the Bronx executive committee, which he chaired, and they anointed Klein as the party candidate anyway. Wagner was subsequently forced to agree. So Klein knows something about executive committees and county leaders: that's how he became a judge.

Esposito is the heir to a boss tradition symbolized by Buckley and his Manhattan ally, Carmine DeSapio. The best example of Buckley's style of leadership was his boast once at a dinner honoring the Bronx district attorney that every assistant DA in the Bronx for the previous 50 years had been recommended by his district leader. "They were not Liberals or reformers," he said, "they were honest-to-God Americans." It was a couple of decades of subservience to that kind of organizational mentality that prepared Klein for his decision in the Esposito case.

I asked Klein if he regarded his former mentor Buckley as a county leader and whether Buckley held the same executive committee chairmanship as Esposito. Klein said yes to both questions, then conceded: "He was in the same position as Esposito." Catching his own slip, he corrected himself: "I may have looked at Mr. Buckley as the county leader. . . . But suppose 50 people call somebody a boss. Suppose the newspapers call somebody a boss. That doesn't mean he's a boss." As one attorney familiar with both the case and the judge told me: "Klein couldn't do anything but decide that way. His whole life has led him to certain feelings about these institutions—the party, the leadership. No one would have to buy a contract to persuade him. The instincts of a lifetime would only permit one result."

If anyone should've known that about Alvin Klein, it was Bob Abrams. Abrams got his start as a Bronx reform assemblyman in the mid-'60s, fighting against the Buckley machine. Klein says that he and Abrams met in Bronx politics and have known each other for years. Pat Cunningham, who came out of the same Bronx club as Buckley and Klein and eventually became Bronx county leader, used to call Abrams the "Hirohito of the Bronx reform movement"—meaning its kamikaze pilot, its cutting edge. It was Abrams's archfoe Cunningham who elevated Klein to a Supreme Court judgeship at the 1972 judicial convention. Indeed, when I first talked with Abrams's aides about the Esposito case, they were openly contemptuous of Klein's machine roots and his shabby legal reasoning in this case. All of this made it only the more surprising when I later read the full court file on the case and discovered that Abrams had acquiesced in the selection of Klein.

Judge-shopping in Manhattan courts begins in something called Special Term Part I, where much civil litigation is processed. Judges are assigned to Special Term on a weekly, rotational basis by Administrative Judge Edward Dudley. As certain pretrial proceedings are filed in Special I, they are marked on the calendar of whatever judge happens to be sitting in Special Term when the papers are ready for what's called "final submission" (that is to say when both sides are ready to have the matter heard). The judge who gets a case while in Special Term may often be the judge who eventually decides it.

Alvin Klein was assigned to Special Term a total of five weeks in his first five years in the Supreme Court, far less than many of his colleagues. He has mostly worked the criminal courts, where he has never had any difficulty recognizing felons or understanding legislative intent. Klein was assigned to begin his first week of service as a Special Term judge this year on May 14. One of the first cases submitted to Klein the morning of his first day on the bench was *Abrams v. Esposito*.

What got the case before Klein was a stipulation signed on May 9 by Abrams and LaRossa, Esposito's counsel, which specified that even though the case would not be ready for submission until June 6, both sides would accept May 14 as the submission date, putting the case squarely in Klein's lap.

The scenario that preceded the stipulation makes it even more difficult to understand why Abrams agreed to it: Abrams filed the complaint on April 10, giving LaRossa the required 20 days to answer or default. The 20 days expired and LaRossa hadn't answered. So Abrams gave LaRossa a five-day extension.

LaRossa filed his motion to dismiss the complaint on May 4 and, in his papers, set the return date as May 14. LaRossa could've picked any day for the next couple of months as a return date. He picked Klein's first day. In leaving only 10 days between the filing of his motion and the date for final submission, LaRossa was giving Abrams the shortest amount of time to reply permissible under the rules of the court. Presented with this rushed deadline and having already granted LaRossa an extension, Abrams had a sound legal basis for requesting and getting an adjournment of the May 14 date, putting the case before a judge other than Klein. A check of the court calendar revealed there were several brighter prospects: Judge Oliver Sutton, whose leanings in a case like this are certainly less predictable than Klein's, was scheduled for the next week; Judge Martin Stecher, one of the city's most respected and independent jurists, was set for the second week in June, almost exactly to the day the final papers really were submitted.

Instead of seeking another date, Abrams executed the stipulation, and on May 14 the stipulation was filed with Klein, giving him custody of the motion. Because the hearing date had been adjourned by agreement, no appearances were made by either side, and there were no submissions of any papers. Abrams met the deadlines set in the stipulation and submitted his final papers opposing the motion on May 31. LaRossa didn't, and once again Abrams gave him an extension.

Abrams's press aide told me they signed the stipulation because "the alternative was to throw ourselves at the mercy of the court" and go before Klein on May 14 "with the possibility that the judge would refuse the adjournment and not give us the time we needed." This explanation, especially in view of LaRossa's delays and the short response time, seemed implausible to the lawyers I asked about it. Abrams's aide added that the attorney general didn't want to ask for an adjournment because *Newsday* editorials had criticized Lefkowitz for his delay in bringing the case, and they didn't want to open themselves to the same criticism. This argument doesn't say much for Abrams's willingness to take possible short-term flak to achieve long-term success. It is also a little silly since the stipulation was signed by Abrams and constituted a postponement anyway. Presumably *Newsday* might've been persuaded that some judge-shopping delays were justified.

Though Abrams's press aides did their best to portray Abrams as having been forced to take Klein, the judge volunteered to me that he "understood that Abrams wanted this case before me." Klein contended: "I wasn't looking for this case. They signed a stipulation to put it before me. It is my understanding that Abrams's office initiated the stipulation because Abrams knew I would decide this case solely under the law as I saw it." After hearing this, I called Abrams's office, informed them of the judge's "understanding," and asked if they'd "initiated" the stipulation. They never got back to me with an answer.

There are only two possible explanations why LaRossa and Abrams might've wanted the same judge: either Abrams miscalculated and, despite Klein's background, thought him a worthy trier of this sensitive matter, or both sides were after the same result.

Proving the Obvious

In an extensive reply-brief and affidavit, Abrams's staff managed to devote no more than a handful of paragraphs to the issue of Esposito's role as county leader. The document went on for pages on the intricacies of the Parr Meadows transactions and submitted an inch-thick stack of documents and exhibits supporting their analysis of these aspects of the case. But their only evidence establishing that Esposito is a county leader was a collection of half a dozen news clips. You don't have to be a lawyer to know the probative value of a *Daily News* story calling him a county leader. Abrams also resubmitted the evidence Lefkowitz originally offered: a 1975 state *Red Book* listing Esposito as a "county chairman." That was all Abrams could marshal to prove the pivotal fact in the case.

I thought he could have done better. I went to the archives of the Kings County Democratic organization at St. Francis College in Brooklyn. Archivist Arthur Konop said that no one from the attorney general's office had ever reviewed any of his records, including the minutes of every meeting of the executive committee from the 1880s to 1969. I started with 1969 and worked my way back to 1920. The record made it unmistakably clear that the titles of county leader and chairman of the executive committee are historically indistinguishable. In these records, every chairman of the executive committee in this century has been described—or has even described himself—as county leader.

The archives' records end when Esposito became county leader. But since then, there haven't been any rule changes that would alter the equation of titles that is already a century old. Nonetheless, I decided to try to see the recent records and called Bill Gary, secretary of the county organization (once listed by Jack Newfield among the 25 worst hacks in city government; *Voice*, December 8, 1975). When Gary did not return my calls, I went to see him at the party's Court Street headquarters. He would not let me in his office, but I did make it into the reception area, where I could see him and he could see me. We shouted back and forth at each other. Gary, who is Brooklyn borough president Howard Golden's former law partner and was editor of the *City Record* under Abe Beame, told me that the minutes of the largest county political party in the state are "not public record." He sneered, laughed, and snapped: "You're not gettin' anything outta here." (The *Voice* has asked the New York Public Interest Group and the ACLU to examine the possibility of bringing suit to unlock the apparently private records of the Brooklyn Democratic Party.)

When I questioned Abrams's office about why they hadn't pursued these records, they called back with an answer that raised new questions. An aide said that Abrams had "substantial, additional evidence" to prove Esposito's county leader role, but refused to say what the evidence was. He just described it several times as substantial and then said they didn't submit the evidence to Klein because "it was not necessary at the initial stages of the case." We all have to wonder what they are saving it for.

Of course, the evidence they chose not to use, as well as the archive records they never reviewed, cannot now be added to their appeal. The Appellate Division will only have whatever evidence Klein had. That makes it at least conceivable that the appeals judges will reach the same conclusion. Of course, they may be more willing than Klein to open the case to a common-sense nose test about Esposito's county leadership. In that case, the paucity of the evidence won't matter that much. But even if the Klein decision is reversed on appeal, Esposito has, at the very least, bought time.

A Background of Relationships

Joe Conason (*Voice*, June 26, 1978) covered the state Democratic convention that nominated Abrams for attorney general. Conason described how reformer Abrams entered the convention with 76 percent of the delegate vote, including the support of almost all the regular party leaders, and then barely held on to the majority he needed. When Governor Carey, Queens county leader Donald Manes, and upstate party leaders subtly moved away from Abrams, and some of them lined up behind Abrams's opponent, Delores Denman, Abrams was able to keep two county leaders behind him: Esposito and the Bronx's Stanley Friedman. When Conason asked Esposito about Abrams becoming a regular, Esposito laughed and said: "He's just come out of the closet, that's all." Esposito explained his persistent support of Abrams as "following his conscience."

Conason also described the increasingly close political relationship between Abrams and Bronx leader Friedman. Friedman, who has spent his career working for Brooklyn regulars like city council majority leader Tom Cuite and Mayor Beame, is the county leader closest to Meade. Their recent two-county partnership is *the* talk in regular party circles.

Judge Klein has a long-standing friendship with Friedman and Friedman's law partner, the omnipresent, sometimes Esposito counsel Roy Cohn. Klein described Cohn to me as "a close personal friend for many years" and said he'd attended several of Cohn's parties.

Klein said, however, that he never discussed the case with either Cohn or Friedman. Cohn said he'd had nothing to do with the case, but the minute I asked him about Klein, Cohn went directly to the question of Abrams: "I never had a case with the attorney general's office," claimed Cohn, "where the AG didn't have a strong say in picking the judge. He usually controls when it comes up." These shifting relationships—Klein, Cohn, Friedman, Abrams, Esposito—form the important backdrop to this case.

The other leading Bronx reformers of the Abrams period— Jay Goldin and Herman Badillo—have become, respectively, an embodiment of the bus-shelter scandal and a silenced, outcast deputy mayor. Their Manhattan and Queens reform colleagues, Manfred Ohrenstein and Jack Bronston, are now collecting legal clients such as shelter-scandal magnate Saul Steinberg. Brooklyn's reform linguist Shirley Chisholm has become a fund-raiser and political bulwark for convicted felon and former councilman Sam Wright, as well as Esposito's brightest black star. Ed Koch, the reformer who beat Carmine DeSapio 16 years ago, has a special relationship with Canarsie district leader Tony Genovesi, who comes from Esposito's home club and has been chosen by Esposito to succeed him as county leader.

And now Bob Abrams has prosecuted Esposito on a dual track. For public consumption, he refiled the Lefkowitz complaint and is now doggedly appealing his loss. But on another level, he has left a trail of subtle omissions and gentlemanly concessions which allowed Esposito to win.

Reform in this town is but a phase in the political maturation process. When those who successfully use it grow up and reach an appropriately lofty height, they allow themselves to become the compromised, but still temporarily respectable, veneer for the same power relationships they previously campaigned to "reform."

5

Amex's Tax-Grab Tower: Probing the Largest Real Estate Deal in New York History

August 30, 1983

W E'VE ALL SEEN THE AD. It starts with the old seventh-grade flashcards, everything from *discipline* to *drive*. Then comes *Shearson/American Express: Minds over Money*. In fact, at Shearson, nothing comes over money. They could have reduced their image to a single flashcard: *GREED*. Earlier this summer they closed the biggest real estate transaction in the history of the city: selling their old headquarters at 125 Broad Street to Canadian developer Olympia & York for $160 million and buying a new one to be built by O&Y for a record-smashing $478 million. Rising now, on the sandy landfill north of Battery Park that took over $100 million in state-backed bonds to create, is Amex's 51-story monument to inventive tax avoidance. Not even Karl Malden could cover what this "corporate pickpocket" is taking from city and state tax coffers to make its visionary new headquarters possible.

Probing the Biggest Real Estate Deal in New York History

The story of American Express's tax-grab tower at Battery Park City has its public culprits: the Koch administration, whose original property-tax abatements for O&Y have wound up benefiting Amex; the Battery Park City Authority (BPCA), whose holdover chairman Richard Kahan had a private financial interest involving Amex at the same time that BPCA was negotiating its Amex deal; and the Cuomo administration, which obliviously handed out $61 million in corporate tax credits to five Amex subsidiaries for relocating into the new Battery Park building.

Koch's generosity to Amex is old hat. Indeed, this time it was accidental. When the city actually adopted an overly generous abatement package for Battery Park in October 1981, Amex was not an announced interested party. That deal was between the city and Olympia & York, the developer of the four-building World Financial Center at Battery Park which subsequently sold one of the sites in the complex to Amex. The end result is that almost half of Amex's new building will get a 75 percent, 10-year tax write-off, while the other half will get a 50 percent reduction for the same period.

The man who made Koch's generosity to Amex notorious was his 1982 gubernatorial opponent, Mario Cuomo. Candidate Cuomo's Amex issue had nothing to do with this property-tax giveaway, since that has only recently been formally passed on to Amex. Instead, Cuomo repeatedly attacked Koch's role in persuading the legislature to repeal the state's 10 percent capital gains tax on large real estate transactions in March 1982. He pointed to a single beneficiary of the repeal, Amex, which announced its deal with Olympia & York right after the demise of the gains tax. He said that Amex, whose president, Sanford Weill, was a leading member of Koch's campaign finance committee, would avoid $18 million in state tax payments because of the repeal. That was 10 percent of Amex's anticipated profit on the sale of its old headquarters.

But the recent decisions of Cuomo's commerce commissioner, William Donohue, and the state's Job Incentive Board (JIB), which consisted wholly of gubernatorial appointees, have made Koch look stingy by comparison. Cuomo insists he did not know the board was giving Shearson/Amex the largest of these 10-year credits on corporate profit taxes ($35 million) until after it had been voted.

Most of the $61 million in credits pivots around Amex's move into the World Financial Center. Until Cuomo personally intervened, the JIB was prepared to give Amex even more. JIB director Llewellyn Farr told the *Voice* that he was recommending approval of Amex's full claim—which would have eventually added up to approximately $85 million. Nonetheless, Cuomo's 1982 "carte blanche for American Express" accusation against Koch now resonates with irony.

The conflict issues ensnarling Kahan, which will be detailed later in this story, are the latest front in a high-stakes development war going on at several levels—between city and state, Koch and Cuomo, Cuomo and the remnants of the Carey years. In recent weeks this war has exploded on several fronts. The mayor attacked Cuomo-backed plans for Times Square and the Queens waterfront. The focal points of Cuomo's aggression have been Kahan and former Carey secretary Bob Morgado, whom the governor recently persuaded to resign as head of the state's Housing Finance Agency. Kahan has so far steadfastly refused to resign as chairman of BPCA, a state authority, before his six-year term expires a year and a half from now. Kahan was appointed by Carey, as was one other current member of the three-member board.

Since Cuomo has been able to fill only one of the $5,000-a-year vacancies, he views it as a runaway agency. His refusal to attend ground-breaking ceremonies on BPCA projects—and Koch's eagerness to attend—is as good an indicator as any of just whose agency it is. Koch, whom Carey backed in the 1982 race against Cuomo, has inherited the Carey remnants centered around Kahan. That is one reason why a deal such as the one just completed—benefiting such Koch allies as Amex and Olympia & York, and involving such familiar Carey players as the former governor's personal attorney Charles Goldstein—could occur in the Cuomo years.

In the middle of the recent battle between Koch and the state over the selection of a development team to rebuild Times Square, the mayor asked Kahan to consider taking over the city's Public Development Corporation. (Kahan ran the state's superpower Urban Development Corporation for four years under Carey.) Not only was the Koch offer an indication of how closely Kahan is tied to the mayor; it was an escalation of Koch's attack on the development wing of the Cuomo administration. Cuomo's UDC president, Bill Stern, has been taking apart the once ballyhooed legacy of his predecessor, Kahan, for months. Stern has assailed Kahan's convention center construction management and his multimillion-dollar trough of legal fees for political firms (particularly Goldstein's). Koch's willingness to hire Kahan was a mayoral rebuttal of months of Stern attacks. Kahan declined, however, and a couple of days later the mayor and Cuomo announced a peaceful settlement of the Times Square dispute.

BPCA's president is Barry Light, who runs the authority on a day-to-day basis and is a protégé of Koch fund-raiser John Zuccotti. It was Zuccotti, who has represented World Financial

Center developer Olympia & York for years, who persuaded the city, right after the 1981 mayoral primary, to grant O&Y its overly generous property tax breaks. Zuccotti got the Koch administration to drop a tougher abatement formula recommended by an investment banking firm retained by the city. A couple of months ago, Zuccotti obtained the mayor's written consent for the BPCA deal between Amex and O&Y, a legal requirement. And it was Zuccotti's friend Light, backed by Kahan's board, who allowed O&Y to begin renegotiating its contract with the authority for all 7.5 million square feet of Battery Park commercial space six months after it was signed. (Zuccotti did not, however, directly represent O&Y in its negotiations with BPCA.)

BPCA's agreement to renegotiate these terms in early 1982 is particularly perplexing in view of the history of the deal that immediately preceded the beginning of renegotiation. BPCA said it picked O&Y in the first place—over a broad field of competitors—because of O&Y's commitment to build and own all of the buildings in the complex. Other bidders wanted to take it a building at a time. In addition, when O&Y and the city negotiated the property tax abatement in October 1981, the city's investment-banking consultants recommended severe penalties if any of the buildings were "sold, financed, or refinanced within 15 years from the commencement of the abatement." This was an attempt to prevent O&Y from a fast turnaround, simply marketing the abatements Zuccotti had won. But Zuccotti got the city to drop that requirement.

A few months after Zuccotti got the city to drop that demand, O&Y was back at the table. The renegotiation ultimately led to the severance of the Amex building from the original four-building package without penalties. In other words, O&Y was allowed to sell the flagship building to Amex at an instant profit.

Tax issues aside, BPCA's renegotiated deal was extremely beneficial to both O&Y and Amex. Under the original agreement, if O&Y wanted to separate one building from the package, they had to give BPCA a $100 million letter of credit, which it would lose should any part of the project be abandoned. The renegotiated Amex deal allowed O&Y to provide a $50 million letter. The letter of credit is the authority's principle security should O&Y default. O&Y was also released from an obligation under the initial contract to complete the construction of one office tower and certain public facilities before any part of the project could be severed.

Under the original agreement, O&Y was obligated to pay the authority several types of annual rent, each calculated according to different formulas, for the 99 years the complex would lease the Battery Park site. Amex was excused from making one type of these rental payments (percentage rent), which could have added millions to the authority's revenue.

Documents obtained by the *Voice* indicate that authority attorneys maintained in early negotiations that these payments should also be paid by Amex. BPCA backed off that position after Amex wrote Light protesting any attempt to apply the percentage-rent provisions to them. Amex contends that as an owner/user of the building it should not have to pay this rent. No one disputes that waiving it was a BPCA concession.

The foundation of the agreement, however, remained the same in both deals. O&Y, and now Amex, would own what's called a 99-year leasehold to the land—an equivalent of ownership minus the obligation to pay property taxes. Both agreed to make payments in lieu of the property taxes, but at significant discounts. At the end of the lease, the property could revert to BPCA. O&Y, and now Amex, would make both rental end tax payments to the authority, which would use them to repay its bondholders. When the bonds are repaid—in approximately 10 years—the city will finally begin to collect its tax payments.

JIB: Don't Leave Home Without It

On April 18, I got a phone call from Glenn von Nostitz, the eagle-eyed aide to West Side state senator Franz Leichter. He told me he'd just gotten the calendar for the next morning's Job Incentive Board meeting and discovered on it a proposed $50 million tax credit for Shearson/Amex, ostensibly to entice them to stay in New York. Von Nostitz was upset because Amex had announced with great fanfare more than a year earlier that it was staying in the state, indeed that it would be moving into the World Financial Center. It was that announcement, including Amex's self-publicized $180 million profit on the sale of its old headquarters as the trade-off for moving into the Financial Center, that provoked Cuomo's campaign attack about the company's Koch-aided tax avoidance. Von Nostitz said he'd tried to alert Cuomo to the agenda item but had been unable to get through.

When Cuomo returned my call, I told him about the Amex item, said he'd criticized Koch for giving the company $18 million, and asked if he was really going to give them $50 million. Cuomo said he did not even know Amex had applied, much less that an approval was calendared. He said his instructions to Commerce Commissioner Donohue, who chaired the board, were to grant only those abatements that met a strict interpretation of the statute. Cuomo had already prevailed on the legislature to abolish the JIB—a tax gouge raided for years by so many corporations that it had become a scandal even the Business Council and the Republican state senate couldn't defend. But the legislature and

Cuomo had given the board until June 30 to finish its business. The last three months would be box office.

"Even the liberal *Village Voice* wouldn't suggest," said an irritated Cuomo, "that the governor should instruct his appointees on an independent board how they should vote on a matter before them."

An hour later, the governor's secretary, Michael DelGiudice, called to read a statement that the governor had abruptly canceled the JIB meeting and had instructed Donohue to carefully review all applications. Von Nostitz had also alerted other reporters, and Cuomo had been besieged by questions. (DelGiudice, who used to work for Shearson/Amex, assured me that he had no involvement in the JIB-Amex issue. Every Battery Park, JIB, or other state official I've interviewed concerning the Amex transaction has confirmed DelGiudice's distance.)

The JIB did not meet again until May 24. Von Nostitz noted that Shearson was not on the agenda. But he called the JIB the day before the meeting just to make certain and was told that Shearson was not scheduled for consideration. The next day, however, shortly before the meeting, the JIB called back and said that Shearson had indeed been placed on the agenda. There wasn't time for Leichter to do anything but rush over to the meeting and protest. By his own account, JIB director Farr was prepared to recommend the $50 million grant in April, but dropped it to $35 million in May. He says he met with Donohue the morning of the May meeting, explained the changes in the recommendation, and was instructed by Donohue to calendar it.

At the meeting, the $35 million was approved for creating 950 new jobs, principally by expanding into the World Financial Center. The $15 million, for the 3,300 jobs Shearson claimed it was considering moving out of the state but decided to keep here, was denied. The JIB rejection of what is called Amex's "job retention" claim was based on its ruling that Amex had "not demonstrated that an out-of-state relocation" was "feasible."

The May decision was essentially repeated when four other Amex subsidiaries—Travel, International Banking, Leasing, and the parent American Express Corporation—came before the board at its final meeting on June 27. By then a fully alerted Cuomo had put Leichter and von Nostitz at a table with the JIB staff, jointly reviewing each application. Some Leichter arguments resulted in reduction of credits; some were rejected. The retention claims of these Amex companies, like Shearson's, were denied. However, they were approved for creating another 744 jobs, all at the Financial Center. If the numbers on these applications hold up when the new Amex building is completed in 1985, these four companies will get $2.6 million a year for 10 years in reductions on taxes. This combined $61 million for Shearson and the other four is a conservative figure. The credit is actually for a fixed percentage of whatever corporate-profit tax they owe and assumes no increase in profits. All the Amex companies are enjoying quarterly profit bursts. That means they'll get the same percentage break on higher profit taxes due over the years.

While the Amex "job retention" theory was a hoax, exposed and rejected solely because of watchdog Leichter, the job creation credits granted were also grossly inflated. Take American Express Leasing Corporation, which got an $11 million credit for allegedly expanding by 37 employees when it moves to Battery Park. Twenty of the new employees are secretaries. The state could directly pay these secretaries $30,000 a year for 10 years and save money. Some companies were turned down at the June meeting in part because there was no real connection between the investment decisions that were made and the jobs that were accidentally stimulated. If ever there was an application that fit that description, it was the Leasing Corporation's.

There was another possible basis for denying the Leasing Corporation, namely that there was no tangible evidence that it was moving into the Battery Park building at all. The four other Amex companies cosigned all the agreements with Olympia & York to buy the new headquarters. Only the Leasing Corporation, which is a mere taxpaying shell for the banking subsidiary, did not. Amex told the *Voice* it was "an oversight."

A curious coincidence in three of the other Amex applications produced additional tax-break dividends. The travel subsidiary pays next to no franchise taxes, only $5,000 a year. The banking and parent companies pay a combined $2.8 million a year. The applications for the three firms indicated that banking and the parent company had lost hundreds of jobs in the year immediately before applying. The travel company had gained hundreds. That meant that banking and the parent company would have fewer jobs at the start of the application period, a lower bottom line. So they could claim they were creating more jobs, giving them a higher percentage credit. Since the travel company started with a higher number of existing jobs, they claimed less job creation and got a lower percentage credit. But travel pays so little taxes anyway, the percentage they got hardly mattered to Amex. Amex admitted to the JIB that the reason for the drop in the number of parent company employees was because some were shifted into the travel company. The JIB would not have had to question Amex's motives to reduce some of the tax benefits gained to this musical-chairs game with personnel numbers.

The Shearson application also contained its excesses. It sought credits both for moving to the World Financial Center and for moving to an unspecified site somewhere in the city. JIB director Farr admitted to the *Voice* that in its 15-year history, the board had never before approved an application for an unspecified location. "It's blank check without an address," said Farr. "We don't approve credits that are that speculative." Farr says this one was approved because it was part of a package with a specific site like the World Financial Center. But when an applicant doesn't even list the optional sites he's considering, there is no way for the JIB to determine just how real the application is.

A vigilant Cuomo administration could have found ways to reduce its carte blanche for American Express. Just by comparing the widely published price tag on Amex's new building at Battery Park ($478 million) with the total eligible investment—property plus equipment—claimed on the five applications ($993 million), it could have smelled something wrong. New equipment alone could not account for such a wide disparity (indeed, $78 million in new equipment to be built by O&Y was figured into the sales price of the building).

But the JIB gave Amex credit for every job created that it claimed. JIB accepted Amex's investment assertions without question, even when the numbers differed massively between the initial application and subsequent letters. Farr and Mary Steffan, the Commerce Department counsel who reviewed the Amex applications, repeatedly emphasized in *Voice* interviews that the state tax department will have to certify Amex's numbers when the relocations are complete. But Leichter's probes have proven that the tax review has been as casual as Commerce's initial study. The tax review will, however, give the governor one final shot at a fair assessment of Amex's claims before state benefits begin to flow.

Beating the Gains Tax

A month before Cuomo took office, Amex started getting nervous about its still-pending transaction at Battery Park. The deal announced back in March had yet to occur, and the candidate who wanted to tax the profits on that transaction would soon become governor. So, Amex's lawyers opened a meeting with O&Y and the Battery Park Authority on December 8, 1982, with the statement that they "wished to expedite conclusion of the current negotiations in order to accomplish a closing prior to year end 1982." According to memos on file at the authority, the lawyer was equally blunt about the reason: "to avoid incurrence of any increase in the transfer tax or capital gains tax effected by New York city or state." The four BPCA representatives at the meeting, all at least technically there to defend state interests, were not recorded as having objected to the goal of beating the tax. One quibbled with the timetable on purely technical grounds.

Throughout early 1983, while a gains tax was discussed in Albany as a new source of city or state revenue, BPCA and the private parties rushed against an unknown deadline. Piles of documents reviewed by the *Voice* confirm the rush. All of the parties say tax considerations were "not the motivating factor." By March every piece of the complicated transaction was in place. A March 15 meeting was called for 9 a.m., with the closing planned right after the board approved the package. But Kahan was the only board member to show up. A phone hookup was arranged with one absent member, creating an invisible quorum, but the lawyers confessed at the start of the meeting that Ma Bell could not make a public meeting legal. Kahan and the absent member voted for the package anyway and said they'd reconvene on March 23 to "confirm" their approval.

There was another legal reason why Kahan should have slowed down, one he mentioned only to Light early in March. He had his own private real estate deal going with Amex. Kahan and Light had quietly consulted an outside counsel about whether this simultaneous transaction barred Kahan from voting. Though the counsel expressed what Light concedes was "serious concern" about the issue and said everything should be put in writing before he could give an opinion, the two plunged ahead without an opinion. Kahan's possible conflict was not disclosed, even to the other two board members, when they actually appeared to vote on March 23.

At this second meeting, Kahan asked the only question posed by a board member before the transaction was unanimously approved. The minutes indicate that Kahan "asked what the status of the capital gains tax law was" and that BPCA general counsel Tom Sullivan "replied that it had not become effective yet."

In between these two panic meetings, Light signed an agreement on March 18, okaying several pounds of binding documents, even though he was not even authorized by a resolution of his board to do so. He says he did so to "stop the lawyers from lawyering, and lock up the deal." The documents were placed in escrow and turned over to O&Y's lawyers. The new Cuomo capital gains law became effective exactly 10 days later. The first time Light formally notified the governor's budget office of the deal was in a letter dated March 28, the magical starting point for the new tax. Light did not mention in the letter that an escrow closing had already occurred. The reason he wrote to budget at all was because the deal had yet to be approved by the Public Authorities Control Board (PACB), an oversight amalgam of the legislature and the budget office whose mandate is to determine that there are sufficient state funds to pay for a project.

After the approval in late April, Amex attorney David Hershberg and an O&Y counsel wrote long letters to the state tax department. As Hershberg put it, the essence of its case was that "a written contract was entered into on March 18," before the effective date of the Cuomo gains tax. "The statute does not preclude the exemption of written contracts that have conditions," argues Hershberg, since these escrow contracts were obviously conditioned on the PACB and BPCA votes. "In fact, all contracts have conditions." Hershberg concluded: "Let me assure you that avoidance of the gains tax was not Amex's motive in the handling of this transaction." Another Amex counsel interviewed by the *Voice*, Mark Cohen, was somewhat more candid. "Of course it was our intention to avoid the tax," he said. In any event, Cuomo's tax department rejected the Amex position, imposed a $9 million tax, and is now faced with the first of what may become several Amex legal challenges to the ruling. Cohen seems confident they will prevail.

Incredibly, while Amex is telling the state tax department that the deal was closed on March 18, the company's applications for JIB benefits contend that the deal was uncertain right up to June 27. The standard for any claim of jobs retained is that there is a possibility the jobs may leave the state. If Amex had closed on the Financial Center, an out-of-state move was no longer feasible. On February 23, in answer to questions raised by the JIB, Cohen filed a sworn statement with the agency "under the penalties of perjury" asserting that an "out of state relocation of the proposed facility continues to be a practicable alternative." The only out-of-state locations mentioned in any Amex application are Piscataway, Morristown, and New Brunswick. The *Voice* contacted the mayors and chambers of commerce in two of the three towns, and the economic development and city planning officials of the third. No one had ever heard that Amex was considering moving there. In conversations with the JIB that continued right up to June 27, months after the escrow closing and even after the final closing on June 15, Cohen concedes he never updated or corrected his February assertion. If an out-of-state option was ever the truth, not even Cohen could argue it was true on June 27.

Shearson vice president Thomas Gengler wrote two March letters to the JIB vigorously pressing the board to put Shearson's application on its April agenda. He wrote on March 25—after the escrow closing—that "the reason for this request is that a Job Incentive Credit can be a material consideration in a decision that Shearson is now finalizing." He said that the World Financial Center deal "should have all the final approvals and signings in the near future," but "not before the Board meeting." The Public Authorities Control Board vote on the Amex contracts was scheduled for three days after the JIB meeting. The final closing was slated to follow immediately. When Cuomo abruptly canceled the April JIB meeting, the final closing was postponed. The deadline written into the escrow agreement was extended another month. Even with these extensions, four of the five Amex JIBs were approved after every one of the hundreds of closing documents was unconditionally executed.

Clearly, Amex wants to eat its cake and have it too. The truth is that Amex never would have moved anything but its most back-office operations out of the state. The retention claim was always a hoax. Amex was committed to the World Financial Center move before it even applied for credits. Despite that commitment, it made itself taxable under the Cuomo gains tax by flirting with the terms of the Financial Center deal throughout 1982, perhaps confident that the new governor would be Ed Koch and that the tax side of the deal could only get better.

Their irreconcilable claims to two different state agencies on the same transaction cannot be explained away, as Cohen tried with the *Voice*. He said the gains tax was for the move out of the old headquarters. And that the JIBs were for the moves into the new headquarters. These were "two separate transactions," he argued, so one could've closed and the other remained uncertain. But Cohen's argument is belied by Amex's own letters to the tax department, which argue that the two transactions "would proceed together." It is the sort of facile reasoning that may provoke knowing, supportive smiles at Amex board meetings. But no one in the rest of the world would believe that Amex could have had one deal without the other.

A Tale of Two Kahans

Richard Kahan, at the age of 36, was already the most powerful public developer since Robert Moses. He had the public entities building Times Square, Battery Park, and the convention center under his control. His reign at UDC had turned it into a statewide economic development engine, creating everything from tax-exempt luxury hotels in Midtown Manhattan to the Carrierdome in Syracuse. It wasn't just his construction techniques that were on the fast track; it was his personal life as well. His relationship with Amanda Burden, the wife of Warner executive and major Carey fund-raiser Steve Roes, was the sizzling talk of the town. In June of 1982 Kahan left UDC and joined the private development firm of Tishman Speyer. The only piece of his once vast public empire that he hung onto was Battery Park. His term as chairman would not end until January 1985.

The Kahan I interviewed last week is a scaled-down version of the Kahan who dominated public development throughout the second Carey administration. To begin with, he is 15 pounds lighter. On a small frame he looks simultaneously lean and drained. It is not just the public beating he has been taking from Cuomo aide Bill Stern that has taken its toll. It is the loss of his job with Tishman Speyer. The timing and circumstances of his departure were very much part of the conflict issue I went to interview him about. In his East Side co-op and at a nearby restaurant, we traveled several times through the intricacies of that issue. He seemed to realize the shortcomings of his own defense—not that he believes he had a real conflict. But he almost had to concede that the full facts do create the appearance of one, and that his and Light's handling of the issue was at best sloppy. At worst, it begins to look like a cover-up.

The place to start is with Kahan's official version of events, a version he now concedes was inaccurate. Kahan wrote Light a letter, dated March 28, after he had voted twice to approve the Amex deal. The essence of the letter is an admission that at the same time as the Battery Park bargaining, Tishman was engaged in ongoing negotiations with Amex, trying to persuade Amex to become a major tenant in a project at 375 Hudson Street (a parking lot where Tishman intends to construct a "high-technology" office building). Kahan wrote: "I am a participant in this project and will receive a financial benefit from it when completed." In his letter, Kahan contended that there was no conflict, however, because he was not involved in Tishman's negotiations with Amex, nor in the authority's direct negotiations with the company. Since the letter, he has added a new argument. Kahan now says that as of mid-February, he was no longer associated with Tishman, merely occupying an office there (he does not even do that now). He says that he also lost his financial interest in Tishman's potential deal with Amex as of February. This reconstructed version of events means that he had no conflicting interest when he voted in March on Amex's Battery Park transaction. He cannot explain why his own letter was so wrong about where he was working.

His argument that he was not involved in the authority's bargaining with Amex is absurd: only he could approve the deal, and Light conceded that he kept board members fully abreast of the details by phone. His contention that he did not directly participate in Tishman's discussions with Amex is meaningless. At any rate, he admits now that he did have something to do with trying to find tenants for the Hudson building, though not specifically with Amex.

What no one can dispute is that Amex's interest in the Hudson building was inextricably linked to its Battery Park move. Amex's applications for JIB benefits refer to an unspecified location where it plans to locate the company's computer center, and possibly its operations facility. These moves, according to the applications, were part of the package of relocations necessitated by the sale of the old headquarters and the acquisition of the Financial Center building.

Kahan's letter was forwarded to Martin Richman, an attorney with the firm of Barrett, Smith. Richman was the lawyer Light had consulted by phone in early March when Kahan first raised the issue verbally. He was the attorney who expressed "serious concern" about the questions raised and said he needed the facts in writing. But he got the facts in writing only after Kahan voted twice. Richman's firm received $3.3 million in legal fees from UDC subsidiaries in the Kahan years, but only $6,000 of it came from Battery Park. The only time BPCA used the firm was in 1981. Light and Kahan justified their decision to turn to Richman—despite the authority's limited prior use of him—by pointing to his prior handling of UDC conflict issues. In fact,

Richman had been in the middle of an earlier UDC brouhaha. Former UDC chairman Richard Ravitch had simultaneously used Richman as both counsel to UDC and counsel to his private construction company HRH. And when Ravitch wanted UDC to build a project beneficial to an HRH project across the street, Richman made the argument to an oversight board that Ravitch had no conflict.

After getting Kahan's letter, Richman recommended, in conversations with BPCA officials, that the board take the vote again, this time without Kahan. So on April 12 the board met again and for the third time passed the deal. This time Kahan abstained. A highly selective version of the Kahan conflict was presented to the other board members. According to Cuomo's only appointee on the board, Richard Sirota, who was present but not yet legally empowered to vote, the Kahan letter itself was never turned over to the members (Light says it was). The in-house counsel's memo given to the board deleted Kahan's admission about his financial interest. Perhaps more importantly, it deleted Kahan's embarrassing explanation for why he felt compelled to vote on the project, namely that "my participation is necessary to have a quorum, since one of the three member positions is presently vacant." In fact, there was no vacancy on the board and could not legally be. The outgoing board member, John Hennessy, would not step down until Cuomo's new member was approved by the senate. He had even voted at the March 23 meeting. Richman says that Light had used the same argument with him back in the beginning of March. Light and Kahan were making billion-dollar public decisions and apparently couldn't count to three.

According to Sirota, Richman's letter referring to Light's clumsy count was not given to the board. Neither, says Sirota, was the $7,300 bill Richman submitted for his brief opinion letter.

Neither was the decision to increase the $7,500, three-year-old ceiling on Richman's retainer with the authority by $10,000, a postopinion increase. Light says they will come before the board in September. Richman did not write his opinion letter until two weeks after the third vote in early April. He found no conflict and said the March vote was "valid and proper." Nonetheless, he said he urged and concurred in the decision to vote again, without Kahan, in April. That, he said, will "put to rest any possible subsequent questioning," about "an appearance of conflicting interest." He cited the applicable sections of the public officers law, including one that barred Kahan from "giving any reasonable basis for the impression that any person can improperly influence him or unduly enjoy his favor." Confronted with that language, neither Kahan nor Richman would actually contend that it didn't precisely describe Kahan's circumstances. Doesn't the fact that, at the same time, he had a financial interest in a private project with Amex form a "reasonable basis" for the impression that Amex might "enjoy his favor"?

This argument does not even have to rest just on his March votes. On October 21, 1982, Kahan voted to permit Amex to take ownership of the building and to permit O&Y to separate the Amex parcel from the comprehensive package. The resolution authorized Light and the attorneys to commence negotiations with that as a goal. In his letter about the conflict, Kahan contended that negotiations between Tishman and Amex didn't start until after that October meeting. He now admits that he was wrong about that claim too.

Jerry Speyer told the *Voice* that the Amex discussions started months before that (he also said they were due to his own close relationships with Amex real estate decision makers). That means that when Kahan voted in October, he was already a participant and a potential beneficiary of Tishman's related Amex transaction. He made no disclosure, not even to Light, at that time. His own letter stresses the significance of this October vote in setting the parameters of the Amex deal with BPCA.

Kahan's inaccurate presentation of the date that Tishman's Amex approach began, coupled with all the other mysterious and secret outrages surrounding the handling of the conflict question, adds to the stench that hangs over this deal. Neither Kahan nor Speyer will offer an explanation for his abrupt departure from Tishman, seven months after he began and shortly after the company gave him a Christmas bonus (a piece of a Chicago building). BPCA repeatedly withheld documents from me about the Kahan conflict. Their attorneys changed the wording of Kahan's letter when they cited it in their own opinion memos. The Kahan letter refers repeatedly to events that had already happened as if they were yet to happen. The case has all the earmarks of a cover-up.

It now appears that Amex will move its computer operations elsewhere. The company is already pressing the city for tax breaks to move, not to Hudson Street, but to the site of the Brinks truck garage near the World Trade Center. If Tishman doesn't get Shearson, whatever conflict existed will produce no payoff. But conflicts are a state of mind at a given moment. Battery Park is Kahan's agency. He made Light its president after Light worked for him at UDC. Kahan's agency gave Amex a great deal. The public and the authority's bondholders were entitled to a single-minded representation of their interests without complications. They didn't get it. The appearances are disturbing enough that they might have gotten the opposite: a trade-off of public benefit for potential personal gain.

Cuomo's Next Move?

The tax-grab items detailed here are hardly the total picture. I have not described Amex's proud plan for turning its $90 million gain on the sale of its old building into a loss for federal tax purposes. Amex announced that it will dump low-yield municipal bonds at a loss to eat up the gains earned on the building's sale. I have not mentioned the state sales tax exemptions sought and won by Amex.

The Amex attitude about its own behavior, expressed by corporate vice president Ida Schmertz, is that it did the city and state "a favor" by staying here. Kahan and Light's attitude is that they turned a desolate landfill into a booming commercial development. There is some truth in both of these contentions. Kahan has what one faithful former employee described as a schizoid personality: "an almost radical, sixtyish sense of social responsibility half of the time and a great attraction to the glamour of the powerful the other half." Despite the recent revisionist history about him, and despite my own opposition to many of the projects he built, he was an effective public professional throughout his UDC years. This conflict suggests he couldn't handle the combined pressure of dual public and private roles.

The Battery Park project itself was a Rockefeller fantasy. It began because of the need to find somewhere to dump the ground excavated from under the World Trade Center. It is unmistakably the most important development project occurring in the city today. It is a new city where thousands will live and work. The expenditure and tax forfeiture of public dollars is creating it. Richard Kahan made all that possible, when he operated solely as a public servant. Each new decision there should be made by those with an insulated, publicly motivated conscience. Each decision should be integrated with total state tax and development policy. It cannot remain a fiefdom, run by the remnants of another era caught between private and public interests.

Research assistance by Todd Friedman and Janna Moore

6

How Ed Koch Handed Over City Hall

February 4, 1986

The labyrinthine corruption scandal reported here dominated the end of Koch's mayoralty and formed the basis of Barrett's first book, *City for Sale*, coauthored with his mentor Jack Newfield. —Ed.

After eight years of charisma and four years of the clubhouse, why not try competence.

—Koch slogan, 1977 mayoral race

AMBITIOUS PEOPLE OFTEN BECOME the thing they hate. History is full of young idealists obsessing about some entrenched evil and then replicating that evil when they come to power. The Ayatollah has become the Shah. George Bush spent the 1970s fighting right-wing extremists and now he wraps himself in extremist icons like William Loeb, Jerry Falwell, and Ferdinand Marcos. And Ed Koch, who first achieved fame by conquering Tammany Hall boss Carmine DeSapio in the early 1960s, has become Carmine DeSapio.

Not the DeSapio who later went to prison, but the DeSapio of the early 1960s and late '50s, who Koch opposed as the personification of patronage, conflicts of interest and cynical abuse of the public trust. Koch has also become the Abe Beame he defeated for mayor in 1977, the incumbent he accused of abdicating governance to the political machines.

This city is now witnessing the start of the largest municipal scandal since the revelation of police corruption in the early 1970s. It's not just that Donald Manes is accused of extortion, or that the deputy director of the Parking Violations Bureau, Geoffrey Lindenauer, has been arrested for taking a bribe in a public urinal. Bronx Democratic leader Stanley Friedman is also under criminal investigation by US Attorney Rudolph Giuliani, Manhattan District Attorney Robert Morgenthau, and the Securities and Exchange Commission. The *Voice* has learned that in December Friedman dumped a large amount of his stock in Citisource—the company for which he got a $22 million Parking Violations Bureau contract in 1984— apparently because he was tipped off about the federal investigation.

The Friedman probes focus on allegations of insider trading and fraudulent misrepresentation of his role in Citisource. (No one has so far suggested that Manes's crew at PVB had the temerity to charge Friedman for *his* contract; it may have been the only freebie Lindenauer, et al. handled). Friedman and Manes are the two county leaders closest to Koch and have been bulwarks of support for his last three races, including the 1982 gubernatorial primary when Manes rejected Queens' hometown candidate, Mario Cuomo, in favor of Koch.

The recent conviction of Queens Supreme Court judge William Brennan for taking payoffs to fix cases from mob defendants, and the separate federal probe of Richard Rubin, the executive secretary of the Queens Democratic party, for taking kickbacks by check for court guardianships and receiverships, suggest that the county party is an organized crime enterprise in a literal sense. The mayor suggests that he thought Friedman and Manes were altar boys until this burst of revelations, but at least two prior Manes-recommended city appointees and one Friedman associate have been involved in similar scams.

The Taxi and Limousine commissioner from Queens, Herb Ryan, pleaded guilty to taking a bribe from an undercover agent in 1982, and Nick Sands, who was apparently recommended by Manes for mayoral appointment to the board of the city's Public Development Corporation, wound up surviving nine bullets in a mob hit and was convicted twice of embezzlement. Not as lucky as Sands was Rick Mazzeo, the Friedman and Roy Cohn–connected distributor of multimillion-dollar leases for city-owned parking lots, newsstands, and other concessionaires. During the first couple of years of the Koch administration, Mazzeo, who managed to put $564,934 into a private company he started while a $15,000-a-year civil servant, ran the real estate section of Marine & Aviation, a subsidiary (like PVB) of the city's Department of Transportation. Mazzeo was convicted and sent to jail once by the feds; but when he faced a second indictment in 1983, his body was discovered in the trunk of a car parked in Brooklyn.

The PVB brand of civic service is inevitable when the mayor awards whole city agencies or sections of them to DeSapio's descendants—party bosses like Friedman, Manes, former Brooklyn honcho Meade Esposito, Staten Island's Nick LaPorte, as well as their top soldiers such as South Bronx kingpin Ramon Velez. Contracting out to the clubhouses is the root cause of the current sensational revelations. A mayor who does not recognize that these career party businessmen are mere vendors of the public weal is wearing blinders.

The continuation of clubhouse patronage was a clause in the Faustian compact that Koch made with much of the city's old-line party leadership during the runoff campaign of 1977, when he got Esposito, Friedman, and others to back him against Mario Cuomo. He's renewed that pact each time he's run, always with the support of every county leader but Manhattan's. Koch's acceptance of clubhouse patronage is what opened the door to corruption, because it based hiring on connections and party loyalty rather than merit. It is hardly surprising that these appointees then began to award contracts and leases based on the same considerations that got them their jobs.

It was Meade Esposito, for example, who gave Koch his worst previous scandal: Alex Liberman, the city's director of leasing, who was the "Man of the Year" in Esposito's Canarsie club and who (almost unnoticed by the media) pleaded guilty in 1984 to extorting more bribes—$2.5 million—than anyone ever previously indicted by a federal prosecutor anywhere in America. Memos filed by both sides in the Liberman case concluded that Liberman "would have been unable to wield such tremendous arbitrary authority without the complicity of others in the Brooklyn Democratic machine." Yet in his current book, *Politics*, Koch describes Esposito in loving terms as someone who "has always been helpful to me," and his administration is still filled with other Esposito appointees. "After Koch was elected, he called us to City Hall," Esposito once told reporters. "He gave us some doughnuts. The powder came off on my pants and he said he wanted to work with us. He catered to us, in patronage, whatever."

The Koch administration has also given Esposito contracts. The prime clients of his small insurance company are city contractors, and they've made Esposito a rich man. "I've been very successful in business," Esposito told the *News* in 1980, "and I owe it all to politics."

No Goodies for Crooks

Throughout the Manes explosion, Koch repeatedly said that the public would forgive anything except criminality. Since the mayor believes he is the embodiment of the public's common sense, he meant that *he* was comfortable with anyone but a crook. That is now the moral standard for a mayor who spearheaded a crusade against DeSapio long before DeSapio became a felon.

The most disgraceful and self-serving indicator of Koch's no-rap-sheet heroes was his embrace of Staten Island {borough president} Ralph Lamberti, who he endorsed for re-election in 1985 even after his own Investigations Commissioner Pat McGinley had publicly reported that Lamberti had committed five misdemeanor violations of the city charter, one of which provided for the forfeiture of his office. A Staten Island grand jury ultimately refused to indict Lamberti, but the record is clear that Lamberti greased the delivery of a 50-acre parcel of prime city-owned land to a developer who was his own private partner. The mayor described Lamberti as "an honest man," a "partner," and a "friend," adding that he was "shocked" by McGinley's charges. McGinley must've been shocked that Koch had become Lamberti's leading media character witness.

Ed Koch is not personally corrupt. And he hasn't turned his entire government over to hacks. Fritz Schwarz, Stanley Brezenoff, Terrence Moan, Henry Stern, Robert Wagner Jr., Gordon Davis, Joseph Hynes, Haskell Ward, and James McNamara are just some of the honest public servants he's empowered. He's appointed many judges of distinction.

But at the same time, he's given the clubhouses custody of agencies like the mammoth Department of Transportation and the Taxi and Limousine Commission. He's given them hidden little shops, where the leases and contracts that feed machines are processed, like PVB, Liberman's leasing office inside the Department of General Services, Mazzeo's Marine & Aviation, some Tax and Planning Commission appointments, the Civil Service Commission, and pieces of such key, obscure entities as Ports & Terminals, the Public Development Corp., and the Board of Standards & Appeals. And then he's looked the other way.

The other way has most often been somewhere in the direction of a mirror. Koch could always look at himself and see clean hands. He could stand in front of a Gracie Mansion mirror with his arms raised triumphantly above his head and know he had done no wrong. He could mistake himself for his government. And then he could turn on the tube. His addiction is power, not money. Lesser politicians develop an appetite for gambling, drugs, women, and a lavish lifestyle. Koch lives on the narcissistic need to watch himself every night on the television news. To be on the news, he has to be in power. And he has long been prepared to allow others to do just about anything if they would permit him to keep power. That is the bargain that is only now beginning to haunt him, because finally it, too, is playing on the television news.

He has manufactured his press conference answers. I-am-not-responsible, he sometimes intimates, because I only appoint commissioners. The commissioners hire everyone else. This is a myth. Mayoral assistant John LoCicero has been publicly identified for eight years as the mayor's patronage chief. What has he been doing all that time if the mayor's claim is to be believed? And what has the best kept secret of the Koch years—Joe DeVincenzo—been doing?

DeVincenzo is identified in the Greenbook as a special assistant to the mayor, but no one except people who hustle city jobs has ever heard of him. A leftover from the Beame administration, DeVincenzo occupies a basement office in City Hall. He sits on the dais of the Brooklyn Democratic organization dinner dance. City personnel officials say he is in charge of something called the mayor's talent bank. One former Koch commissioner told the *Voice*: "I couldn't hire anyone without the Joe D. letter." He has been processing jobs for Koch—everywhere in city government—since Koch became mayor. A half dozen sources have told the *Voice* about having to go to Joe D., even for raises.

Remember Candidate Koch, running against Cuomo, in 1982? Remember how he decided to play hardball after Cuomo rapped him in the first debate? Remember that Koch made a TV commercial about Cuomo's aide Bill Cabin, who had hidden five no-shows on the lieutenant governor's payroll, copped the checks himself, and gotten indicted? Remember Koch snarling that he ought to be impeached if he ever carried five phantoms on his payroll? The same Koch is now saying he never met Geoff Lindenauer. He says he neither selected nor knew the PVB crew—an entire agency handling millions in city funds. He says he just looked at the revenue bottom line and saw it going up. He says he always thought Stanley Friedman was in the holy water business. He says it's "news to me" that Anthony Ameruso, the transportation commissioner who oversees PVB and several other past and future scandals, is identified with the Brooklyn Democratic organization. He says it's also news that Ameruso has stacked his agency with hacks from every county party.

Our mayor, after 25 years of public life and two books about politics, is a babe in the woods, a shock absorber. He can only shake his head in surprised chagrin. He can only argue that the question is not whether his government *caused* this scandal but what it is now doing to cover it up.

A few lines have been elided here because the microfilm was illegible. —Ed.

The mere existence of the Michael Dowd contract, earning $2 million from the city in six years, is the best evidence of just how much the mayor will tolerate to satisfy powerful friends. Koch names Dowd in his own book as the man who managed Cuomo's 1977 race and hired a private detective to probe Koch's sex life. Yet the mayor who says he never forgets a slight has, indirectly, been making Dowd rich. Once Manes was given an agency, he was allowed to reward whomever he would reward. The legendary long memory gave way to Manes's large pockets. Everything else dissolves when Koch's power needs are at stake.

The Koch Machine

Pol-businessmen like Stanley Friedman are so arrogantly confident that the voters will never get in the way of their public profits that they put themselves up front in the collection business, seemingly the last place a politician would want to be. The letters we get dunning us to pay our parking tickets have become the unlikely prism through which we can all finally see, with sudden clarity, the nature of our leaders and our government. But PVB is only one of the machine haunts in the Koch years. Here are a few others:

- Top Koch officials have been leaking stories that Transportation Commissioner Anthony Ameruso is on his way out for at least the last four years. They said it because they thought it was true. Then, magically, Ameruso would ride out the rumors. He was appointed commissioner when Koch became mayor. Koch ignored the advice of his own screening panel, which opposed the appointment of Ameruso, who comes out of the Boro Park club of Brooklyn beep {borough president} and county leader Howard Golden. His other rabbis are Esposito and Bronx congressman Mario Biaggi. Ameruso not only survived the Mazzeo scandal during the first couple of Koch years, he then went job hunting for the discredited Mazzeo in other city agencies.

Ameruso was the target of two 1981 probes by the State Investigation Commission. SIC reports obtained by the *Voice* (and written about in a 1983 NYC column) say that the investigation "focused on the awarding by the NYC DOT of the midtown tow-away contracts to TRW Transportation Inc." and on the granting of "no parking anytime signs" to the mob-owned SPQR Restaurant in Little Italy.

A few sentences here were illegible. —Ed.

At a press conference last week, Koch emphatically denied that he'd ever been urged to appoint or retain Ameruso by any Brooklyn political leader. But Esposito told the authors of *I, Koch* (a biography written by the *Times*, *News*, and *UPI* bureau chiefs): "There were rumblings that Tony was going to be dumped. I saved him by telling Koch that he's my guy, he's a good man, don't drop him."

- Taxi and Limo chairman Jay Turoff, a Brooklyn regular out of the Bensonhurst club led by Howie Golden aide

Marcy Feigenbaum, was originally appointed on the final day of the Beame administration in 1977. But Koch reappointed him in 1982, making him his own. The SIC is currently in the midst of a year-long probe of Turoff, investigating a possible hidden interest he may have in a car service and an allegation that he has several lines of credit in Atlantic City casinos. Other Koch appointees to the nine-member commission include party regulars Douglas McKeon from the Bronx and John Russell Sr. from Staten Island.

• Housing Preservation and Development commissioner Anthony Gliedman is an active member, coordinating election day activities, of Canarsie's Thomas Jefferson Club in Brooklyn. He is close to both Esposito and district leader Tony Genovesi. "I recommended him for a job," Esposito told the authors of *I, Koch* about Gliedman. "I spoke to LoCicero and told him to take care of this guy because he's good." When another club member, Mo Silver, lost his state job in 1983 and went to work for the nonprofit Wildcat Services Corporation, he immediately began negotiating new contracts for Wildcat with Gliedman, who employs his wife, Sheila Silver, another club-member. Gliedman's agency has also delivered countless housing projects and community consultant contracts to neighborhood groups controlled by machine loyalists including multi-million-dollar sponsorship deals to hacks like former city councilman Luis Olmedo, who recently got out of jail on federal extortion charges, and Ramon Velez, the well-heeled prince of Bronx poverty who is Friedman's prime minority property.

A few paragraphs that discuss allegations against Ramon Velez were elided here. —Ed.

- Two days before Manes was discovered on Grand Central Parkway*, Koch named a new chairman of the screening panel that recommends city marshals to him for appointment. The chairman, Peter Rivera, who says he has a "friendly and cordial relationship" with Velez, is a contributor to Velez's sidekick, Assemblyman Hector Diaz, and represented Velez's wholly-owned subsidiary, City Councilman Rafael Castenaira Colon, in an election law matter last year. Rivera's partner represented a Velez backer charged with assaulting the wife of a candidate running against Colon. Rivera, who has a $7 million collection contract with the city's Health and Hospitals Corporation, and has also been appointed to the Off-Track Betting board, says he is tied to Latin pols unconnected to Velez, like Bronx State Senator Israel Ruiz.

City marshals are among the juiciest organization plums— potentially six-figure jobs that require nothing more than a high school diploma. New York is virtually the only major city that relies on such bounty hunters to collect court judgments. Their annual income (as much as $300,000) is determined by how many people they evict, how many salaries they garnish.

A lifelong opponent of the marshal system, Koch introduced a bill to abolish it when he first became mayor, lost in the assembly,

---

* Donald Manes, Queens Borough President, attempted suicide on January 10, 1986, by slashing his wrists. He was found in his car on the Grand Central Parkway. He died by suicide on March 13, 1986.

and then gave up. After Stanley Fink became speaker {of the state assembly} in 1970, Koch never even asked him to back an abolition bill. Instead, Koch adopted the window dressing of a screening panel. *Voice* stories over the years have listed the numerous new marshals who've climbed out of clubhouses, as well as the party ties of some of Koch's panel members. The most prominent duo were Carlos Castellanos and Elba Roman, two Luis Olmedo-designees, both of whom were suspended for pocketing collections and not reporting them to the city. Castellanos also wound up nabbed in the Olmedo extortion case and trooped off to the federal pen with the man Koch used to call his favorite councilman (another shock).

Of course, in recent days, Koch has made ex-Queens marshal Sheldon Chevlowe even more notorious than Castellanos, calling him "a bag man." It was at Chevlowe's funeral that Manes allegedly approached Dowd and asked him to switch the payoffs from Chevlowe to Lindenauer. As *Post* stories have established, Manes tried to penetrate the screening process Koch created for marshals with a few phone calls to City Hall. Chevlowe's wife was quickly appointed, rushed past hundreds of other applicants.

- The Department of Transportation (DOT) is loaded with high- and low-level patronage. The agency's chief counsel, Robert Shaw, is a Friedman appointee, out of Stanley Simon's Riverdale club. The job was handled in classic patronage fashion—Shaw replaced another Bronx jobholder, George Salerno, who won a more significant state post. The chief of Legal Affairs is Michael Mondshein, an active Jeff Club member from Brooklyn. Deputy Commissioner Julian Prager, who's now overseeing PVB, has been active in the Village Reform Democratic Club, an invention of Koch and LoCicero's designed to counter the anti-Koch Village Independent Democrats.

Felice Saccone, an assistant commissioner who now handles all of DOT's leasing and facilities management, is also active in Village Reform Democratic Club, together with his wife Joanna. Both are close to LoCicero and, ironically, to Carmine DeSapio. Saccone and DeSapio repeatedly share tables at the dinner dances of the Brooklyn and Bronx Democratic Parties, and stayed for a private dinner together after the Manhattan organization's recent Tavern on the Green affair. Sources indicate that Joanna Saccone babysits for DeSapio's daughter's child. Felice Saccone was originally named to replace Mazzeo as real estate director in Marine & Aviation in 1980, but he has been promoted twice since and now handles the entire agency's facility portfolio.

• DOT Assistant Commissioner Leonard Piekarsky, a Friedman friend and primary day worker who is also a member of the Rockaway club in Queens, became Saccone's boss at Marine & Aviation in 1980, which was renamed the Bureau of Ferries and General Aviation in the aftermath of the Mazzeo scandal. Piekarsky replaced Leon Tracy, another Jeff Club captain who was tainted by Mazzeo and burned in a series of city comptroller's audits. Though Piekarsky made substantial improvements in the agency, he also delivered at least one notorious concession to a Cohn/Friedman-represented newsstand firm, after negotiating the terms with a Cohn associate already under indictment in a videotaped bribe case involving an Amtrak contract in Washington. Piekarsky says he didn't know about the indictment at the time.

Paragraphs on patronage in the ferry service, the department that inspects potholes, and the civil service commission were cut here. —Ed.

- Ted Teah, a partner in Stanley Friedman and Roy Cohn's law firm, is a Koch-appointed City Planning commissioner from the Bronx. And planning commissioner John Gulino, whose appointment in 1978 was vigorously opposed by the American Institute of Architects, is the former law chairman of the Staten Island Democratic party. Gulino shares his three-story office building on the island with LaPorte's county headquarters, and he is the lawyer for several developers doing business with the city.
- Harold Fallick, another Brooklyn pol out of Marcy Faigenbaum's clubhouse, is an assistant commissioner at Ports & Terminals and processes some contracts. Throughout much of the first Koch term, the agency was notoriously tolerant of lease abuses and rent arrears at a city-owned pier facility by operators tied to Tony Scotto, the convicted Longshoreman union leader and Gambino crime family member. The ILA and its leaders have given the once-scornful Koch $59,000 since 1978.
- Steven Spinola, the president of the increasingly powerful Public Development Corporation (PDC), was selected after getting votes of approval from both Manes and Esposito. PDC's vice president in charge of the sale of city-owned property is Margaret Guarino, a longtime Esposito ally whose husband is active in the Jefferson Club and is a regular contributor to Golden and the Brooklyn party. Spinola was taken to a pre-appointment interview with Esposito in his Brooklyn office by Guarino. "Meade said he

would put in a good word for me," Spinola told the *Voice* in 1983. Two sons of Guarino's brother-in-law, who runs funeral homes with Guarino's husband, were murdered in mob hits in 1982, one while acting as a pallbearer. Federal organized crime strike force sources told the *Voice* that Anthony Guarino, Margaret's brother-in-law, is an associate of Tom Lombardi, a capo in the Genovese crime family.

Staten Island beep Lamberti's land-grab for a business partner was quietly processed through PDC. And minutes of a clandestine 1985 meeting obtained by the *Voice* reveal that Ramon Velez and his partners Lugovina and Batista tried to steer a piece of the city property out of the agency that controlled it and into PDC, because they believed they could get Spinola to turn it over to them.

Responding to press accounts, Koch asked DOI this week to investigate another PDC negotiated deal: Manes' delivery of the air rights over the municipal parking garage behind Queens Borough Hall to developer Joshua Muss. Muss, who plans to build a 23-story tower there, gave Manes a $10,000 contribution at the time, exceeding the $5,000 legal limit. A related Muss company and employees gave over $21,000 since 1981 to Brooklyn's Golden (one contribution of $7,500 was also illegal), who's spearheading a Muss-developed hotel for downtown Brooklyn through PDC.

****A few paragraphs further enumerating Brooklyn club house influence were cut. —Ed.***

- Koch is the third mayor to allow Esposito to turn the 261-acre, city-owned Brooklyn Navy Yard into an Esposito playground. Every pier and every naval vessel that docks there for repairs is insured by Esposito. Esposito's firm {the microfilm is illegible for a line} and broker for a minimum of $50 million worth of insurance covering the drydocks, and shipyard building leased on a 40-year basis by his principal client, Coastal Drydock, headed by Charles Montanti. Esposito personally pressured David Lenefsky, the Koch-appointed chairman of the yard's board, to deliver the no-bid, extraordinarily favorable lease to Montanti, who's been the subject of two federal probes. Lenefsky told the *Voice* that Esposito did not disclose his insurance interest in Montanti's contract when he called to complain about "why it was taking so long to get the negotiations finished."

Both Coastal and the city corporation that runs the yard have been heavy patronage employers as well, with Coastal carrying another Weiner in-law as personnel director and a longtime Esposito district leader employed as the Lenefsky board's secretary. Koch did not name Lenefsky to begin the clean-up of the corporation until a couple of weeks after he was re-elected in 1981—leaving the management of the Navy Yard firmly in the hands of Esposito cronies until then. A Brooklyn Supreme Court judge who was asked to rule on a pay claim submitted by the yard's executive director through most of the first Koch term said that conditions there, which led to several indictments, made "the corruption of the Tweed Courthouse architects look amateurish."

One top executive at the yard during the early Koch years, Charles LoCicero (not related to John LoCicero), was an associate in the Colombo crime family; his father was a consigliere in the same family and was machine-gunned to death. Hired ten days after he finished a six-year jail term, LoCicero got a series of rapid promotions until he held two of the five highest executive posts there. LoCicero was eventually indicted in 1980 on 190 counts of bribe receiving, grand larceny, forgery, falsifying business records, and theft of services, but he is still a fugitive. One of his scams involved the theft of hundreds of thousands of dollars in Navy Yard checks written to fictitious individuals and contractors that were endorsed by the hot dog vendor who parked his wagon at the yard. The vendor turned the payments over to LoCicero. The LoCicero scandal was a second or third wave at the yard (a previous executive director was convicted of conspiracy to sell $1.6 million in stolen cashiers' checks); but nothing deterred the Koch administration from treating the port as Meade's motherland. Even Lenefsky's current board and administration has its Esposito players and favors.

Four More Years

For years Ed Koch has prospered by manipulating the press, baiting blacks, taking credit for things he didn't do (like solving the fiscal crisis), and governing effectively from the point of view of the richest third of the city. But the scandal that started with a slashed wrist could change everything. It has, at least temporarily, persuaded the public that its government is in trouble. What will it mean for Koch in the end?

We put that question to one of the city's most astute power-brokers this week. His reply was: "No fourth term. And a very messy third term." The PVB scandal has put things in perspective. It's illuminated the recent past. It's revealed a flaw in Ed Koch's character that may become his fate. A year from now he will look at the government of this city and not see a lot of the present faces. He will look into a mirror and see a face that has aged, that has sagged, like Dorian Gray's.

No fourth term is what this is all about.

Research assistance by Janine Kerry Steel and Leslie Conner

Wayne Barrett, My Broder from Another Mother

Gerson Borrero

WAYNE HAD A REPUTATION for not being an easy person to speak with.

Most people felt that he was interrogating them. With a weekly deadline always looming, there was no wasting time on trivial chit-chat. No *boberías* for Wayne.

And yet, he maintained decades-long relationships, both with colleagues like me and with sources. People spoke to him, confessed to him, revealed secrets. He had some of the best sources in New York and put them to use against the abusive and corrupt powerful in politics, government, and business.

What those sources received in response was accurate reporting. That style of precise language and explanations of his pursuit gained the respect from those that would often start out either petrified of an inquiry by Wayne or suspicious of his motives. They may have had problems with his interrogative style, but the serious and factual reporting eventually overcame those fears.

I spoke to Wayne on an almost daily basis. Whether talking about sports, politics, or the latest scoundrel on his radar, there was always passion and purpose.

Whenever Wayne had questions about a Puerto Rican elected official or Latino *políticos* or community leaders or activists, he would ask for a complete background, specific connections to others in my community and the broader political structure. Our brotherhood was far from perfect. We had many political disagreements, but none severe enough to cause a permanent rift.

Well, there was the one exception. It was about baseball. He never understood or forgave me for being a Yankee fan. It went beyond his devotion for the despised Boston Red Sox. He was just brutal in his beat downs about my love for the Bronx Bombers. "How could you as a Puerto Rican who believes in independence of your island be a fan of the Yankees?!" That didn't shut me up; I retorted that "Fidel [Castro] is a Yankee fan." I got tired of being beat up and opted for not talking baseball with him. Yup, I punked out.

I wasn't the only one who wilted under Wayne's oratorical assault. The current governor of New York also punked out at least once, Wayne told me. "He wasn't responding to me. He just stayed quiet." It was like Wayne was a reminder to the younger Cuomo that he couldn't BS him, and that Wayne was probably on the right side of the argument.

Wayne was often harsh, but he believed in redemption. I learned this when he said to me one day, "I went to visit Hevesi yesterday." The former New York state comptroller had served prison time, in part because of Wayne's reporting. I couldn't believe it, and we spent a long time in a back-and-forth on his reasoning. I confess that I never fully understood why he would visit Hevesi at his home. But like the flip side of sources trusting Wayne to be accurate, Wayne never wrote anyone off.

After a lifetime of covering NYC politics, Wayne and I had no shortage of topics to discuss. But there was the one time that

I became so infuriated at Wayne that I screamed at him and told him to never again talk to me about this subject. No small talk, just facts, he reported it without drama: "I'm not going to live to write about the next Mayoral election." And once again, my broder from another mother was right.

Gerson Borrero is a longtime amigo of Barrett's, former editor in chief of *El Diario NY*, a political commentator at NY1, and a political editor and host at HITN.

7

How Ramon Velez Bleeds New York: Señor Big

December 31, 1985

THE SOUTH BRONX'S LEGENDARY public sponge, Ramon Velez, is once again New York's most powerful Puerto Rican. Though Velez hasn't held elective office since he lost his city council seat in 1977, he's rebounded from the scandals that dogged him then and is back as the city's undisputed king of salsa poverty. During his almost 20 years of influence, the South Bronx has become the nation's poorest congressional district, with infant mortality and unemployment rates that would shame Caracas. At the same time, Velez, with a yearly income of at least $221,000, has become the nation's richest poverty plutocrat.

Velez's power is rooted in the $16 million annual budget of the dozen community groups he controls, his personal ties to the White House and City Hall, his interlocking interests with the businessmen who run Bronx Democratic and Republican politics, and his dominance of the community's premier showcase event, the Puerto Rican Day Parade. His supportive role in the recent Reagan and Koch campaigns, as well as his endorsement of the narrowly reelected Bronx borough president Stanley Simon over Latin assemblyman Jose Serrano, have now placed Velez at the

While reporting on South Bronx poverty baron Ramon Velez's siphoning of affordable-housing funds, Barrett and photographer Susan Perry Ferguson followed the big man to Puerto Rico. He attacked them with a broom. The photo hung in Barrett's office ever after. (Photo courtesy of Susan Perry Ferguson)

head of the postelection receiving line, an old-style ward leader poised for a quantum leap in his poverty profits.

Velez was one of a hundred guests invited to the first official state dinner at the White House after the 1984 election (honoring the visiting Grand Duke of Luxembourg, a ruler whose kingdom is half as populous as Velez's). Kathy Villaponda, the White House liaison to the Hispanic community until she recently resigned, said Velez had been to the White House "several times" and was included in briefings with the president. Steve Taracido, chairman of the Republican National Hispanic Assembly, said that Velez sponsored a Bronx rally for the Republican ticket in 1984, did commercials and appearances on Spanish television, and was one of 16 members of the National Steering Committee of Democrats for Reagan/Bush. "Ray is very much involved in Republican politics at all levels," said Taracido, noting that Velez, who controls several Bronx Democratic district leaders, is still a registered Democrat.

When a mudslide killed hundreds in Puerto Rico this October, Ed Koch, Velez's other prime political ally, called a press conference, announced the formation of a relief committee, and named Velez to head it. The mayor hugged Velez three times during that press conference, extending those remarkable dangling arms of his around the largest bellyful of antipoverty gluttony in the nation, shamelessly forgetting his own 1977 campaign denunciations of Velez as a "poverty pimp." Velez took full advantage of the moment, asserting that Koch had designated him "the deputy mayor for Puerto Rican affairs" and noting that no prior mayor had ever so honored him, a proclamation of his own rehabilitation. At the start of Koch's first term in 1978, the administration cut off millions in funding to two Velez-controlled antipoverty groups, the Hunts Point Community Corporation and the Puerto Rican Community Development Project, based on "evidence of possible fiscal fraud." While several Velez associates in these programs were successfully prosecuted, federal and state authorities probed Velez for years without indicting him.

Velez runs the city's largest individually controlled empire of housing, day care, mental health, drug, alcoholism, economic development, home attendant, and senior citizen programs as if they were McDonald's franchises, taking a slice of the public subsidy from each for himself. In a 1984 filing with the state attorney general's office, he reported collecting $209,000 in salary and pension as president of the city-funded Hunts Point Multi-Service Center. He has yet to report his 1985 income, but his salary jumped from

$47,000 to its 1984 level in just two years. Though the city pays this salary and the tab for most of the programs Velez administers, neither the Human Resources Administration nor the mayor's office could come up with a résumé for him or even tell the *Voice* if he is a college graduate (his mother told me he is not). He drives a 1985 Buick registered to the South Bronx Community Management Corporation, a housing group he chairs that has an annual $1.4 million contract to maintain city-owned buildings. The woman he lives with is the director of another Bronx poverty program and drives a Volvo registered to the Multi-Service Center.

In addition to his Hunts Point salary and perks, Velez draws an estimated $12,000 in $1,000-a-meeting stipends for chairing two South Bronx companies that receive funding from Bronx Venture Corporation, a nonprofit consulting company with government contracts that Velez also chairs. Not satisfied with these bloated earnings, he's become an antipoverty entrepreneur, setting up for-profit development corporations that are now busy collecting enough government projects to make him a one-man free-enterprise zone. He has put his entire empire on a computer and pays an accountant six figures in public dollars to keep the books for the dozens of corporations he runs.

A month-long *Voice* investigation of Velez has uncovered startling new facts about his assets, business partners, and personal life. The highlights of the *Voice* findings are:

- Velez has amassed a real estate empire here and in Puerto Rico worth over a million dollars and including at least 16 properties. Four Velez condos are located on the Condado, the most expensive beach land in San Juan. While the 450,000 people of the South Bronx still await that neighborhood's revitalization, Velez has sunk a fortune, largely taken from his earnings there, into luxury development a thousand miles away.

- Velez has compromised the heart of the city and state redevelopment effort in the South Bronx by becoming a secret partner in a private real estate deal with the city's top planner in the South Bronx, Jorge Batista. The two became partners a month after the mayor appointed Batista president of the South Bronx Development Organization early this year. Batista's state- and city-funded $3 million agency is charged with renewing the blighted neighborhood. Despite his conflict-of-interest business ties with Velez here and in Puerto Rico, Batista's SBDO is aiding Bronx projects sponsored by Velez and a third partner in these private deals, longtime Velez associate Frank Lugovina. Since assuming the presidency of SBDO, Batista has also quietly become a director in Lugovina's development corporation, which is currently involved in several joint projects with Velez.

- In February, Velez divorced his wife of 15 years, Caroline Velez, and married the 25-year-old Osana Chacon Rios in a private ceremony in San Juan. He left his new wife there, returned to New York, and resumed living with his former wife, Caroline. Caroline still makes frequent public appearances with him, sat at his side on the reviewing stand of the Puerto Rican Day Parade in June, and was photographed with Velez and the mayor at a scholarship dinner-dance months after the divorce. The divorce and marriage papers were filed in small towns outside San Juan, where they were less likely to attract public attention.

  Velez's closest associates in New York were not told of the divorce. Neither was Velez's mother, whom we interviewed in his hometown of Hormigueros. Caroline Velez signed the divorce papers and was given sole ownership of their 10 condominium apartments in San Juan. However, the new wife, Osana Chacon, who has since given birth, uses at least two of these condos and has helped rent one of the others to a tenant. Chacon's brother, Jose Chacon, was hired this year to manage the new Felisa Rincon de Gauthier Houses in the South Bronx, an $8.4 million, 108-unit federal housing project sponsored by the Hunts Point Multi-Service Center. (Various Bronx public payrolls have long carried both children from Velez's first marriage, his brother, and other family members.)

- Velez owns a gutted, unsealed, three-story building at 425 East 141st Street in the Bronx, which he bought in his own name from federal housing authorities in 1979. The building, located next to a church and on an otherwise viable block just a few doors from a junior high school, appears to be a shooting gallery for Bronx junkies. Dealers openly sell drugs in front of the building. Another Bronx property Velez has owned since 1979—a four-story occupied tenement, at 3196 Third Avenue—has 22 code violations, as well as frequent heat and hot water problems. One pregnant tenant, nervous about the safety of her soon-to-be-born child, said her apartment is overridden with mice and rats. Though Velez signed a stipulation in the divorce proceeding saying that all properties he acquired during the marriage would be listed and divided, he did not report at least these two properties and the Bronx home he and Caroline have been living in since 1973. Velez owns this property in his own name alone.

- Though barred by a standing 1977 court order from any association with the Puerto Rican Day Parade, Velez practically owns it. A state judge directed Velez to dissociate himself from the parade because he was caught dipping into its half-million-dollar till for personal loans. But Attorney General Robert Abrams, who is charged with enforcing the court order, has taken no action, even though Velez has openly presided as chairman of the parade's fund-raising banquet at the Grand Hyatt, accompanied the parade's executive committee on a promotional tour of Puerto Rico, and positions himself annually in the front-row-center spot of the reviewing stand. Abrams's office says they are now investigating these violations, but they have not audited the parade's books since Abrams took office in 1978.

In 1984 Velez got the parade committee to dedicate the parade to Dr. Ronald Bauer, the first non–Puerto Rican ever so honored, even though Bauer's World University in Puerto Rico had already been shaken with the scandal that has since resulted in its closing. Bauer had previously given Velez an honorary doctorate that the 52-year-old Velez wears as if he'd earned it. The General Accounting Office accused Bauer of pocketing $2,000 a month in expense money, taking $544,613 in Veterans Administration payments for veterans who weren't at the school, and transferring $9.4 million in federal funds to affiliated schools in three countries—most of which went bankrupt. Three university administrators were charged with 67 counts of grand larceny, but Velez now chairs an island-based committee that is trying to get the university reopened with Bauer at the helm.

• Despite his awesome public earnings in New York and his prominence in city government and politics, Velez claims to be a bona fide resident of Puerto Rico. He and Caroline swore in the divorce documents that they'd been residents for at least a year, the legal minimum to qualify for a divorce there. While Velez has neither a New York driver's license nor an automobile registered to him here, he has both in Puerto Rico, using addresses at opposite ends of the island. He's also had a gun permit in Puerto Rico since 1979, which was granted him on the basis of his claim that he is the head of a household living in San Juan. Sources close to Velez says he goes to Puerto Rico approximately once a month.

There is a full federal tax exemption on at least that portion of a resident's income earned in Puerto Rico, as well as tax breaks for residents that can reduce the tax liability on their New York income. There are also possible local tax advantages available to residents. Because of the confidential nature of tax returns, it is unclear whether Velez has taken advantage of these breaks.

The only legal evidence of his Bronx residence is his voter registration card, which says he lived for eight years at 648 Jackson Avenue, a tenement building located next to the Hunts Point Multi-Service Center. Several tenants told the *Voice* that a young woman has lived alone in the apartment Velez is registered to vote from for at least a year, and that another tenant, also not Velez, lived there before her. Half a dozen tenants who know Velez by sight, some of whom say they've seen him going in and out of the Multi-Service Center, say he doesn't live in the building. "I've never seen him in here, and I've lived here 11 years," says Carmen Marcano, who lives a floor below Velez's claimed apartment. Caroline Velez has used the address of Velez's political club as her voting address for years (her antipoverty program is located on the second floor of the same building). Neither is registered at 326 Swinton Avenue, their Throgs Neck home far from the impoverished neighborhood he dominates.

A Reliable Autocrat

These charges have surfaced at a time when Velez is beginning to break into economic and housing development projects in the South Bronx at a megabuck level. The resourceful opposition of former South Bronx Development Organization president Ed Logue minimized Velez's development activities for years. But Velez's federal allies at the Housing and Urban Development agency drove Logue out in late 1984 when they defunded SBDO and gave their $1.5 million portion of SBDO's basic operational budget to three groups, including the Velez-chaired Bronx Venture Corporation. Logue's replacement is the accommodating Batista. And in October 1984, just a few weeks before the election, HUD selected the Hunts Point Multi-Service Center as the sponsor of a $6.5 million Section 202 project, involving 99 units of housing for the elderly.

Bronx Venture was also awarded consultant contracts this year from the city's Community Development Agency and Public Development Corporation totaling $250,000, to supplement the half million in Logue's former federal funding that Velez is using to develop commercial projects. The PDC money was earmarked as a priority budget demand of borough president Simon, whom Velez backed against his own onetime protégé, Jose Serrano—a sign that Velez's arrangement with Bronx Democratic leaders is paying dividend.

Last year Velez incorporated a for-profit consultant and real estate corporation, Ravel Associates Ltd. This year he opened an

office for Ravel at 2804 Third Avenue, a prime commercial building owned by Bronx Venture and gloriously rehabbed at government expense. When we went looking for Velez in the Bronx on
two separate days, his car was parked in front of Bronx Venture,
and sources close to him say that he is spending less and less time
at the Multi-Service Center and more and more at Bronx Venture
and Ravel. Ravel is now involved in several joint ventures with
corporations run by Velez's associate Lugovina. He and Lugovina are scouring the Bronx for sites and funding, confident of
federal, city, and county support. He is even trying to cement
relations with state officials whose mortgage and housing agencies
are increasingly critical elements of development packages. Velez
became a sponsor, and Lugovina a vice-chairman, of the recently
formed Hispanic fund-raising committee for Mario Cuomo,
attempting to woo a distant, if not hostile, governor.

Koch, Bronx boss Stanley Friedman, Simon, and Velez's federal allies seem as indifferent to his greed as they are to his dem-
agoguery and explosive bile (see "The Story Behind the Story,"
reproduced below). He may be an occasional embarrassment, but
he is a constant functionary, a reliable autocrat. Instead of having to deal with the mounting frustrations of the borough's 75
percent black and Latin minorities, they only have to trade with
kingpin Ramon, indicted state senator Joe Galiber, and a handful
of lesser hustlers atop the agonized sea.

A loser the last three times he ran for public office, Velez got
2,280 votes of the 15,000 cast when he ran for Congress in 1978,
a fourth-place finish that apparently persuaded him to give up his
electoral career. Since then, his South Bronx Democratic Club
has elected a local councilman, assemblyman, Democratic district
leaders, and school board members. But the white politicians who
entrust him with control of so vast a community institutional

base are not responding to these meager signs of grassroots support (indeed, Velez's councilman, Rafael Castaneira Colon, barely won reelection this year, getting slightly less than 30 percent of the vote in a crowded field). They empower him precisely because he won't let the agencies he runs empower Latins. He has refused, for example, to back any of the three Latin candidates who've opposed Simon since 1979, undercutting the chance to elect the first Puerto Rican on the city's Board of Estimate since the '60s. "I can't bite the hand that feeds me," he candidly told *El Diario*.

The *Voice*'s latest look at Velez is a veritable travelogue of scandal. Stretching from small country towns where conflict-of-interest deals with big city bureaucrats are buried, to San Juan condos and other island properties apparently acquired in part with his income from South Bronx poverty programs, it is a tourist tale begging for the sunlight of newsprint.

An Engineer's Dream

Guanica, Puerto Rico—It was a warm Saturday morning last February, and Ramon Velez was riding down an almost impassable, rock-covered road. He watched the green hills around him dip gradually, first onto a sandy beach and then into a tranquil inlet. Velez had arrived in Guanica the night before—a sleepy town on the southwestern tip of the island, depressed after the closing of its sugar factory years ago, but one of the only ports in Puerto Rico deep enough for cruise ships. A Velez functionary had organized the four-day excursion to Guanica, involving some 50 South Bronx leaders, but Velez had left most of his guests at the hotel while he took a car a mile or so down the dirt road. The car passed four-foot-tall, cactus-like yucca plants; the elegant, tiled ruins of a retreat house where Catholic bishops used to gather and meditate; and a still-active salt mine nestled in the corner of the bay. Off to the side was a rotted, abandoned hulk of a truck, with two words in English painted in large letters on the side: BAD BOYS.

He'd brought the woman he would divorce in four days, Caroline Velez, to see what he sensed was an engineer's dream, the natural topography for a luxury hotel and villas: gentle slopes descending into quiet, caressing water. He'd also brought his consultant, Antonio Fuentes, and the two partners who planned to join him in this venture.

One partner was predictable: Frank Lugovina is a Velez protégé who has risen to a level of real estate sophistication transcending that of his mentor. A member of the state's Banking Board and the city's Water Finance Board, Lugovina is now the codeveloper of a $39 million Battery Park City housing project—a far cry from the years of hustling for a piece of the burnt-out Bronx to build sandbox-sized low-income apartments. A Hugh Carey appointment in 1982 to chair the state's billion-dollar mortgage agency (SONYMAE), Lugovina was forced out a year later by the new governor, criticized for an expense-voucher raid on the agency that included junkets for top executives and their wives to Martha's Vineyard, Reno, and Palm Beach. His development firm recently got a $2 million construction mortgage for a Bronx housing project from the upstate Troy Savings Bank, which received $6 million in SONYMAE deposits during Lugovina's term, and he's become an investor in a small, Puerto Rican–run bank that received SONYMAE deposits during his term that were three times as large as those given to established Latin banks. Convention-center contracts were taken away from one of his firms in 1983 when the attorney general ruled that the contracts were in conflict with Lugovina's state position.

The other partner was Jorge Batista, a member of the state Board of Regents and chairman of the city's Loft Board. Landing Batista as a partner was probably a bigger prize to Velez than the project itself. A month earlier, Batista had started at SBDO. His unsoiled reputation and the multimillion-dollar public agency he ran were already becoming conduits for deals back in the Bronx— deals a lot more concrete than the speculative vision the three talked about that day on Guanica's untouched beach.

Accompanying Batista on the Guanica beach was the first person he hired when he took over SBDO in January—chief engineer James Manoussoff, who'd previously worked for Batista at a Bronx hospital. Batista, who runs SBDO as a $50,000-a-year consultant expected to work 800 hours a year, got Manoussoff a similar consultant package, $45,000 a year for 750 hours. While Batista's two city posts (SBDO and the $30,000-a-year loft-board job) earn him a commissioner's salary and, according to top city officials, are supposed to add up to a full-time position, Manoussoff is part-time at SBDO. He is permitted under his contract to perform other consultant services so long as they don't conflict with his SBDO obligations. A few days after the Guanica trip, Batista wrote a planning memo to Velez and Lugovina listing Manoussoff as the New York consultant on the first phase of the Guanica project—a plan to get federal senior-citizen housing funds to build a Section 202 project on the inland side of the property.

The plan, as Batista explained in the memo, was to set up a business corporation and "execute a shareholders agreement among R. S. Velez, F. Lugovina, and J. L. Batista so that each of us has the right to acquire one-third interests in the Bishops Point Development Corp." (Velez's consultant Fuentes, using the Bronx Venture address, was one of three signatories on incorporation papers filed for this company in Puerto Rico a couple of weeks after the Batista memo.) Bishops Point would then, according to the memo, enter into a lease with an option to buy the Guanica land. Batista also suggested that another company, the nonprofit La Providencia Inc., be incorporated in Puerto Rico (it was) and that a board of directors "be negotiated by R.S.V. with local political, governmental, community and religious leaders." La Providencia would be established as a tax-exempt corporation eligible for the Section 202 housing subsidies and would then seek funding for what Batista estimated in the memo would be 60 to 75 single-family houses for seniors.

An option letter was prepared by Batista in late March and sent to Oscar Valle, a real estate agent in Mayaguez, Puerto Rico, who represented the family that owned the Guanica property. It offered $300,000 for the property, a third at closing and the remainder over a five-year period. The theory was that if HUD granted the 202 allocation, La Providencia would buy that portion of the 300-acre site needed for the housing project from Bishops Point, paying top dollar and using federal funds. Bishops Point would use its profits on the federal sale to complete the payout plan with the original owners, acquire the rest of the site, and begin the hotel project.

Federal regulations require that the nonprofit sponsor of a 202 project be unconnected with the owner of the land. The arrangement planned by Velez and his partners was an attempt to circumvent that arm's-length requirement. Since Puerto Rico and New York are covered by the same regional housing office, the three were confident that they had the contacts to get a 202 approved (indeed, Velez had obtained a 202 allocation for the Bronx project just a couple of months earlier).

Caroline Velez, Manoussoff, Fuentes, and the three partners toured the beach that day with Lugovina's wife, the realtor Valle, and a Puerto Rican builder related to Fuentes named Miguel Reyes Fuentes. (Reyes Fuentes had signed the incorporation papers for Bishops Point and La Providencia.) Both Valle and Reyes Fuentes freely discussed the visit that day and the participants in the proposed deal. So did the real estate broker for the buyers, Ernesto Martinez. A longtime housing activist in New York whose Puerto Rico real estate interests are managed by Valle, Martinez was the spark plug for the deal. After learning of the availability of the property through Valle, Martinez used intermediaries to interest Lugovina and spoke to Batista himself. Lugovina, he says, then "brought in Velez." Martinez says he was told that "any deal Lugovina is a part of, Velez has to be a part of" and that this arrangement "works both ways."

Before the trip to Puerto Rico, Martinez went to a meeting at Lugovina's Bronx office. "It was Batista who told me that they were going into the deal with Velez," said Martinez. "Batista said they'd be one-third partners. They said that whatever Jorge, Frank, and I agreed to, Ramon would agree. After that meeting, they went down to Puerto Rico together."

"Batista's letter was never answered," says Martinez. "They offered $300,000 and the daughter wanted to sell, but the uncle was sticking out for $900,000. The partnership is still interested. There is no time limit on that offer. Oscar says we just have to wait." While I was reporting this story, the recalcitrant uncle died. Madel Pirallo, whose mother is the principal owner of the property, says that she heard months ago that "three or four Americans made an offer" for the property, but was never told the details, "probably because my uncle thought it was too low." Valle offered the same scenario as Martinez, saying he was "still representing the owners" and hopeful of making a deal.

Martinez and others also recall one other player in the proposed Guanica deal, the then mayor Liduvino Garcia Salcedo, who joined Velez, Batista, Lugovina, and some of the others in a discussion of the project back at the hotel, after their February visit. A few months later, Garcia was indicted in San Juan Superior Court on three corruption charges involving a kickback scam with contractors. Martinez says that he'd talked with Garcia before the Puerto Rico trip, asking about water and power lines, roads and construction permits, and that Garcia was "cooperative." The contractor Reyes Fuentes, whose family is a dominant and reputable force in Guaynabo, on the eastern side of the island, recalled Garcia discussing the availability of exceedingly cheap Department of Agriculture bulldozers at the meeting that day in the hotel and his own control of their use. Martinez simply noted: "It's quite customary to make all sorts of deals with the mayor for this heavy equipment."

Mayor Garcia reportedly announced that "when everything was finished, a piece of land would always be appreciated," and Velez, Antonio Fuentes, and he went off for a private conversation. Efforts to talk with Garcia in Puerto Rico were unsuccessful, but the government's investigator on the case said that he'd heard about the proposed beach deal and Garcia's involvement in it. Garcia will go on trial soon, and is also facing a federal investigation.

Velez, Lugovina, Batista, and Manoussoff refused to talk to the *Voice* (Velez rather emphatically). But after weeks of stonewalling, Batista did offer some minimal answers through a spokesman, Ethan Geto, head of a private public relations firm retained by SBDO. He flatly denied that he had ever been a partner in a business deal with Velez or Lugovina, adding he'd also "never profited" from one. He said the draft option letter obtained by the *Voice*, which listed the three as "principals and owners," had been "doctored." He said he'd signed the option letter as a lawyer for Velez and Lugovina, and that the letter had the same sentence listing principals, but mentioned only those two. Batista refused to provide a copy of his version of the letter, nor could he counter the planning memo written by him which expressly said that the three would be partners on the project. Even his defense, that he was a lawyer for Velez and Lugovina after he took over SBDO, is an admission of a conflict relationship, though less of a conflict than if he were a principal.

*** *A detailed discussion of the business relationships between various entities in the real estate transaction has been elided. —Ed.**

Empire in the Sun

The Guanica project fit comfortably in Ramon Velez's expanding portfolio of Puerto Rican ventures, though none of the others were similar conflict transactions. Instead, these deals represent simply a siphoning off of Velez's South Bronx earnings to build a poverty-purchased empire in the sun.

In February 1983, when Velez was just entering the world of six-figure salaries, he bought a three-and-a-half-acre vacant strip of property in the center of Boqueron, a resort town near Guanica, from an engineer named Armengol Iglesias. The purchase price was $63,000, which Iglesias says Velez paid in three installments by personal check. The last payment was two months ago. Velez also retained Iglesias to design the 25 private homes he plans to build on the site and has paid him twice for getting the project through two crucial phases of the local planning process (he will not say how much). Iglesias was also listed in the Batista memo as an engineering consultant on the Guanica project.

The Boqueron land dips down a hill to the beach, just like the Guanica property. Iglesias owns 25 contiguous acres, also vacant, where he plans to build, possibly with Velez, a luxury hotel. Just like in Guanica, the projected income from Velez's initial housing project might make the hotel possible. Santos Ortiz, the mayor of nearby Cabo Rojo (which administers the tiny town of Boqueron) and a longtime friend of Velez, said that the planning commission had given Velez's project preliminary approval. Iglesias said the final plans will be finished in a few months and that Velez, who took sole possession of this land in the divorce proceedings with Caroline, will sell the homes before they are built.

This summer Velez attended a ceremony in Boqueron, when New York housing commissioner Anthony Gliedman presented a city fire truck to the town. The truck was bought for $10,000— raised here and in Puerto Rico—after a fire destroyed seven homes in the town because it took too long for trucks to arrive from Cabo Rojo. The truck is now parked in a makeshift garage right behind Velez's property. Ed Pagan, a local realtor whose firm represents Velez, told me that after the ceremony, Velez sat down with a group of local businessmen to discuss quickly buying another piece of Boqueron property opposite the elementary school. Pagan said that the group told Velez that the site was likely to be selected by the education department as the site for a new high school. Velez and the group were apparently considering a quick turnaround and a fat profit on the school sale. It is unclear if a deal was ever made. I called Oscar Morales, a Boqueron businessman close to Velez who reportedly participated in both the discussion and the selection of the school site, but he hung up when I mentioned the school property.

The only other Puerto Rico properties Velez kept as sole owner after the divorce were a hundred-acre farm in Las Marias and a six-figure, two-story private home in Mayaguez. The Mayaguez house was the first property Velez is known to have bought in

Puerto Rico, way back in 1972. One of its apartments is still lived in by his first wife, who refused to answer most *Voice* questions. This house is only a few miles away from the small house in Hormigueros where Velez's 81-year-old mother, Maria Ramirez Velez, lives. When a photographer and I visited the mother's house with a translator from the University of Puerto Rico, Mayaguez campus, we were met by Velez's sister, who is in her mid-fifties. We explained that we were doing a story on her brother, and she took us into Mrs. Velez's bedroom.

Dressed in a blue cotton housedress and white cotton socks, Mrs. Velez sat on the edge of her bed. A bare lightbulb lit the room. A portrait of her husband, who died three years ago, hung on the wall. A fan, an aluminum walker, and a single chair were all that occupied the room. Her round, cherubic face lit up when she told us how Ramon got "interested in politics as a teenager" and led a procession "praising the Popular Democratic Party." She said he "liked to study a lot" and wanted to be a lawyer, but quit school to fight in the Korean War. She was proud of his achievements in New York, said she'd visited him there three times, and that he had helped her get medical treatment through the Multi-Service Center.

Asked if he'd helped buy the house she how lives in, she said: "No. His father and I spent our life savings on this house five years ago, $15,000. The house we were living in was old and falling apart." Asked if he'd ever offered her a place to live in Puerto Rico, she said he hadn't. She said that he didn't own any property here, but that he'd invited her to stay with him in New York. She said she lived solely on Social Security. She and Velez's sister talked warmly about the person they believed was Velez's wife, Caroline. The mother described her diabetes, arthritis, and heart condition and said she was constantly in and out of hospitals.

The rest of Velez's identifiable property on the island is in San Juan. Though these properties were awarded to Caroline Velez in the divorce, the titles, which list Ramon as co-owner, have not been changed. Velez bought his first condo in 1975, adding others in 1977 and 1978. His most active year was 1982, when he purchased three in the space of a few weeks—though his salary at the time was only $47,000. Typically, his purchase of a one-room apartment in the Astor Condado, a condo across from the beach along the prime strip of hotels, cost $36,000 and was financed with only an $18,000 mortgage. He bought a 6,000-square-foot duplex penthouse at the top of the luxury Centrum Plaza in Hato Rey for a recorded $100,000, including a $28,000 cash payment. That price is extremely low for the building, which is located just a block from the main headquarters of Banco De Ponce and Banco Popular, along what's called the Golden Mile. Velez reportedly had a Jacuzzi, given him by a New York contractor, hauled 12 stories up for the duplex.

Velez rents many of these condos, and his tenants, most of whom are quite happy with him as a landlord, told us they send checks, made out to him personally, to his post office box in the Bronx. He keeps the Centrum Plaza, the Astor, and the apartment we visited him in, at the Chateau Lagoon, for his personal use. He acquired the Lagoon apartment in April 1984 for $55,000, assuming a $38,000 mortgage and paying the rest in cash. It was the second apartment he'd bought in the building, which is also located directly across from the hotel strip and the San Juan convention center.

They Stoop, He Conquers

In the late '70s, dozens of Velez employees were subpoenaed before a federal grand jury that had targeted him, but no indictment ever resulted. The assistant US attorney handling the case, Richard Weinberg, never successfully prosecuted a major corruption case before or after taking on Velez. Weinberg is listed only three times in the annual reports covering his five years in the prosecutor's office and only once as the lead attorney on a case—a small food stamp prosecution. Weinberg didn't prosecute many cases because he became one of the office's top appellate attorneys, rising to appellate chief. As he worked his way up in the appellate section, he brought the Velez case with him, according to then US attorney Robert Fiske. Appellate attorneys write briefs, not indictments, and Weinberg, who quickly assumed a leadership role in the section, had other demands on his time. The Velez case died when Weinberg left, in September 1979.

Beating the probes of the '70s has given Velez a kind of immunity. He is seen in the streets of the South Bronx as impregnable. A half dozen of the people who live in the building where he claims to live, next door to the Multi-Service Center, curse him but regard him as if he were larger than life. "No matter what you do," said one, "Ramon Velez is going to wind up with his share of the money." In the South Bronx, he is as unavoidable as rubble. Even a Jorge Batista stooped to deal with him. The people have rejected him, and yet he still rules. It will take a bulldozer to move him—a mayor, a prosecutor, a governor, a newspaper publisher, a TV producer. Without that kind of combination, the kingpin will roll on, until he finally decides to take his Bronx winnings to Boqueron. And sit on his hill, gazing into the sunset.

The Story Behind the Story

The untouchable Ramon Velez, who once boasted that he'd survived 150 investigations, was recently indicted for the first time. After a lengthy probable-cause hearing in a San Juan courtroom,

Judge Alba Del Valle Galarza set a January 7 trial date for Velez on three misdemeanor assault charges, each of which carries a maximum of six months in jail. The charges were a result of his recent attacks on *Voice* staff in Puerto Rico—including an attempt to strangle me in a stairwell and a broom-swinging barrage against me and *Voice* photographer Susan Ferguson.

Velez was represented by four attorneys, including a former San Juan district attorney, and attempted twice to get the hearing adjourned. As allowed under Puerto Rican law, Velez and his attorneys remained in the hearing room throughout the proceeding, were granted a wide latitude in cross-examining Ferguson and me, and made emotional appeals to the judge, describing the case as pitting "Americanos against natives." (In New York, defendants and their attorneys are not permitted to participate in grand jury proceedings.) Though a three-hour adjournment was granted Velez so he could produce witnesses, neither he nor any other defense witnesses chose to testify.

Prominent supporters sat with him during the day, including a former judge, the ex-head of a bankrupt San Juan university, prominent businessmen, and former island senator Ruth Fernandez. A Velez relative showed San Juan reporters a letter of support Velez received from Ed Koch. *San Juan Star* reporter Robert Friedman reported that the mayor had written that he was "no fan of Wayne Barrett" and that he wished Velez well "in this particular case." The mayor later told the Spanish daily *El Diario* that it was a private letter to Velez and refused to comment on the indictment.

The attack occurred in mid-November, when I was reporting this story, visiting Velez's many Puerto Rico properties and interviewing his tenants, relatives, and associates. Velez was simultaneously spending a week and a half there and, as his subsequent statements to the press have indicated, kept getting feedback from people I'd interviewed. He knew we'd visited most of his condos. He was staying in one of the few we hadn't. When we arrived at this condo along the Condado in San Juan and rang his buzzer from an outside gate, he stuck his head out the window, saw us, then buzzed us in, waiting for us at the top of a narrow stairwell he knew we had to walk up. After I knocked on the door leading from the stairwell to the hallway, Velez suddenly burst from behind it, threw his immense weight at me, and knocked me to the floor.

He held me in a stranglehold and swore repeatedly that he would kill me. For at least a minute, I believed he intended to and could. Ferguson grabbed him from behind and thrust her fingers in his eyes, forcing him to loosen his grip. Then he chased us out to the courtyard of his building, brandishing a broom and shoving Ferguson's camera into her face. A crowd gathered and he began screaming, "Communists! Homosexuals!" When I accompanied the police to Velez's apartment after the incident to identify him, his brother Tutu, who'd joined him there, warned me in front of six cops: "You'd better run and you'd better hide."

His assault on us was Velez's way of responding to a prying press. Former WNEW-TV reporter Steve Bauman, whose stories led to federal probes of Velez a decade ago, weathered death threats and Velez press releases accusing Bauman of taking $50,000 bribes from Velez opponents. At the same time that Bauman was exposing Velez, the *Voice*'s Pete Hamill wrote an extraordinary article demonstrating how Velez's rise to power was linked to the still unprosecuted and mysterious murder of Edwin Rivera, a Velez opponent who was run down in front of 30 witnesses outside a Bronx public meeting by a car that dragged his body 50 feet. Not long after Hamill's article was published, a number of his close friends and relatives were called by individuals who told them he'd

Ramon Velez curses the photographer after attacking her with a broom-
stick. (Photo courtesy of Susan Perry Ferguson)

been killed in Brownsville. Since his friends knew that Hamill was
in Brownsville that day, they panicked.

Earlier this year, Velez shoved *Voice* photo editor Fred McDarrah, when McDarrah tried to take his picture at Koch's reelection
announcement. When I visited Velez's South Bronx Democratic
Club on election night in 1982 with Joe Conason and a *Voice*
photographer, Bronx Democratic leader Stanley Friedman had
to intervene to prevent Velez and his sidekicks from physically
throwing us out of the club. And in April 1985, Velez's 31-year-
old son from a previous marriage, Ramon Jr., drove his car directly at a parked car carrying *Voice* reporter William Bastone and
a photographer, chasing them off the road and down a sidewalk.
This attack occurred after Bastone had returned to his car following an unsuccessful attempt to interview the younger Velez on the
street.

Velez has the same respect for his political opponents as he has for a free press. Herman Badillo, who recalls that bullets were fired through his campaign headquarters when Velez ran against him for Congress in 1976, has been on the receiving end of Velez innuendo for years, including a scurrilous letter from him published in *El Diario* a few months ago. Former city councilman Gilberto Gerena Valentin, who beat Velez in 1977 and lost to a Velez-backed candidate in 1982, is suing Velez for libel. After Valentin's opponent, Rafael Castaneira Colon, defeated him in a special election, Velez went on Spanish radio to thank the voters and plunged into an extraordinary diatribe against the 67-year-old Valentin.

Velez said Valentin "represents infamy, the lie, hate, abuse against women, atrocity," and lamented that Valentin "now unfortunately goes to Social Security." ("What we want to do," Velez suggested as an alternative to Social Security, "is to make a public monetary collection to get him a one-way ticket to Iran.") Screaming that Valentin was a "child molester" and a "bandit," Velez described himself as "a Puerto Rican man that will not sell his country to strange interests, be it Russian or Iranian, Communist or Socialist. I am a patriot, not a traitor like Gerena Valentin."

Velez described Colon's win as "the biggest victory of my life," promising the radio audience during his rant against Valentin that justice would finally prevail under Colon. Two months later, the *Voice* revealed that Velez's new city councilman owed $13,189 in child support payments to two wives and six children that he'd left on welfare. The city quickly moved to force him to pay. Colon used a phony name in the child support case, a phony union label on campaign literature, a phony Cuomo endorsement, a phony Bronx address, and a phony Fordham law degree. Ramon's son went on Colon's payroll immediately, though he was a full-time employee of Citibank for the same 26 months that he drew city council checks.

Since the Rivera murder in 1969—and the investigations that kept it alive in the press through much of the '70s—fear has been a prop of the Velez machine. The ballyhoo in the Latin press about his recent assault on *Voice* staffers, while sharply critical of Velez, may also be feeding the legend of his fury. To complement his strong-arm reputation, he has an ex-cop bodyguard, once suspended for excessive force and now employed by the Teamsters and Velez. In 1982 Velez slapped his councilman Colon in the face on election night in front of the victory-party crowd when Colon forgot to thank him in his acceptance speech.

Velez is a warrior king who rewards loyalty, punishes those who stray, and assails his enemies. No wonder the mayor admires him.

Research assistance by Janine Kerry Steel and Jennifer Zaina

8

Has Stein Broken the Charter?
May 15, 1984

While Ramon Velez and Bronx political boss Stanley Friedman were lining their own pockets with money meant for their struggling neighbors, Manhattan borough president Andy Stein, for the price of a campaign donation, was redrawing the map of Midtown for New York's biggest developers. The city was being remade—for those who could pay. —Ed.

PIONEER ANDY STEIN, this week's East Side congressional candidate (17th congressional district), has been exploring the frontiers of the campaign finance laws, particularly since his reelection as borough president in 1981. While the Board of Ethics has long been troubled by city officials who take campaign contributions from those doing business with the city, it has decided that these contributions don't constitute, in the words of the city charter, a "valuable gift, whether in the form of service, loan, thing or promise." The board has tolerated these contributions (rather than treating them as gifts and forcing recipients to forfeit public office) because the money doesn't go into the pocket of the official and thus is not a personal benefit.

However, ever since Stein was reelected, his campaign finance committee has been collecting hundreds of thousands of dollars, mostly from developers and contractors doing business with the city. The committee then conveys the contributions to Stein personally. With each payment to Stein, the committee reduces a $520,000 debt to him for loans he'd made to his 1981 campaign. A *Voice* examination of Stein's financial filings with the Board of Elections has isolated many instances in which a corporation or individual has contributed funds that merely passed through his finance committee, sometimes for as briefly as a few hours, and then were transferred out of the committee to Stein personally. In addition to repaying the bulk of Stein's loan, the committee has also paid Stein over $42,000 in interest. Stein's counsel points out that the committee's interest payments to Stein were less than the interest that Stein was forced to pay the bank, Manufacturer's Hanover Trust, which made a personal loan to Stein in excess of $600,000.

The loan and interest payments raise new questions, not only about the borough president's possible violation of the gift section of the charter, but also that he may have broken the charter's emphatic ban against a city official having "any financial or other private interest, direct or indirect, which is in conflict with the proper discharge of his official duties." Stein's attorney, Tom Schwarz, and his publicist, Marty McLaughlin, offered a similar response to the issue, arguing that any intimation of wrongdoing was "in effect arguing that no one who runs for office should ever make a loan to their committee because it can't repay the debt with contributions." No other candidate for city office has loaned any substantial amount of personal funds to their campaign in recent years, much less repaid their own loan with contributions collected from city contractors and developers.

The *Voice*'s analysis of specific contributions and apparent quid pro quos focuses on the 1982 period (the 1983 and 1984 contributions suggest a similar pattern). Stein's lawyer and publicist were offered the details of each of the following questionable instances, but chose not to respond beyond McLaughlin's assurance that "our attorney tells us everything is on the up and up."

- Before and after the City Planning Commission recommended serious tightening of midtown zoning policies during early 1982, Stein was the Board of Estimate's "strongest advocate of relaxing restrictions on midtown," according to one top city source who supported the commission's new limits on density. Virtually every major developer supported Stein in this unsuccessful effort to thwart the changes. Prior to the May vote on the commission's proposals, Stein "engineered the layover" of the item for a month, said two city officials. This gave one particular developer, Solstead Associates, the opportunity to get construction underway on its new East 48th Street office tower. Because of Stein's delays, the Solstead project wound up covered by the old zoning regulations, permitting much greater density than they could've obtained if the new rules applied. Solstead then gave $10,000 to Stein's committee, on July 29, 1982, and another $10,000 on November 15. Stein personally received $28,000 from the committee in the same months.

- Stein's advocacy of lax zoning on the East Side dovetailed with a virtually simultaneous contagion of developer generosity. On February 11, 1982, Zachary Fisher contributed $5,000 at a time when the cash balance in the committee's account had hit a low of $1,000. The committee's next transaction, 11 days later, was a transfer of $5,000 to Stein personally. On March 18, Donald Trump added $20,000 to the kitty and, four days later, Stein withdrew $10,000. Both the Fisher Brothers and Trump are major East Side developers with a continual stake in that area's zoning.

Later that year, Stein became the prime champion for the Fishers' unsuccessful attempt to wipe out landmark designation for the Lever House and replace it with a 40-story office tower. He rounded up all the other borough presidents for the showdown Board of Estimate vote, but lost to Jackie Onassis, who got Comptroller Jay Goldin to cast the decisive vote against it. In 1979, Stein did everything but pour the concrete for Fishers' Park Avenue tower, arranging zoning variances, tax breaks, street changes, air rights, and community board support. The Fishers gave Stein $45,000.

Trump's $46,000 total, most of it given before the election, also corresponds with specific Stein acts on behalf of Trump Towers—including an affidavit Stein provided in State Supreme Court supporting Trump's attempt to win a $50 million city tax break for his casbah for oil sheiks. And who can forget the mayor's poignant description of Stein's courting of Housing Commissioner Tony Gliedman—in Stein's apartment—on Trump's behalf.

In addition to these contributions during the zoning debate, Stein was deluged in its aftermath by developers like Harry Macklowe ($20,000, split between June and August), Donald Zucker ($10,000 in July), George Klein ($10,000 in August), the Milsteins ($25,000 in summer money), and Peter Kalikow ($5,000 that September). By October, the Sylvan Lawrence family and company, one of whose principals loaned Stein his spectacular vacation house in East

Hampton for the 1979 summer, came through with another $10,000 (their eventual total exceeded $77,000). It would, of course, be a mistake to attribute these contributions solely to Stein's performance on the zoning changes. That performance was part of a fabric of virtually unwavering support for the specific projects of all these developers, and others. During the final six months of 1982, while the committee was collecting these real estate thank yous, Stein personally received $136,000 in six separate loan repayments.

- On March 3, 1982, John Kluge, the head of Metromedia, gave $20,000 to a depleted Stein finance committee, which had returned to its $1,000 balance. The same day Stein withdrew $15,000 from the account. As the *Voice* and *New York* magazine reported in 1981, Kluge was then pressing the city for a five-story addition to Metromedia's East 67th Street building, including a penthouse for him and his new bride. Though CBS newsman Morley Safer and other neighbors fought the expansion, Stein's office lobbied hard behind the scenes in Kluge's favor. Kluge's project barrelled through the community board, whose members are largely appointed by Stein. In 1983, Kluge added another $5,000 to the Stein kitty, giving him $45,000 total.

- During the same period of the Fisher, Trump, and Kluge contributions, while the Board of Estimate was beginning formal consideration of the special theater-district provisions of the new midtown zoning plan, Alvin Nederlander Associates Inc. contributed $5,000 to Stein. Nederlander was the owner, according to the *Daily News*, of 10 of the 44 theaters covered by the new theater-district designation. The Nederlander contribution came at a time when the committee was at low ebb again, with barely a thousand in the tank, and preceded another loan payment to Stein.

Nederlander fiercely opposed the special demolition permits proposed by the planning commission, which would've set up a restrictive process before any of the 44 theaters could be destroyed. Nederlander wanted the owners to have maximum flexibility to do with their theaters as they would—from air-rights sale to demolition. He argued that his organization financed their shows by borrowing against individual theaters. If banks couldn't demolish, they wouldn't loan, he said. Council president Carol Bellamy, supported by Stein, forced a change in the planning commission's proposal and put a sunset provision on the new zoning regulations of one year.

Nederlander and other owners were named to a Theatre District Advisory Council, which is still preparing new regulations to govern development issues there. One city official recalled that Stein repeatedly pressed the Koch administration to deal with Nederlander's "problems." After the changes he favored were amended to the new zoning code, Nederlander kicked in another $11,790 to Stein's committee in September 1982. Stein withdrew $32,500 as a loan repayment the same month. In March 1983, on the first anniversary of his initial contribution to Stein and shortly before the sunset provisions expired, Nederlander gave another $5,000. The committee repaid Stein $35,000 that month.

Research assistance by Julie Hack and William Bastone

9

Patronage Outrage
May 5, 1998

Most of the names in this article are unfamiliar even to dedicated news readers, and it was written years after the other pieces in this section. It is included here because it is maybe the quintessential Barrett article: employing all the tools in his reporting arsenal to show the fatal consequences of political graft. —Ed.

THE SCHOOL CONSTRUCTION Authority project officer at the Brooklyn school where a child was killed by falling bricks in January was hired—despite a long arrest record and dubious qualifications—because of his political connections to the Pataki administration.* An SCA probe has found that the officer's failure to require the contractor doing roof work at the school to erect a wood-covered sidewalk shed may have contributed to the death of 15-year-old Yan Zhen Zhao, the *Voice* has learned. Gary Marrone, 43, who got his job through family ties to the state Conservative Party, quit the SCA on April 8 after the *Voice* began raising questions about his oversight at P.S. 131 in Borough Park. Marrone had day-to-day responsibility

---

* George Pataki, governor of New York, 1995–2006.

for the safety of the job site and resigned just as SCA inspector general Peter Pope completed an investigation of his performance.

Pope's still-secret findings have also led, according to SCA sources, to the recommended dismissal of Marrone's immediate supervisor and the demotion of another top agency executive. These personnel moves, however, have not yet been formally announced. Board of Education officials all the way up to Deputy Chancellor Harry Spence, who sits on the three-member SCA board, have been critical of Marrone, with Spence noting that "the principal told me she could never find him."

Investigators concluded that Marrone even allowed the contractors to take down a portion of the fencing around the school in what they said was precisely the area where Zhao was killed and another child was seriously injured. Brooklyn district attorney Charles J. Hynes recently indicted the contractors on manslaughter and criminally negligent homicide charges, attributing the girl's death to their failure "to provide shedding or to close the sidewalk in the area of construction."

When Hynes announced the indictment at a March press conference, he said that "the ineptitude of SCA employees" at the school did not rise "to the level of criminal conduct," but that it "came pretty damn close" and "better not happen again."

Marrone's wife, Fran Vella Marrone, is the $68,346-a-year special assistant to Paul Atanasio, the only SCA trustee appointed by Governor George Pataki. In late 1995, shortly after assuming her position, Mrs. Marrone began pushing SCA president Barry Light to hire her husband, according to sources at the agency. Light declined, citing an explicit SCA bar against hiring relatives. But within five weeks of Light's February 1996 departure, the agency hired Gary Marrone.

Fran Marrone is the Bay Ridge Conservative Party district leader, a member of the state party's executive committee, and vice-chair of the Brooklyn party. Atanasio, too, has been associated with the party for years—running once as its congressional candidate in Bay Ridge. Both are close to Conservative Party boss Mike Long, who told the *Voice*: "I don't remember if I recommended Fran or not for the SCA job. If I didn't, I wish I did." Marrone and Atanasio were prominent guests at the party's annual dinner at the Sheraton two weeks ago, at which Pataki was given its highest award.

Atanasio, an investment banker who has secured billions in state bond underwriting since Pataki took office, retained Long as a $5,000-a-month consultant at his firm, Chemical Securities, in January 1995. Long, the owner of a Bay Ridge liquor store located around the corner from the state party headquarters, had no underwriting experience. But the 328,000 votes Pataki attracted on Long's ballot line just two months earlier more than accounted for the new governor's margin of victory. Atanasio was also executive chair of New Yorkers for Term Limits—an offshoot of the Conservative Party—and Fran Marrone was a committee staffer, drawing a total of almost $50,000 in salary between 1993 and 1997.

Gary Marrone was arrested in three different cases in Florida in the '80s and once in New Jersey in the '70s. His only conviction was on a 1985 misdemeanor fraud charge in Sunrise, Florida, though a 1983 obstruction charge was listed as having been "turned over to another agency." In 1986, he was charged with calling the Sunrise cop who'd arrested him a year earlier and telling him: "I'm going to get you for what you did to me. I am going to kill you. I'll be out tonight looking for you." In that case, the local district attorney "declined prosecution."

Marrone's 1985 arrest included a disorderly intoxication charge—which was dismissed when he was convicted on the fraud count. Documents reviewed by the *Voice*, however, reveal that P.S. 131 principal Dr. Virginia Bartolotti believed he had a drinking problem during the work at her school. In a 1997 letter to her deputy superintendent, Bartolotti complained that "no one at the SCA" did anything about Marrone "even when I reported the fact that the site manager was drunk in my office while on duty and while at one of those meetings I'm referring to."

Bartolotti's 1996 logs indicate that she'd seen Marrone "drunk" once and "smelled liquor on his breath" on another occasion. The principal noted that she reported both events, but was told that Marrone maintained that "the smell was from a medication he was taking." She and other witnesses at the school were grilled by SCA investigators recently about these incidents.

Bartolotti and the school's custodian, Robert Steiger, also repeatedly called Marrone's supervisors, noting his persistent absence from the job, with Bartolotti insisting that nothing would improve unless Marrone was replaced. Bartolotti told the *Voice* that though the SCA protocol required Marrone to appear daily, he was at the school only "occasionally," and left her with "no direct means of getting to him." Marrone lives only 10 minutes from P.S. 131.

The $57,000 project-officer position ordinarily requires "a baccalaureate degree from an accredited college," but Marrone had only two and a half years at Miami Dade Community College, and left without an associate degree. Minimum qualifications for the SCA post do permit the hiring of someone who has "a satisfactory combination of education and experience," suggesting that Marrone's claimed seven years of construction experience as a "project manager" may have been used as the basis for hiring him.

The most recent job on Marrone's résumé was with Hercules Construction, a company that was barred from doing business with the agency and was under federal investigation for bribing and defrauding Board of Ed and SCA officials at the time of Marrone's hiring. Hercules president Gregory Rigas—another associate of Mike Long who contributed the legal maximum years earlier to Atanasio's congressional campaign—pled guilty to two federal felonies four months after Marrone left the company to join the SCA. Rigas agreed to pay $189,000 in restitution to the agencies he'd defrauded, most of it to the SCA.

Marrone's résumé describes him as project manager for Hercules's New York City Housing Authority work from 1992 through 1995, and Rigas was charged with filing false certified payrolls with NYCHA for precisely that period. The SCA inspector general's (IG's) office played a pivotal role in developing the criminal case against Rigas.

Rigas was also accused of setting up Aim Construction—a phony WBE (Women's Business Enterprise)—to win affirmative action contracts. NYCHA records indicate that after Hercules was forced to drop the allegedly fake WBE in 1994, Rigas briefly replaced it with Builder Nine, a company that listed Fran Marrone as president and Gary Marrone as vice president. Sources indicate that the Marrones may have tried to certify the company as a WBE—an irony in view of the Conservative Party's fierce opposition to set-aside programs. Gary Marrone still drives a car with a "BUILDER9" license plate.

In addition to Gary Marrone's questionable hiring, Fran Marrone's employment at the agency may violate the city charter, which bars employing "a member of the state committee, an assembly district leader, or an officer of a county executive committee of any political party" in any position "with substantial policy discretion." Since the state legislation that created the SCA makes its employees subject to this charter provision, the agency's brass reportedly challenged Fran Marrone's hiring in 1995, arguing that she held all three party titles. But lawyers at the agency ruled that her position did not involve substantial discretion.

Fran Marrone has bounced from one political job to another since walking into Long's Brooklyn party headquarters two decades ago—working for State Senator Chris Mega and the state Crime Victims Board as well as the term-limits committee. Her only other known employment was as an officer of construction firms run out of the family home, one of which still has an Internal Revenue Service lien against it.

It is unclear how she got the SCA to waive its rules and hire her husband. The agency's HR-15 procedural rule expressly states that it "will not hire relatives of SCA employees to prevent any favoritism or conflict of interest," and lists "spouse" as the first familial relationship whose hiring "would violate the Authority's Nepotism Policy." SCA officials declined to answer questions about why Gary Marrone was exempted from this prohibition. Citing the ongoing work of the agency inspector general and the city's Department of Investigation, an SCA spokesman denied access to either Gary or Fran Marrone's résumé. The *Voice* did manage to obtain some résumé information from other sources, however.

Not only did Gary Marrone's connections at the highest levels of the SCA get him the job; they apparently insulated him for months despite the mounting criticism of his P.S. 131 performance. Bartolotti's "many, many calls" to the missing Marrone's supervisor had no effect on Marrone's assignment, or the supervisor's willingness to sign Marrone's time sheets. The district superintendent, Francis DeStefano, said the construction supervision was "terrible" and that the SCA "wasn't being responsive to a school community that told them the job wasn't being done right."

Ellie Engler, an industrial hygienist for the United Federation of Teachers who was frequently at the school, said that 70 percent of the top-floor classrooms were damaged by water leaking from the roof, teachers and students were exposed to asbestos, gates and doors to the pitched roof were left open, and that the SCA did little about any of it. "We tried to register complaints with the SCA, and the SCA didn't listen," Engler said. Finally, in October 1997, Randi Weingarten, the UFT president, went to the school and got Deputy Chancellor Spence to meet with teachers, parents, and the principal.

"There was an uproar in the school," Spence says. "I promised I'd do everything I could to clean it up. I went back to the SCA and told them it needed immediate attention and supervision. As a result of that intervention, the project officer was removed." Though Marrone was reassigned from the school on October 17—well before the Zhao incident—the subsequent investigation blasted him for a 17-month failure to insist on a sidewalk shed, and for his willingness to allow the fence to be removed from the area where the child was killed.

Zhao was outside the school on January 9—waiting for a friend—when two bricks holding down a tarp over the entrance struck her on the head and cut a 10-year-old girl standing nearby. "We believe there should have been a shed there the entire time," Buildings Department spokeswoman Ilyse Fink said when the incident occurred.

An SCA spokesman was also quoted in January as saying that the fence was taken down because, even though the roof work was ongoing, masonry work on that side of the building was finished. Sources in the DA's office say that SCA officials specifically declared that a sidewalk shed would have to be built as part of the job at a bidders conference in January 1996—prior to Marrone's arrival at the agency. Yet Marrone never required one.

Patronage has become synonymous with Pataki over the last three and a half years. An extraordinary *Daily News* series has suggested that even paroles may be purchased.

Paul Atanasio, the Pataki appointee at the heart of the Marrone scandal, has made Bear Stearns, his current employer, the number-one bond house in state government. Atanasio's first big killing in the Pataki era was at the Port Authority, where he secured a $100 million noncompetitive offering. The Authority executive director who approved the deal was George Marlin, the onetime mayoral candidate of the Conservative Party.

More recently, Atanasio won the senior management position on the $7 billion Long Island Power Authority bond issue, the biggest in history. Bear was also the agency's financial adviser structuring the offering. LIPA deputy director Patrick Foye is another active Conservative Party leader who, according to Andrea Bernstein in the *New York Observer*, encouraged Bear's selection as adviser.

As damning as this big-bucks influence peddling is, the public price tag does not include a young life. But at the SCA, it may well have.

It apparently was clear a year ago that Gary Marrone was not doing his job at P.S. 131, and everyone around him was afraid to act. If they had, Yan Zhen Zhao might still be alive.

Research: Tracie McMillan and Jarrett Murphy

PART III
Prince of the City

"For a moment, up against a real adversary, he did not look embattled by his own demons. His jaw relaxed. He listened. The unpracticed smile returned— less tooth, more lip. His eyes had a lightness to them. Even the shoulders did not stoop protectively. His new tragedy and test appeared to have surgically removed the distrust and cynicism that ordinarily grip him, and he became, at least momentarily, a whole and engaging man. It was enough to make those of us who've known him for a couple of decades wonder if he could rediscover himself."

—From "A Kinder, Gentler Rudy?"
May 2, 2000

The Journalist and the Prosecutor

Tom Robbins

WAYNE BARRETT wrote three books starring Rudy Giuliani. Together, they totaled almost 1,400 pages. That's not even counting the hundreds of articles he pounded out in the *Village Voice* and elsewhere in which the prosecutor turned politician was either hailed or fileted. Of the books, first was *City for Sale*, the story of New York's municipal corruption scandals in the 1980s that Wayne and his mentor, Jack Newfield, wrote together. Then came *Rudy!*, the deeply critical biography that Adam Fifield helped Wayne compile after Giuliani was elected mayor of New York. A few years later came *Grand Illusion*, the scorching investigation into Rudy's handling of 9/11 that Wayne coauthored with journalist Dan Collins.

Giuliani the prosecutor was the undisputed hero of the first one. The next two offered distinctly more jaundiced views of the man once dubbed "America's Mayor." After Giuliani's election, Wayne often caught flak from liberals who blamed him for helping create the aura of integrity that Giuliani rode into office. As Rudy's City Hall punished the poor, gave police free rein, and installed political hacks in the agencies, more than a few people wondered how it happened that Wayne and the lefty *Village*

Voice had initially bestowed their seal of approval on the crusading prosecutor. And while Wayne never said so explicitly, he clearly took it personally when the politician he'd helped mold began turning into his opposite.

It's an occupational hazard facing even the most skeptical reporters that we sometimes fall hard for those who stride grandly across our beat and whom we come to greatly admire. And there's no question but that for several years, one of those Wayne Barrett admired more than most was Rudy Giuliani.

It would have been surprising had things gone otherwise. After taking office as Manhattan's top federal prosecutor in 1983, Giuliani began pursuing many of the targets that Wayne was hounding in the *Voice*'s pages. Other prosecutors chased evidence first revealed in the *Voice*. But Giuliani took things farther and faster. He also expressed the same visceral disdain as Barrett for those who violated their oaths of office. As the stories in this collection illustrate, Wayne seethed at the venality of those whom he saw as trading on public trust for private gain. Back then, so did Rudy.

There were other links. Both Barrett and Giuliani were products of Catholic schools. Both had once considered entering the seminary. As young men, both had viewed Robert Kennedy as a personal hero. Both had chosen careers where the financial reward was modest in exchange for the ability to tilt their lances at wrongdoers. Just as important, when Wayne talked, Rudy listened. That was no small thing. In City Hall, Mayor Ed Koch openly scoffed at the *Voice* and its reporters. As a result, much of the city's press corps tended to shrug when the *Voice* reported that scandal was afoot in city government. Giuliani, however, read those stories closely. And he wanted to know more. He met often with Wayne and Jack, testing his theories and seeking theirs. An avid seeker of publicity, Giuliani courted many members of the press. But his relationship with Barrett and Newfield was different. It was a two-way street, where the prosecutor was often the one taking notes.

City for Sale dubbed the US attorney a "priestly prosecutor." It cited the life lessons he had learned from his working-class father—the same father Wayne would later discover had been a mob-tied stick-up man. Wayne and Jack even gave Rudy the last word: "It's inevitable there will be reform," they quoted him saying. If it sounded more like a vow than an observation, that was the idea.

Barrett and Giuliani were never social friends. They spoke often and shared many dinners, but the focus was shop talk. When Rudy launched his campaign for mayor, Wayne determined to keep his distance. Not that he didn't support some of the reforms the Republican was pledging. During the 1989 election, he wrote tough stories on both candidates. He told me later that he wasn't sure whom he was voting for until he got into the voting booth. In the end, his hand reached for the lever for Democrat David Dinkins, who was about to become the city's first black mayor. For Barrett, a white man raised in a southern Virginia town where racism was smotheringly pervasive, the issue of racial justice had come to define his life. During the late 1960s and 1970s, he and his wife, Fran, had chosen to live in Brownsville, one of Brooklyn's poorest neighborhoods and overwhelmingly black. When the teachers' union went on strike in protest against a bid for community control in nearby Ocean Hill and Brownsville, Wayne went to work teaching kids.

Giuliani lost that first election by a narrow margin and almost immediately began organizing a new campaign for 1993. This time the emphasis was less on civic reform, more on law and order and all the other subtexts of race in a city always wobbling between its best and worst instincts. I'm not sure exactly what turned Wayne's thinking about Rudy Giuliani, but I know his change of heart began when he realized Rudy was no longer running as the reformer but as the white guy against a vulnerable black incumbent. Once Giuliani was elected to office, the chasm only grew. Barrett watched as many of the same players he and Rudy had once agreed were prime candidates for investigation won City Hall favors.

Wayne always believed he had played it straight in writing about Giuliani, even when he was extolling his record. The prosecutor wasn't his target in those days, and Wayne hadn't scrutinized his past as he did later. When Wayne began researching his 2000 biography of the then two-term mayor, he realized that he had missed some crucial chapters. One of the most telling was Giuliani's handling of the Haitian refugee crisis in 1982, when he was at the Justice Department. Even before he started typing, Wayne told me how disturbed he was at what he found: in a precursor of today's Trump-ordered migrant holding pens, thousands of Haitians were being detained in scandalously filthy conditions awaiting extradition back to Haiti. Giuliani personally met with the brutal dictator they had fled, Baby Doc Duvalier. He then reported back to his bosses that there was no political repression in Haiti, thus no reason to grant asylum. Meanwhile, boatloads of Cuban refugees were put on the fast track to legal status. Rudy's response to the hapless Haitian refugees, Barrett realized, was a window into what was missing in the man, a moral sinkhole that had only grown larger with the years. That ailment helps explain the Giuliani we see today: a hollow man who gleefully serves as top legal gun for a rogue president, a man whose scams should have been on the radar of the old racket-busting prosecutor Wayne once knew.

Tom Robbins was a longtime *Village Voice* colleague and good friend of Wayne Barrett. He is investigative journalist in residence at the Craig Newmark Graduate School of Journalism of the City University of New York.

10

How Rudy Giuliani's Budget Will Destroy the City

Memo to Rudy

March 14, 1995

Barrett's castigations of Rudy as he grew into a craven, hollow version of himself carried a pale of mourning. He'd know the better man Rudy might have been. —Ed.

DEAR RUDY:
    When you announced your new four-year financial plan a few weeks ago, you invited anyone with other ideas about ways to close the city's immediate $2.7 billion gap to step forward. Though sometimes you seem as open to the advocates of budget alternatives as you were in the '80s to defense suggestions about what to present to a grand jury, it is time, regardless of your defensive disposition, for differing visions to surface.

While you prefer to portray the budget's bitter medicine as unavoidable, it is in fact a compendium of conscious choices. You have made constituency choices, partisan choices, class choices, age choices, even ethnic choices. All budgets do to a degree, but yours are the least evenhanded of any budget in the modern history of the city. Unless you redistribute this pain, your mayoral legacy will be a city divided along the very lines of your budget choices, wracked by a despair and suspicion unseen even when it teetered on bankruptcy 20 years ago. Unless you stand up to the unmistakable targeting of this city in Washington and Albany, you will not take the oath to guard it again, as surely as Mario Cuomo's 72 percent tally here last year demonstrated that New Yorkers understand, as you once did, that George Pataki will do nothing but hurt us.

You have faced hard choices with courage throughout your public life. It was not just ambition that propelled you to take on Mike Milken and the Lords of Wall Street; it was a reverence for justice in the face of unimaginable wealth, and an unflinching will. You prosecuted Robert Wallach, the best friend of the attorney general you worked for as US attorney, because no one could get to you. You turned your back on a powerful US senator from your own party who sent whispered messages to you on behalf of mobsters whose death threats could not deter you. You prosecuted a state senator from the same party, and tried unsuccessfully to dispatch him as your wired emissary to the Albany lair of a legislative body that was then the state GOP's only foothold of power. You nailed the son of Brooklyn's most powerful Republican leader.

The reward for these on-the-merits choices was a $13 million smear campaign in the 1989 mayoral primary of your party, the most vicious vilification of a candidate ever attempted in this city's politics. Your endorsement of Mario Cuomo last October, flying in the face of the same foreboding partisan forces that damaged you in 1989, was a redeclaration of your own independence. Emphasizing that you were supporting Cuomo because he was "his own man" revealed just how central it is to your own self-image to stand by your gut, to resist the tide, to be led by profoundly personal purpose.

Since you were never a partisan prosecutor, your promise to be a nonpartisan mayor, reiterated in two fusion campaigns, had a ring of credibility that has only now become faint. Having withstood the Meese, D'Amato, Anderson, Lauder, and other Republican tests of your grit, why bend now to Gingrich and a Peekskill shill?

There are transcendent moments in the life of a great city, and in the careers of its leaders, and this budget year is surely one. You are faced, in some respects, with the same overarching choice that Koch and LaGuardia—the two predecessors you most identify with—also confronted early in their mayoralties. In a 1987 *Dissent* essay, Irving Howe recounted how Ed Koch "realized," during the Reagan years, "that to remain a liberal would mean to pit himself, maybe hopelessly, against the powers of Washington," and so the one-time Mississippi marcher accommodated himself to the times, eventually coming "to enjoy the violation he was staging of his earlier self." Koch was to Reaganism, concluded Howe, what LaGuardia "had been to Roosevelt's New Deal—the municipal broker for the dominant social force in the country."

A budget that adds $400 million to the $800 million in welfare and Medicaid cuts already proposed by a suburban governor is, at root, a continuation of this conduit tradition, an amateurish attempt to mimic the meanness of the national mood to the detriment of a city you are charged with protecting. A public posture that implicitly welcomes a gouging Pataki tax cut that you debunked only last October may help doom the city not just this year but over the next half decade at least, to a starvation diet of Albany aid, squeezing every service from schools to universities to transit to health care that requires a minimal return on the investment New Yorkers make in their state government. A bow to Gingrich's new crime-bill proposal and abject silence in the face of all the damage his Contract {with America} will do to us have combined to create the image of a cowed mayor, cantankerous only with those too small to defend themselves, "a bully to the weak and a toady to the strong," as Jack Newfield once described Ed Koch.

If you think these shifts will make you one of them again, your lifetime of penetrating prosecutions taught you nothing about the darkness that blankets these soulless men. They hate you for the same reason I have long admired you: a proud honesty that separates you from a political culture encased in cynicism. Whatever message they sent you of forgiveness and threat, do not believe or fear it. You have fought them all your life and they will never accept you.

No knowledgeable critic demands that you respond to this crisis as David Dinkins or any classic Democratic liberal would. No reasonable observer can quarrel with the fact that the people of this city elected you, albeit marginally, because they wanted a mayor who would face these chronic deficits decisively at last, who might give us a year, by the end of his term, when we did not have to read the panic headlines that seem to come with every annual chart presentation in the Blue Room. No realist would expect you to shut precincts or add general business taxes.

But neither were the people of this city told—at any time in your continuous campaign for mayor that began in 1989—that you would countenance a multiyear budget plan that offered hundreds of millions of dollars in tax breaks for co-op and condo owners, financed with what could be lifted from the pockets of the poor and the sick. Though downtown was dead when you ran 16 months ago, you never intimated that you might make it a virtual tax-free zone to bail out a generation of overdevelopers—even as you so decimated the City University system that the Borough of Manhattan Community College, located in the heart of this giveaway zone and attended by one of the nation's largest black student bodies, would have to shut its doors to a third of its ordinary incoming class.

An inside-baseball discussion of Rudy's relationship with the Liberal Party, a minor party in New York that held significant political power because it cross-endorsed some Republican candidates (including Rudy), was cut here. —Ed.

I raised your favorite sound-bite stats with an aide of yours, especially the claim that even after reductions in the basic needs, rental, and other allotments for dependent children, the city's maximum payments to the poor would still be among the nation's 10 most generous. Pointing out that our cost of living was twice the national norm, I insisted that your reassuring shibboleth ignored the highly relative and relevant value of what that grant can buy, and he said determinedly: "If that leads to people making the decision that they'd be better off getting welfare in other places where the cost of living is lower, fine."

Paragraphs on the contents of a 39-page plan for fiscal and economic recovery developed by candidate Rudy during the campaign have been cut. —Ed.

The Rudy of 1989 launched his campaign with an announcement speech that noted that each time Koch attacked "those less fortunate by exaggerated and cruel characterizations," New York lost "a bit of its soul." Calling homelessness "a matter of conscience," you pledged to "end" it with small shelters and permanent housing, deriding the fact that the Koch administration only acted to aid the homeless when sued. "I will not need a court to respond to the suffering of New

Yorkers," you said. "Common decency, conscience, commitment—all of which I offer and will provide—compel us to do better. As mayor I will make a real commitment to the homeless." The only commitment now appears to be a resolve to make more of them.

Repeatedly citing your own role in recommending the appointment of the first Puerto Rican US attorney, Benito Romano, you made a "commitment that my administration will reflect the diversity of our city," promising to "recruit and bring into the government blacks, Latinos, Asians, women" so that "everyone sees a direct connection to the governing of this city." Before you took on the "color-blind" lens that has led in your government, as it inexorably has everywhere it is invoked in American culture, to regimes of comfortable look-alikes, you understood that empowering every group in a diverse city was a way "to end the alienation" and build "a government of inclusion."

*** *A further recounting of Giuliani's campaign promises was elided here. —Ed.* ***

My favorite memory of the 1989 Rudy, however, was your response during a WNBC-TV debate with cosmetics millionaire Ron Lauder, who referred to the homeless as "disgusting." Though you were in the midst of a Republican primary and competing for conservative votes, you interrupted him. "Ronnie really doesn't understand suffering in this city. He has no idea what it's like. Suffering to him is the butler taking the night off. We have people in this city who are suffering. We need to be compassionate about it."

*** *A discussion of homeless and drug-treatment policy and the electoral strategy of his 1993 campaign has been elided. —Ed.* ***

The fact is that I needn't reach back half a decade to find a different Giuliani. You are not even the mayor you were when you delivered your State of the City speech in January, or endorsed Cuomo in October. Throughout that period, the city's balance of payments with Albany and Washington was a constant centerpiece of your governing pitch, pointing out forcefully that this city produces billions more for state and federal government in taxes than it receives in benefits. Now that you are endorsing less, even asking those who are shortchanging us to go back to the drawing board and find more to take away, you have made it city policy to widen the very gap you bemoaned only moments ago.

I could not believe the upside-down candor of the top aide I talked with, who methodically explained to me how Pataki's brutal Medicaid cuts were "five times the budgetary relief" for the city than the long-sought but now abandoned state Medicaid takeover would have been. Reducing a question of fairness to one simply of cost, he said that the cuts have made "immaterial" the city's effort to get the state to pay the same share of Medicaid as every other state does.

A mayor whose constant theme is economic development is now rejecting billions in intergovernmental aid that is the lifeline for half the city's neighborhoods, where hospital, home-care, school-lunch, and Human Resource Administration jobs are the routes to upward mobility, and where even cash payments like welfare sustain the jobs in local commercial strips and at the corner bodega. The city council finance staff calculated last year that our savings on the 4,000 HRA jobs you cut was $ 7,400 per worker, while each slashed position was formerly drawing two to three times that in federal and state subsidies. Your budget, and the state and national priorities you are quietly acceding to, will put the employed bulwarks of struggling communities on the dependent rolls of the support system you disdain so much that you are cutting it, too.

Never before—not even when New York faced bankruptcy and our welfare grant really did exceed federal poverty levels—has any government of this city ever seriously considered an assault of any magnitude on the programs that federal and state governments pay for so overwhelmingly. Everyone understood that to do so made no economic sense even if these initiatives of Democratic and Republican administrations were belittled, as you do without providing any real evidence so far, as mere jobs programs. Everyone understood that blocking federal social-service dollars would turn many neighborhoods with economies of scarcity into battlegrounds for scraps, raising the temperature of a city already overheated with class and race tensions.

Your Budget Is the Least Evenhanded of Any in the City's Modern History

But forget compassion. Forget even the fragile stability of these neighborhoods. How is it that the Republicans in Washington understand that all politics is regional, that the Contract with America has less to do with ideology than with geography, and our mayor doesn't? A large part of the battle in D.C. is over the shifting balance of payments caused by a recent decline in defense allocations to the Southern and Mountain states, and the need for a party based in those states to lay claim to the disproportionate share of federal dollars they've long been accustomed to receiving. That's why the Republicans are prepared to finance defense increases (talk about a jobs program!) with social-service cuts.

*** *A discussion of federal funding and Food Stamps and several highly detailed proposals for targeted tax increases was cut here. —Ed.* ***

A budget that asks nothing of many while selectively savaging the poor does not convince this city that it is in real trouble; spreading the sacrifice will.

You have to deeply want to change the direction you've taken in the last few weeks to adopt much of my package. You have to recognize that you cannot become mayor of all the people if you do not. I believe you can because in the 10 years I've known you, it has always been ideas and people, not ideology or partisanship, that grabbed your attention. This plan is a low point in your public career, reminiscent of the day you surprised yourself and backed Alfonse D'Amato's 1992 reelection bid. If it is the plan of the man who backed D'Amato, against all of his own best instincts, you must make it the plan of the man who, two years later, endorsed Mario Cuomo, pushed forward by all that is caring and courageous within you.

You have to reread your Cuomo endorsement speech and remain true to its premise. That is both good budgetary advice and good political advice. Recast as a Cuomo Republican, you may be unbeatable in this town, ready for the necessary combat with a governor you correctly described four and a half months ago. You cannot let your government be shaped by the tainted tabloid duo of the *Post* and *News*, whose every editorial sentence is a lesson in class warfare, sold to the struggling, but written in service to the comfortable.

A paragraph about Giuliani's first-year budget was elided. —Ed.

I remember you the day in New Haven in 1986 that you convicted Stanley Friedman, the maypole of a city circled with corruption. You were so worn by a trial you risked everything to handle yourself that a blood vessel had burst in your eye, and your cheek was covered with red shaving scars. No one I knew worked harder, moved, no doubt, by a desire to lift your own career, but also out of a rooted conviction of right and wrong. Our generation did not come to power to cancel every effort at what is good that was clumsily crafted by our fathers and mothers. We did not come through the '60s to make Newt's or George's revolution. There is still time for us to become builders, not wreckers.

Research: Marcus Baram and Denise Kiernan

11

The Color of the Cuts

June 20, 1995

The pages of the *Village Voice* in the months after the Gingrich Revolution were full of alarm at the cruelty and extremism of the new congress, aware that the country was undergoing a monumental shift in its understanding of the purpose of government. Barrett's articles focused on the racial politics behind the economics, from prison expansion to winnowing public hospitals. He raised an alarm on matters the country is grappling with now, a quarter century later. —Ed.

FOR TWO COLOR-BLIND GUYS, it's uncanny how often the Republican mayor and governor keep hitting black and brown targets with their 9mm budget blasters. Elected with over 35 percent of the Latino vote, Rudy Giuliani would prefer no doubt to find a way to narrow still more the racial scope of his fiscal fire, but the interconnectedness of minority life in this town won't permit it. The ethnic dimension of these punishing policies is only one of the plausibly deniable, yet nonetheless real, occurrences of a spring budget season in New York when nothing has bloomed but paradox.

Competing for months over who could take more shots at those cycling dependents riding out of the government bank with bags of Medicaid and welfare loot, Rudy and George {Pataki} pretended not to notice that the $800 million to $1.2 billion they were chasing was disproportionately going to minorities. In a last-ditch effort to get assembly Democrats to join this Medicaid/welfare assault, Rudy threatened to fire away at middle-class programs like libraries and the arts if he didn't get what he wanted, but everyone seemed to know instinctively that his last white target was Mike Milken, two jobs and two campaigns ago. Sure enough, the mayor who constantly berates the Board of Ed for its worst-case-scenario menu of cuts dropped his "middle-class" contingency plan overnight and went back to the welfare well for tens of millions more in savage savings.

The new Rudy plan, just announced last Friday, also seeks another $100 million out of the blackest and brownest of targets, the Health and Hospitals Corporation. Even though the nurses' aides collecting bedpans are camouflaged in white, it is the city's most minority workforce, serving the city's most minority patients, and ever since Rudy and George came to power, they and their cleaning and feeding cohorts in city hospitals have been sitting ducks for gunslingers at City Hall and in Albany. The same mayoral candidate who endlessly assailed the city's Off-Track Betting Corporation as the "only bookie" losing money (when it was in black hands) is so busy privatizing public health care he's forgotten his pledge to get the city out of the patronage-producing (mostly white now) racehorse business.

Derided as if it were the city's only "jobs program," HHC has become the best example of the Giuliani administration's "disaffirmative action" policies. In the mayor's closely confined universe of all-white decision makers, it is just one more color-blind coincidence that police and fire are the city's whitest agencies and that these jobs programs keep hiring.

Getting cops out from behind their desks so we can save money with cheaper civilians is such a no-no to the Tough Guy Mayor that all the editorial boards and auditors and observers who screamed for it last year aren't even bothering to return to the still-true theme. Firefighters, too, have been hoisted on the untouchable "public safety" petard, so that even their attrited vacancies are slated for refilling, as if they, like cops, are part of the mayor's elastic electoral mandate.

Also back on the butcher's-block table in the mayor's new wave of cuts, as well as singled out in one more discriminatory state appropriation formula, is the Board of Ed, whose per capita pupil expenditures are lower than Peekskill's but still far too high for these partners in precision budgeting.

The kids at the turnstiles who may become the first in the nation to pay to travel to public school—perhaps more, with the MTA {Metropolitan Transit Authority} deficit, than the current transit fare of $2.50 a day—are disproportionately black and brown. (Lucky us, though, we have squads of quality-of-life cops ready to handcuff them if they try to jump the turnstile.) Art and music will vanish from public school classrooms; so will junior varsity sports. Referee Rudy will blow the whistle on the games that give so many kids a lift. He will not notice, of course, the color of the ninth-grade hand no longer going up with a jumpshot.

As a transparent distraction from the devastation of his school cuts, the mayor has also simultaneously launched a campaign to put the board's sexually overactive security guards (minority) under the aegis of the only growing public or private enterprise in the city, the Billieboys at NYPD, who can be counted on to be white and to prefer a beer to a babe.

In all the tightfisted clamor about this proposal, the media has barely noticed that the outgoing school security chief, much quoted because he now favors the Rudy Remedy, has also quietly conceded that the main reason his unit failed is because he had only 60 supervisors for 3,000 guards. He said he begged for more but instead had to make a 20 percent cut as a result of last year's Giuliani budget.

What happened to the Board of Ed's legendary administrative bloat? Can it be that the only way to get enough supervision over this unarmed army in the schools is to annex it to 1 Police Plaza, where desk-job bloat is still beautiful? Could court officers and school crossing guards be next? What about those renegade Port Authority police or the Park Rangers? Is the Pentagon safe?

The City University is the blackest and brownest major public university system in America. The mayor who likes to tell us again and again how high our Medicaid and welfare benefits rank nationally—distorting the welfare figures when he does—never mentions that tuition at CUNY community colleges is higher than it is at 95 percent of similar institutions across the country.

While his and the state's budget push community college tuition even higher, no one but City Comptroller Alan Hevesi mentions that it is already twice the national average. If picketed or questioned by angry or even pleading students, the-mayor-who-has-never-met-a-tax-on-wealth-he-didn't-want-to-cut tells them sternly that paying more to get a college degree will be a good, reality-check lesson for them. Presumably, that's what every injustice with a decided yet presumptively accidental racial edge is, at least in the Giuliani civic classroom.

The workforce reductions at the Human Resources Administration—the hardest-hit city agency—and the decimation of the Youth Services hit minorities harder than anyone else.

The combined state and city blows at foster care, day care, and preventive care target the very households GOP rhetoric already maligns every day.

The extraordinary neighborhood-by-neighborhood analysis released weeks ago by Hevesi's office specifies the exclusively minority communities that will lose tens of millions in economic activity as a result of these budgets, up to "about 20 per cent of their total neighborhood economies." Yet George and Rudy rationalize every spending and tax cut they propose as an economic stimulus, oblivious to the reality that we are a city and state with two economies, and that the urban factory, for example, is now a hospital, and when you kill it, you kill a community.

As indifferent as he is to the collapse of Bronx and Brooklyn neighborhoods where health care is the largest employer, the new governor has no difficulty recognizing and refinancing the economic engine that drives many of the upstate communities that elected him. Though too short on cash to deliver much this year, Pataki manhandled the assembly into a secret, 10-year, sentencing-reform agreement that will, by the time he is seeking reelection, lead to hundreds, if not thousands, of more jail cells in counties where his votes are. A new or expanded prison to Oneida County is what a hospital is to the Bronx—a centripetal employer with a magnificent multiplier effect. He even wrote into the budget a requirement that the new drug treatment facilities required by the sentencing changes be built in his electoral heartland.

The wonder of Pataki's economic stimulus package for upstate is that the bumper crop that feeds it are black and brown felons. The tighter the downstate crunch, shoving an increasingly desperate urban underclass toward crime, the bigger the upstate prison population explosion. Eighty-two percent white, the state's 21,000 prison guards can be counted on to rush to the polls in

1998 to pull the lever for the policies that an assembly estimate indicates may produce $20 billion in new cells over the next two decades.

No one has any evidence that the tougher sentences for violent felons—the Citizens Budget Commission says the governor's new sentences may double incarceration time for up to 30 percent of the population—will actually reduce crime. All we know is that it satisfies the hunger for punishment as surely as it shifts state resources regionally.

Combined with the Medicaid and welfare cuts, the coming prison boom, not expected to get fully underway for a couple of years, will accelerate the redistribution of state resources away from the city and to the already blessed upstate bastions of the supposedly antigovernment GOP. It follows and no doubt will repeat the "success" of the largest prison expansion in any state ever, pushed by Mario Cuomo and the Republican senate in the '80s. Why is it that some Wars on Poverty, no matter how often they fail, can be tried again and again, with even bigger bucks?

There is, as well, no limit to the money even a broke governor can find to repave and rebuild upstate highways and bridges, even while he calls a halt to bonds for transit projects in the city and joins the mayor in an assault on the MTA budget that will undercut maintenance in a system already on a deadly collision course.

Pataki has even turned the racial legacy of his party's last elected predecessor, Nelson Rockefeller, into a cynical joke, making the Urban Development Corporation the prime funder for suburban pools and upstate stadiums. Created in 1968, with Rocky twisting arms long distance while marching in Martin Luther King's Atlanta funeral, UDC was supposed to be the single greatest force for housing and community integration in the country. Instead, the new gang in Albany plunders it for bond-financed booty, much of it targeted for the well-off. That they have to turn to UDC to pay for these projects is a paradox—launched at a time of such terrible cutback—because there will be no money in the 1996 state till for them once the first-year tax cut for the rich goes into effect.

What's most astounding, after this roll call of discriminatory state and city choices, is that the mayor and governor can declare, with straight and even scolding faces, that their actions will have no or little effect. Rudy denounces as "doomsayers" those who merely want to hold him accountable for what he is doing to the scapegoated. He will not let truth enter the cocoon. He attacks the critics who suggest other ways to salvage the budget. He cozies up to the unions that may help reelect him, not adding a dollar to their expected budgetary contribution. He pretends he has an ideology when all he has is a scorecard. His fake friend Pataki screws up that pained country-boy grin and pats himself on the tax cut–death penalty back.

Neither of them may actually know a poor person. Neither has seen the sun go down in Brownsville, where all that was hopeful is dying. There are faces in this city that cannot be seen from where these men sit. But they know a bully when they see one. They know liars too. And Rudy is right about one thing: They do not need a CUNY degree to know when someone is coming after them.

Research assistance by Dierdre Guthrie, E. Assata Wright, Sheila Maldonado

Cheap Lives

Tracie McMillan

I N 1998, as I was nearing the end of eight months
working under Wayne Barrett at the *Village Voice*,
he handed me a task that changed my life. I no longer have the
yellow legal pad where I tracked my work, or a copy of the dot-
matrix notes I printed out from the green-screen computer and
left piled on his chair. But I can see it anyway: a handwritten
check-box and the phrase "Call Sheila Williams."

Barrett told me to call Ms. Williams because of a tragedy: her
20-year-old daughter, Sonya, had died in a 1991 stampede at City
College. Police had failed to control the crowd at a basketball
tournament featuring celebrity rappers, and nine young people,
all black, had died. They had lain underfoot as a police captain
instructed 66 officers, including eight already inside the gym, not
to act—even as college officials and 911 callers begged for help.
A police radio communication from the incident included an
officer's assessment of the students inside: "They're not humans.
They're animals."

The families of the dead students filed wrongful-death lawsuits
against New York City, the state, a private security company, and
the event's promoters: Sean "Puff Daddy" Combs and Dwight
"Heavy D" Myers. Shortly before Barrett must have asked me to
call Ms. Williams, a judge had approved a $3.2 million settlement.

When Barrett handed me that task, he would have told me that the Giuliani administration refused to pay anything until the judge ordered the city to take responsibility. In response, New York offered 2.5 percent of the total, so little that the other defendants threatened to settle separately. In the end, the city paid 5 percent: $166,000.

And then, Barrett would have told me why he was writing about this case: Mayor Rudolph Giuliani had recently held a press conference to announce a different, much higher profile wrongful death settlement. This was the city's response to 80 plaintiffs[*] charging police negligence and violations of civil rights in the 1991 Crown Heights riots. The city paid those plaintiffs $1.35 million,[†] with the mayor directly apologizing to the family of Yankel Rosenbaum, the riots' single fatality, for the city's "clearly inadequate response."[‡]

It wasn't Barrett's style to tell me to ask Ms. Williams personal questions: how it felt to lose her daughter, what the loss had meant, what her truth was. Instead, he told me to ask what she thought about the divide he saw, and named. For her family, she said, "Giuliani did nothing....I don't know what reason there could be other than discrimination."[§]

What Barrett probably didn't tell me, but ended up writing, was that the problem wasn't just racist city bureaucrats—it was racist media attention, too. "Saturation press coverage helped

---

[*] Reported in the *New York Times* on April 3, 1998.

[†] Note that other accounts put the settlement at $1.1 million, such as this *Times* piece: www.nytimes.com/1998/04/03/nyregion/mayor-apologizes-for-city-response-to-crown-heights.html.

[‡] *Ibid.*

[§] Wayne Barrett, with research by Tracie McMillan and Jarrett Murphy, "Cheap Lives: How Rudy Stonewalled the Families of Nine Dead Black Students," *Village Voice*, April 21, 1998.

create a moral imperative to compensate the Crown Heights victims," wrote Barrett. "But the media never even covered the CCNY lawsuits, walking away from the story immediately."*

Barrett wrote that story for politicians and citizens in New York, and maybe it changed things in some small way there. For me, helping report it created a shift, slow moving but tectonic in scale, in how I understood racism, and its centrality to honest journalism.

I'd grown up, like most white Americans of my era, knowing that racism was wrong. But this was an opposition to overt, articulated hatred. In college, I was learning about racism's complexities and its flip side, white privilege. On that settlement story, I learned something far more powerful: racism can be measured in dollars and cents, as much as lives lost. I've been learning to calculate its cost ever since.

Tracie McMillan is author of the *New York Times* best seller *The American Way of Eating*. She is working on her second book, *The White Bonus*, about the cash value of whiteness in America, for Henry Holt. She interned for Wayne Barrett in 1998.

---

* *Ibid.*

12

Rudy's Milky Way: An Administration "Of, for, and by White People" Has No Time or Room for Blacks

January 19, 1999

With special reporting by Nicole White

H IS WORLD IS AS white as Seinfeld's, a slice of the city so comfortably one-dimensional that even the popular star of the ongoing Giuliani serial cannot see his own, peculiarly un–New York, isolation. Not since the days of Vincent Impellitteri nearly half a century ago—through the tenures of Robert Wagner, John Lindsay, Abe Beame, Ed Koch, and David Dinkins—have there been so few black faces in high places in a city administration. Never before has 80 percent of any ethnic group rejected the reelection campaign of an incumbent mayor, as exit polls said blacks did in 1997, preferring a white woman they barely knew who had no chance to win.

And never before have more of a mayor's targets—squeegees, cabbies, street vendors, public-hospital workers, welfare recipients, police-brutality victims, CUNY students, and the dispersed elderly ill {the} from Neponsit nursing home—been so consistently of one hue while his beneficiaries—cops, firefighters, hotel

operators, express-bus riders, tax-break developers, Staten Island-
ers, and Yankees and Jets owners—been so consistently another.

All his life Rudy Giuliani has occupied a milky universe—
raised in a blanched Nassau suburb, educated at insular Bishop
Loughlin High School and Manhattan College, shuttling twice
between the colorless cubicles of the Justice Department in Washington and the US Attorney's Office in Manhattan, practicing law
at three mainline firms where not just the shoes were white.

As a kid born in Brooklyn, he rooted for the all-white Yankees
while Jackie Robinson crossed the color line at Ebbets Field, just
a couple of miles away from his home. He so craves the familiar
he married his own cousin. He quarantined Haitians in Florida
camps for the Justice Department. The first home he ever bought
was an apartment in the East 80s, and he has never lived, like so
many white New Yorkers, on a block alive with human diversity.
The only two blacks he regularly talks to at City Hall today are
both named Rudy, but neither Crew nor Washington has been
able to help him past his racial wall.

Now focused on a Senate race just a year or so away, he knows
every button to push to reach white voters but did not, even with
a bottomless campaign treasury in 1997, buy a millisecond of advertising in any black medium. One of four mayors who replaced
black incumbents in recent years—including those in L.A., Chicago, and Philadelphia—he is a national emblem of urban reas-
surance, a tamer of the tribe. He always has his defeat of the city's
first black mayor as a ready excuse for black hostility to him five
years later, an alibi that saps any obligation to bridge what has
become a gulf of fearful proportions.

Blacks are a grand abstraction to him. He rarely hosts town
meetings in their neighborhoods. He frequently lectures them
about everything from their child-rearing habits—attacking a

mother for allowing her teenage son to be out bicycling at 2:30 a.m. when a cop gunned him down—to their work ethic. He's spent the year riding the sky from one Republican capital to the next, engulfed by a party so fair it cannot be fair, telling Arizonans in April that Phoenix feels "like home" and that "the issues" in that 5 percent–black town "are very much the same" as in 25 percent–black New York. He is never heard discussing racism or poverty as if they are real facts that a mayor could actually combat.

He is too busy crediting himself for crime reductions to ever mention that the communities ravaged a decade ago by crack and guns might have had something to do with the decline, helping to deliver themselves from a culture of death. He is certain that work resurrects the dependent even when it takes good mothers away from their children to push brooms on city streets without any promise of a genuine job. Not only is he ready with a knee-jerk benefit of the doubt virtually anytime a cop goes head to head with an African American; he does not appear to have a doubt.

In his first weeks in office in 1994, Giuliani refused to meet with Al Sharpton and others over a police raid at a Harlem mosque. It worked so well he's been rejecting black guests or invitations ever since. He said no when David Dinkins asked him to his home for dinner after a war of words over Crown Heights. The new borough president of Manhattan, Virginia Fields, who ran on the Liberal line with him last year and is known for her warmth and equanimity, begged for a meeting during the recent Million Youth March controversy and was instead denounced as a "coward," along with the rest of the African American leadership.

Carl McCall, the highest-ranking black official in state history, takes trips to Israel with a Republican governor, but was stood up when he tried to arrange a sit-down with the mayor. Neither did Rudy have time for the cabbies, who are now mostly African and

South Asian, even when they believed by the thousands that his new taxi rules threatened their livelihoods. A *Voice* survey of 35 black leaders, 30 of them elected, identified many who'd reached out to the mayor on issues ranging from AIDS funding to the Harlem march, usually without so much as a callback.

The city's Equal Employment Practices Commission, a quasi-independent body that is supposed to monitor minority hiring, said in its annual report in 1996 that it "looked forward to a meeting with Rudy Giuliani" to discuss the draft of a new equal opportunity plan. Even though the city charter requires both a plan and a mayoral consultation with the EEPC, according to Abe May, the commission's executive director, "none ever occurred." Jointly appointed by the mayor and the council, the mildly critical commission Rudy would not meet with is, to this day, chaired by Charlie Hughes, the scandal-scarred D.C. 37 union president who appeared in Giuliani television ads in 1997.

Yet Priscilla Wooten, the city councilwoman who endorsed Giuliani last year and was the only leader surveyed by the *Voice* to praise him without caveat, tells the story of how her husband was recently awakened from a daytime nap on the porch of their East New York home by a tap on the shoulder. Wooten's husband "thought he was dreaming when he saw Rudy smiling in his face," the councilwoman said. All it takes is a lot of amens, and Rudy is, after all, willing to minister to a select black flock.

As painfully apparent as this chasm is, the *Times*'s endorsement of Giuliani last year did not make a single cautionary mention of race. When Reverend Calvin Butts, a prominent Harlem minister, branded the mayor a racist this May, a *Times* editorial characterized Giuliani's relationship with minorities merely as one "marked by clumsiness and needless tension."

While the *Times* has acknowledged that blacks "feel bruised and excluded" by the administration, the paper of record has yet to examine Giuliani's antiblack underside in any comprehensive or ongoing fashion. Remarkably, black management drew far more attention in the less-polarized Koch era, and David Dinkins absorbed three nonstop years of media body blows as a supposed anti-Semite. Yet the whiteout of the Giuliani story— in the *Times* and elsewhere—has marginalized blacks, misinformed whites, and allowed Rudy to continue to portray himself like he did in his now laughable 1993 campaign slogan, as the mayor of "one standard, one city."

The *Times* has brilliantly dissected Giuliani's welfare agenda, for example, but it hasn't connected these policies to his overall impact on blacks, thereby contributing to the color-blind camouflage concealing the administration's seemingly irresistible targets. The paper's excellent coverage of Giuliani's overnight evacuation of the Neponsit nursing home in Queens last year, resulting in daily $3,050 fines by federal health authorities for violations of commonsense safety regulations, did not mention that most of the evicted residents who appeared at a city council hearing were elderly blacks living with every kind of affliction.

When the Council of Black Elected Officials convened in Harlem shortly after the Million Youth March to assail Giuliani as "unconscionable" and to claim he'd given their request for a meeting "the back of his hand," no city daily wrote a word. The council includes officials representing 2.5 million people.

Black voices of outrage are seldom aired. Distilled facts are presented again and again in story after story. All that's missing is the context of continuous attack that most black New Yorkers now understand instinctively.

Indeed, Rudy has managed to so bury the race question—converting anyone who raises it into a proverbial arsonist—that even his liberal opponent last year, Ruth Messinger, seldom dared. Only the brutality issue is regularly presented in unavoidably racial terms.

But even there, Giuliani's incident-by-incident indifference, the sacking of his own post–Abner Louima task force, his resistance to a twice-passed council bill for an independent commission, and his police commissioner's rejection of abuse cases substantiated by the Civilian Complaint Review Board have hardly become a media censure of him. White editorial boards forget black agony over this five-year mountain of CCRB complaints, which increased again in the data that was released last week, when they write their periodic paeans to the mayor.

Rudy kept at his side a deputy mayor whose "watermelon" reference to a black-owned financial company and "two-white-men-have-run-New-York-for-200-years" comments were called "racist" by the *Times*. He said nothing during an on-air appearance with his then friend Bob Grant when Grant called Congressman Charlie Rangel a "pygmy." Asked by the *Washington Post* to defend his record on minorities, he said: "They're alive, how about we start with that," which he later explained as a reference to plunging homicide rates. He was once quoted as saying that it would be "a good thing" if poor people "left the city," conceding that driving them out of town through welfare cuts was "not an unspoken part of our strategy; it is our strategy."

In his first months in office, he eliminated the special assistants who acted as liaisons to particular ethnic groups, including blacks, but the worst-kept secret at City Hall was that one of his top aides continued to perform that function with the Jewish community for years. He also wiped out Dinkins's set-aside program for women and minority contractors, promising to increase minority contracting without any formal preference program. He has never offered a scintilla of evidence since then that he's done that.

Giuliani has hired 1,500 investigators to scrutinize the desperate claims of the welfare poor even while he's cut the inspectors and attorneys who insure housing-code compliance to a mere 243. He's created a test for homelessness that requires shelter seekers to prove they aren't warehousing castles.

These are the barely noticed racial anomalies of life in Rudyland. They flit on and off our pages and our screens. But they are, in a city where blacks have long since transcended Ralph Ellison's telling title, a constant challenge and concern.

We are a better city than Rudy will let us be. Municipal governments are not corporations judged only by bottom-line stats of tax and welfare cuts. There is a love here he can't feel, one that is not just tough.

Research assistance by David Kihara, Will Johnson, Coco McPherson, Soo-Min Oh, and David Shaftel

13

Raging Bull
February 16, 1999

Amadou Diallo, an unarmed man, was shot by police 41 times in the early morning of February 4, 1999. His death, one in a string of high-profile police killings of black men while Giuliani was mayor, prompted outrage and weeks of protest. More than 1,200 people, including many elected officials, were arrested in civil disobedience at NYPD headquarters. Barrett's reporting documented the ratcheting up of police aggression under Giuliani that preceded these killings. —Ed.

H E STOOD IN THE closetlike vestibule of his Soundview home, reaching for the keys in his pocket, his eyes filled with terror at the four barking white faces just feet from him with guns as large as history. This newly arrived African, who chose America, would be greeted by a welcome wagon of 9mm bullets in the darkness of the night. Every mother in New York descended from a slave could see her son, every man himself.

The mayor suspended judgment. He asked for patience. A two-story house became a pockmarked memorial visited by thousands and yet the mayor, who's never missed a water-main break, stayed away from the 41 holes in the heart of his city.

Within 14 hours of Amadou Diallo's death, Rudy Giuliani left town for Pennsylvania to regale a banquet room of white Republicans with the story of how he'd tamed New York. His shadow, the same police commissioner who'd canceled a trip to a national police conference to be at his side the week before the 1997 election, flew almost as quickly to California for a five-day parley, and the mayor said the trip was okay. "It wouldn't make sense to interrupt him," Giuliani explained as angry crowds gathered near his fenced-off City Hall, "unless there was an actual crisis going on, which there isn't."

The mayor met with a delegation of African leaders, and when one told the press that he {the mayor} had expressed sorrow over this "regrettable mistake," his press secretary rushed to correct the diplomat, insisting he'd never called it a mistake, only a "tragedy." Then he manufactured body-count charts he thought could answer a cry no number could silence and, pointer in hand, delivered a lecture on NYPD restraint.

He had talked for years about how well he understood police officers. He'd told us that four of his uncles were cops. At the funerals of policemen and firemen, he had repeatedly spoken of them and their families as the special people of New York, the best of our time. Tin-eared now, he could not hear Diallo or his family. He could not feel the pain of so many of the people of his city because, in truth, these were not his people.

Black men died at the hands of New York police long before Rudy Giuliani took office. They will continue to die if he moves on to become Senator Cop. But the mayor who has made himself synonymous with the NYPD cannot be surprised if a city that credits him, at his own insistence, for the department's anticrime success also blames him for its savage excess. He cannot evade a share of responsibility for police aggression when it kills the gentle if he tours the land seeking plaudits when it supposedly stops criminals in their tracks.

Beginning with his demagogic 1992 appearance at a police riot near City Hall to protest David Dinkins's creation of the Civilian Complaint Review Board (CCRB), Giuliani has a record of contributing to a climate of brutality that now grips every community of color in New York:

When the Abner Louima incident threatened his reelection campaign in 1997, he appointed a 28-member task force, saying he believed that "there is a real opportunity, one that only gets presented to you for a period of time, to permanently change the way in which the Police Department relates to the communities in NYC." Five months after the election, he dismissed the task force's one-inch-thick report, saying its recommendations "made very little sense," agreeing to adopt only the one that called for changing the title of the NYPD's office of community affairs to community relations. "That's a good change," he said.

CCRB complaints have risen from 3,580 in 1993, the last year of Dinkins, to 4,975 in 1998, a 39 percent increase. While complaints soared to a high of 5,618 in 1995, they dipped to a low of 4,816 in the middle of the mayor's 1997 reelection campaign, climbing upward again last year by 4 percent. A *Dateline* investigative crew using black "testers" twice found contemptuous resistance when they tried to file a complaint at a precinct in 1997 and 1998.

Though a city commission that investigated police misconduct recommended the creation of a permanent independent monitor, Giuliani has twice vetoed and bottled up in court city council–approved bills to create one. "A much better way to improve the police department," argued a mayor who'd once headed federal probes of corrupt cops, "is to get it to investigate itself."

The largest increases in CCRB complaints between 1993 and 1997 involved allegations about invasions of privacy. Premises searched went from 29 complaints to 166; persons searched from 232 to 502; property damaged from 157 to 223. Unholstered-gun complaints went from 38 to 66, and threats of arrest climbed from 166 to 402. Only four complaints were filed about the firing of police weapons in 1993, compared with 26 in 1995 and 20 {each} in 1996 and 1997.

A Brooklyn grand jury declined in 1997 to indict two cops who'd fired 24 times at an unarmed black man sitting in a car, but issued a muted report criticizing the Street Crime Unit that subsequently killed Diallo. Though Brooklyn DA Joe Hynes is a Giuliani fan, the mayor assailed him for "engaging in a little more of a political exercise than an exercise in revealing facts." The report's nine recommendations died on its pages, though many, such as the finding that officers in the unit had "too much discretion," may be hauntingly relevant to the Diallo shooting.

Disturbed that one of the cops had emptied his 16-shot Glock, the grand jury concluded that "the goals of the NYPD with respect to controlling the number of shots fired" in situations like this had "not been achieved." It was also upset that there was "no formal criteria or testing" for assignment to the street crime unit. Citing the NYPD director of training, who said that precinct commanders look for "characteristics like arrest activity, a willingness to be proactive, somebody that is assertive," the grand jury faulted the department for not giving all the officers in the unit specialized training.

The latest CCRB report, covering January to June 1998, found a 58 percent increase in police beatings compared with the first six months of 1997, as well as a 27 percent hike in "drag/pull" allegations and a 39 percent jump in pepper-spray incidents. Even the Giuliani-appointed CCRB concluded that the recent rise was "troubling."

When eight congressmen, led by the senior Democrat on the House Judiciary Committee, John Conyers, held a public hearing on police brutality here, the mayor denounced it as a "political rally" though it was deliberately held after his reelection. The Department of Justice and the US attorney testified, and 1,000 people attended, but Giuliani ignored Conyers's public appeal to "please, Mr. Mayor, give me a minute or two." After one speaker went off on a momentary rant about Jews, the mayor quickly used the incident to denounce Conyers et al. for "not standing up to bigotry."

When 16-year-old Michael Jones was fired at 17 times by cops, one of whom also emptied a Glock, the mayor repeatedly assailed his mother while Jones lay in a hospital with six bullet wounds. Blaming the shooting on the fact that Jones was riding his bike armed with an ominous-looking toy gun, Giuliani said: "Adult supervision would have prevented the gun. It would also have prevented being out at 2:30 in the morning for whatever purpose, and I don't think the purpose for which he was out was a salutary one." There was no evidence that Jones, who survived, was involved in any criminal activity.

A New York Civil Liberties Union review of Police Commissioner Howard Safir's handling of CCRB complaints found that the mayor's constant companion had "in effect nullified" 66 percent of the tiny number "substantiated" by the agency. CCRB investigations confirmed only 5 percent of complaints, passing them on to Safir for disciplinary action. He did nothing on more than two-thirds of the cases. When Safir did act, 60 percent of the time he imposed "the most lenient disciplinary measures"—a verbal warning or forfeiture of up to 10 vacation days. The irony is that Safir himself has three appointees on the CCRB and, as the agency observed in its own report, "panels of the Board almost always substantiate a case with the concurrence of a police commissioner designee."

Giuliani dissed a 1996 Amnesty International report that reviewed 90 police brutality cases as "exaggerated," saying the organization had "a viewpoint." He stonewalled a request from Public Advocate Mark Green to examine the department's handling of substantiated CCRB complaints, saying that Green's "motivations are political," and tying up Green for two years in still-ongoing appeals that have already lost before five judges. The mayor also threw out the "political" defense at comptrollers Alan Hevesi and Carl McCall when they tried to audit the NYPD, forcing McCall to sue and stalling Hevesi for three years.

When a Bronx judge acquitted Francis Livoti of the chokehold death of Anthony Baez, Giuliani called the verdict "a careful, well-thought-out, legally reasoned opinion." Livoti was later convicted in federal court. When a cop with seven civilian complaints in four years, three of which had been substantiated by the CCRB and involved excessive force, shot a squeegee at point-blank range last year, the mayor saw it as "an ambiguous situation" with facts that "argue for the police officer" as well as for the homeless man who lost his spleen.

The facts that argued for the cop were the victim's half dozen minor drug-possession convictions over the prior decade, prompting the mayor to liken the shooting to one of a low-level drug dealer. "It doesn't mean we're going to stop enforcing the law against drug dealers," said Giuliani, pledging that his celebrated war against squeegees would continue.

The mayor opposes residency laws for city cops. His corrections department strip-searched all 53,000 misdemeanor arrestees for 10 months in 1996 and 1997, until stopped by a lawsuit. Court claims against the city for cop misconduct rose 74 percent between 1993 and 1997. Giuliani's first four budgets—including the one issued three months before the Louima incident—cut funding for the CCRB. Had the cuts not been restored by the city council, he would have cumulatively removed $2.4 million from a $5.2 million agency. Shortly after the Louima incident, Giuliani added $1.5 million to CCRB's budget, only to call for a $588,000 cut a week after his reelection. The mayor's most insidious defense of the police is to float the notion that those who criticize cops in incidents like Diallo are "cop bashers" who evince a form of "prejudice" no different than racism and anti-Semitism. Nothing disturbs the NYCLU's {New York Civil Liberties Union's} Norman Siegel more: "To equate hundreds of years of oppression based on immutable racial traits with criticism of the tactics and practices of individual police officers," he says, "is to show how disconnected Rudy Giuliani is to this issue." It is a disconnect of denial, a disconnect of convenience. The mayor is fond of attacking every criticism as political. But it is he who has positioned himself as New York's Mighty Whitey, playing to the national avatars of a party that long ago abandoned Lincoln. It is he who has justified the "benefit of the doubt" he gives cops by contending that "crime would not have gone down as much" if he "let police officers hang out there" and stayed neutral until all the facts about an incident are known. It is he who, on his way to Washington, will leave this city bitterly partitioned, with blacks and whites blind to each other.

Research assistance by Coco McPherson, Soo-Min Oh, and Ron Zapata

Killer B and Me

Peter Noel

I N THE NEARLY 30 years I had known Wayne Barrett, I felt that the man I affectionately called "the Killer B" had wholly "Africanized" me.

This is not a confession, but an epiphany about a series of teaching moments that would disrupt my radical politics and relationship with Barrett for years to come. It was not until I considered the formative impact that Barrett's solidarity and friendship with Black radicals in Brownsville, Brooklyn, had on him that the man's influence on me made much sense.

Barrett, after all, understood the overt, covert, and denialist nature of race and racism in America and nuanced every argument about its racial politics with his own brand of "pragmatic Barrettism." But when he deep-dived into your shallow battology, things turned ugly, fast, which brings me to the first lesson he taught me.

Lesson No. 1. I was a Trinidad-born iconoclast and still deeply entrenched in the waning Pan-Africanist movement when I arrived at the *Voice* in 1990. Early on in our relationship, when I believed it was I sensitizing Barrett to the ideologies of freedom fighters in Africa and their advocates stateside, it was he who raised concerns about their revolutionary rhetoric rendering me useless to the *Voice* if it wasn't properly contextualized in my local reporting.

"The rebellion is on 125th Street and in Flatbush," he said, or shouted something to that effect as he handed me the book *Axioms of Kwame Nkrumah*, the revolutionary who brought Ghana out of British colonial rule. It remains my personal manifesto and guide to understanding politics.

Lesson No. 2. After Barrett found out that the controversial leader Roy Innis, who had ties to some of the most repressive regimes in the motherland, had invited me on a junket to Nigeria, in 1991, he presented me with scenarios of the blowback I'd receive from African Americans at home who were openly critical of that country's human rights record and who themselves had been targeted by Innis. I nixed the trip, and, as he advised, began to focus instead on the new postapartheid revolution Mandela was leading in South Africa and the lessons, if any, that Black liberation movements, from Harlem to Bed-Stuy, had learned from Mandela's leadership. In 1994, Barrett successfully lobbied for my plum assignment to cover Mandela's historic election to the presidency.

So, was Wayne Barrett more capable of acknowledging Black people's plight when other white journalists wouldn't? Racism was the lens through which he viewed the paradigm shift of New York City ethnic politics, and he especially parlayed this clear-eyed analysis into coverage of each mayoralty. In the early '80s, Barrett pummeled Ed Koch for triggering three rounds of congressional hearings into rampant police brutality in Black neighborhoods. But to me his racial consciousness was most evocative during the administration of Rudy Giuliani. Barrett had exposed a Giuliani base of supporters who were fearful of devaluing their whiteness by making allies of communities of color. In 1993, after I told him I was all-in against Giuliani's looming ascendancy, he pulled my coat regarding a huge package the *Voice* was planning to publish about Giuliani's now demonstrably racist campaign to take back white control from the city's first Black mayor. Though Barrett felt he and Shaun Assael had written the definitive exposé about "Rudy's Questionable Contributions," he joked that my story "Why Blacks Fear Giuliani" (which later would form the basis for my book on Giuliani's terroristic crackdown on Black lives) should lead the field of stellar writers.

In the late '90s, Barrett and I teamed up again after the Street Crimes Unit—a Giuliani, mostly white goon squad, claiming to "own the night" by terrorizing the Walking While Black—had gunned down Kevin Cedeno, Amadou Diallo, Patrick Dorismond, Patrick Bailey, and Malcolm Ferguson. When Giuliani shamelessly argued that the killings, and the sadistic torture of Abner Louima, did not define his leadership style, Barrett's searing postmortems showed that the incidents were not just an aberration but part of a pattern and practice of "Giuliani Time."

But Barrett and I both acknowledged that we'd become frenemies: we just didn't always agree on how much influence progressive whites like him should have over the struggle for Black self-determination and empowerment. We had a nasty fight after which we didn't speak for years. One summer day, I saw him on a Brooklyn street and shouted, admirably, "The Killer B!" Barrett's trademark, suck-back laughter evinced a spirit of camaraderie as we reconciled and sat down for a hearty lunch topped off with a barbed debate about Black asymmetric politics. I wish we were still arguing.

Peter Noel was a staff writer at the *Village Voice* from 1990 to 2001. He is the author of *Why Blacks Fear "America's Mayor": Reporting Police Brutality and Black Activist Politics Under Rudy Giuliani* and is at work on a book about police criminalizing and killing Black men and boys in 1980s and 1990s New York.

14

The Yankees' Cleanup Man
May 1, 2007

> "Over a sweater, he [Giuliani] wore a navy-blue suit,
> the fly of the pants unzipped. He accessorized with
> an American-flag lapel pin, American-flag woven wal-
> let, a diamond-encrusted pinky ring, and a diamond-
> encrusted Yankees World Series ring (about which an
> innocent question resulted in a 15-minute rant about
> 'fucking Wayne Barrett,' a journalist who manages to
> enrage Giuliani even in death)."
>
> —Olivia Nuzzi, in *New York* magazine,
> December 23, 2019

This is the then 12-year-old article that still rankled
the former mayor. A classic Barrett piece in its ob-
sessive arcana, this ran when Rudy was leading the
pack of 2008 GOP contenders. —Ed.

THE GREATEST LOVE AFFAIR of Rudy Giuliani's
life has become a sordid scandal.

His monogamous embrace of the Yankees as mayor was so fer-
vent that when he tried to deliver a West Side stadium to them
early in his administration, or approved a last-minute $400 million

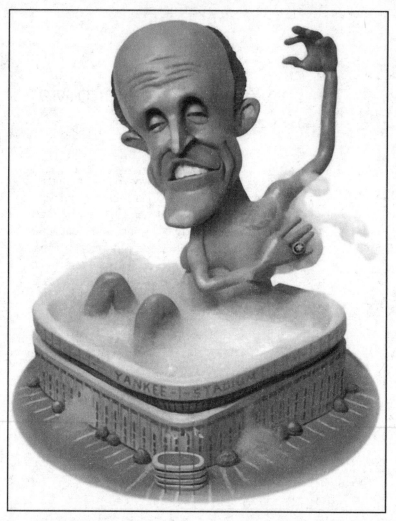

Barrett's castigations of Rudy as he grew into a craven, hollow version of himself carried a pale of mourning. He'd known the better man Rudy might have been. (Illustration courtesy of David O'Keefe)

subsidy for their new Bronx stadium, New Yorkers blithely ascribed the bad deals to a heaving heart.

It turns out he also had an outstretched hand.

Sports fans grew accustomed to seeing Giuliani, in Yankee jacket and cap, within camera view of the team's dugout at every one of the 40 postseason home games the Yankees played while he was mayor. His devotion reached such heights that at the 1995 Inner Circle press dinner, he played himself handing the city over to George Steinbrenner in a lampoon version of the Broadway musical *Damn Yankees*, succumbing to a scantily clad Lola who importuned him on behalf of the Boss to the tune of "Whatever Lola Wants (Lola Gets)." Mike Bloomberg understood years later that the song was no joke; he nixed Rudy's stadium deal in his first weeks in office.*

It is only now, however, as Giuliani campaigns for president, that we are beginning to learn that this relationship went even deeper. Giuliani has been seen on the campaign trail wearing a World Series ring, a valuable prize we never knew he had. Indeed, the Yankees have told the *Voice* that he has *four* rings, one for every world championship the Yankees won while he was mayor. *Voice* calls to other cities whose teams won the Series in the past decade have determined that Giuliani is the only mayor with a ring, much less four. If it sounds innocent, wait for the price tag. These are certainly no Canal Street cubic zirconia knockoffs.

With Giuliani's name inscribed in the 1996, 1998, 1999, and 2000 diamond-and-gold rings, memorabilia and baseball experts say they are collectively worth a minimum of $200,000. The Yankees say that Giuliani did pay for his rings—but only $16,000,

---

* But ultimately, Bloomberg made tremendous giveaways to the Yankees, subsidizing the new stadium and underwriting white-elephant parking garages. —Ed.

and years after he had left office. Anyone paying for the rings is as unusual as a mayor getting one, since neither the Yankees nor any other recent champion has sold rings to virtually anyone. The meager payment, however, is less than half of the replacement value of the rings, and that's a fraction of the market price, especially with the added value of Giuliani's name.

What's more troubling is that Giuliani's receipt of the rings may be a serious breach of the law, and one that could still be prosecuted. New York officials are barred from taking a gift of greater than $50 in value from anyone doing business with the city, and under Giuliani, that statute was enforced aggressively against others. His administration forced a fire department chief, for example, to retire, forfeit $93,105 in salary, and pay a $6,000 fine for taking Broadway tickets to two shows and a free week in a ski condo from a city vendor. The city's Conflicts of Interest Board (COIB) has applied the gift rule to discounts as well, unless the cheaper rate "is available generally to all government employees." When a buildings-department deputy commissioner was indicted in 2000 for taking Mets and Rangers tickets, as well as a family trip to Florida, from a vendor, an outraged Giuliani denounced his conduct as "reprehensible," particularly "at high levels in city agencies," and said that such officials had to be "singled out" and "used as examples."

City officials are also required to disclose gifts from anyone but relatives on forms filed with the COIB, something Giuliani did not do with any of the rings. Giuliani certainly used to sound serious about the need for full public disclosure. In 1989, he denounced his mayoral opponent, David Dinkins, for failing to disclose frequent-flier tickets to France given to him by a friend, even though the friend did no business with the city; Giuliani called it an example of "arrogance and disrespect for legal and ethical obligations."

And there's another, more recent, and closer-to-home example of arrogant nondisclosure noted publicly by Giuliani. When former police commissioner Bernard Kerik pled guilty last year to charges involving a city contractor's gift to him of a $165,000 apartment renovation, Giuliani said that Kerik had "acknowledged his violations." As part of a $221,000 plea deal, Kerik agreed to pay a $10,000 fine to the COIB for accepting and then failing to accurately disclose the renovations. Not only are Kerik and Giuliani's concealed gifts of similar value, but Kerik, like Giuliani, made a partial payment for the renovations—$17,800, far less than full value.

More ominous for Giuliani, Kerik's prosecution came eight years after the renovation of his apartment began, an indication that the ordinary statute of limitations doesn't apply to the continuing reporting requirements of the COIB. In addition, Giuliani reportedly paid the Yankees as recently as 2004 for one of the rings, another reason why an investigation might still be timely. It is also a violation of state unlawful-gratuity statutes for a public official to "solicit, accept, or agree to accept any benefit" from a business like the Yankees, which leases the stadium from the city.

If Giuliani neither received the rings, nor was promised them while in office, he would not have violated these rules. In repeated exchanges with the *Voice*, a Yankee spokeswoman was vague about when Giuliani actually received the rings, though she suggested that Giuliani might have obtained them when he paid for them— which would have been well after his mayoral term ended in 2001. Alice McGillion of Rubenstein Associates, the public relations firm that represents the Yankees, said that in 2003, Giuliani paid $13,500 for his 1998, 1999, and 2000 rings, and in 2004, he paid $2,500 for his 1996 ring. She said that the team had only "transmittal" documents that confirmed the payments and that, from those documents, it could be "reasonably deduced" that he didn't receive the rings until then.

McGillion acknowledged that she had no other evidence besides the records of payment to lead her to believe that Giuliani received the rings years after the championships were won. She declined to respond to two sets of emailed questions about whether it was the team's contention that rings weren't made for Giuliani until 2003 and 2004, or if they were maintaining that his rings had actually been manufactured during his mayoralty and held by the Yankees, with his assent, until after he left office.

Although the Yankees replaced Joe DiMaggio's lost rings in 1999, making new ones years later is almost never done and would have been an exceptional favor. Asked if the Yankees would make a ring several years after a World Series win for a new recipient, David Fiore, the ex-CEO of American Achievement, the Texas-based manufacturer of the team's rings, said: "Not after the fact; they're all awarded at the same time. If you lose it a couple of years later, we will replace it."

Giuliani's protracted delay—paying for a 1996 ring eight years later—might well be seen by the IRS, COIB, or other investigators as an indication that he recognized the impropriety of receiving them while mayor, or, as Giuliani used to describe it in his prosecutorial days, an "inference of guilt." If the rings were promised and made for him while he was in office, though not actually delivered until after his term ended, that could still involve violations of the gift or gratuity statutes, according to investigators.

Four sources, two from the manufacturer and two from City Hall, have told the *Voice* that a ring was made with Giuliani's name on it in 1996 or early 1997. The City Hall sources also recall him receiving the ring at that time. In addition, one of these sources, joined by two other ex–Giuliani staffers, says the mayor did not take possession of the three additional rings until much later. The best recollection of these aides is that he got these rings as a package near the end of his term in 2001, just as his administration closed a number of critical deals with the Yankees. While the Yankees could offer no explanation for why he paid for three rings in one year and the 1996 ring a year later, the chronology cited by the sources suggests one. He paid for the three he received together, and then later remembered to pay for the one he'd gotten long before. He paid $2,000 less for the 1996 ring than he did for the others—another indication of how disconnected from market factors this reputed sale was, since many ring experts believe that the 1996 ring, which ended a nearly two-decade Yankee drought, is the most valuable of the four.

McGillion also declined to answer questions about the tax implications of Giuliani's rings, which may explain the late payments. Bill DeWitt III, one of the owners of the St. Louis Cardinals, says the team, which won the championship last year, issued 1099-MISC (miscellaneous income) forms to employees and nonemployees who received rings, but the Yankees have never done that. At the time of the Yankee wins, IRS rules required the reporting of gifts of more than $10,000 by either the donor or the recipient (the threshold was recently raised to $12,000). DeWitt says that estimating a ring's value for tax purposes gets "a little gray and murky," and a Cardinal spokesman says that the club actually boosted employee salaries to cover taxes they might have to pay on the rings.

Three tax attorneys tell the *Voice* that Giuliani's payments may have been intended to lower the value of the gifts below the IRS thresholds. That would mean that neither the Yankees nor Giuliani would have to report the transaction. The belated payments then may have been a postdivorce or pre-presidential-campaign attempt, on the advice of tax counsel, to avoid dealing with the actual timing and true value of the rings.

Frequently ensconced in George Steinbrenner's eight-seat 31A box and four Legends 31AA seats next to the Yankee dugout while he was mayor, Giuliani and his many guests were also repeatedly given Yankee jackets, caps, autographed balls, and other gifts. "He would require gifts at every game," says a former close Giuliani aide, whose account is supported by both a Yankee source and an ex-cop assigned to the mayor. He even wanted a fitted cap with the World Series logo and other special caps, and the equipment management had to reach into the players' uniform case to find one for Giuliani's large head. The Giuliani group also raided the closet in Steinbrenner's office, even taking DiMaggio jackets with red piping for the mayor and guests. "They finally turned the spigot off in 2000 and said we just can't do it anymore," the aide recalls. The cop remembers jackets and balls—some signed by all the Yankees—stuffed in the back of the city cars they used to drive back from the stadium.

The Yankees say Giuliani paid for at least some of his tickets, though he did not pay when "he attended in his official capacity." They declined to specify which games were official, or to answer detailed questions about the other largesse. Several friends who sat with Giuliani at games, like Emergency Management Director Jerry Hauer, say they were never asked to pay. "I don't believe he paid for our seats," says Hauer. "I don't think anybody paid for them. It would have cost him a fortune." Russell Harding, one of three members of his family who went to Yankee games with Giuliani and the head of the Housing Development Corporation, wrote in an email disclosed after his arrest on charges of bilking the city for hundreds of thousands of dollars: "I never have to pay for things like that...especially Yankee tickets...just one of the perks I get with my job....And knowing the mayor doesn't hurt either." Russell's brother Robert (both are sons of Liberal Party boss Ray Harding) was actually in charge of the Yankee Stadium negotiations for Giuliani.

With tickets for Giuliani's box and Legends seats selling for $50 to $200 for regular-season games, and with Giuliani and an average of eight guests attending a minimum of 20 games a year, the eight-year price tag for the mayor, including the far more expensive postseason games he never missed, would have been an estimated $120,000. That's quite a load on an average salary of $150,000. Obviously, any substantial tickets and assorted gifts to the mayor or his city employee guests would also have run afoul of the $50 COIB limit.

The Yankees say that Mayor Bloomberg has purchased four season tickets in Section 53, behind the Steinbrenner box that Giuliani still uses, and pays even when he attends in his official capacity. Bloomberg does not allow anyone on the city payroll to use his seats because he regards it as granting an improper benefit to a subordinate. (The Yankee spokeswoman declined to characterize the difference between how the two mayors dealt with seating at the stadium.) Giuliani's periodic payments for some of these tickets may also have had a tax motive. Had he paid nothing for the seats, he would have had to treat the entire Yankee goodie bag as income.

Giuliani's sense of entitlement about the Yankees was so deep that he frequently used a police boat to haul himself and his guests to games, using either the slip near Gracie Mansion or the Wall Street/South Street one near City Hall. In his own book, *Leadership*, he revealed that the first Yankee game he ever took Judi

Nathan to was David Cone's perfect game in July 1999, almost a full year before he announced at a press conference that she was his "very good friend." Judi and her girlfriends became part of his stadium entourage, just as his previous very good friend, Cristyne Lategano, had been in the earlier years. When Giuliani's wife, Donna Hanover, barred Lategano from the box if her son Andrew was at the game, the young press aide sequestered herself in Steinbrenner's suite, extending Giuliani's reach to the home-plate section of the stadium as well. Judi, too, eventually became a presence in the Steinbrenner suite.

At one point, according to the close aide, George Pataki's office asked if the seats could be "split in half, either horizontally or vertically" so the governor could get access. "Absolutely not," was Rudy's answer. What about just two of the seats? Another no. Asked if he'd ever sat in the prized seats, Gene Budig, who was American League president for most of the Giuliani years, tells the *Voice*: "I got to sit in [the] seats a couple of times when he wasn't there, but never with him. The seats were practically in the dugout." The prominence of the seats and the success of the team quickly catapulted Giuliani into prime-time sports-hero status. He even managed to get himself interviewed on camera in the locker-room champagne celebrations of the great victories, running right in through the dugout after the game. That was in addition to his regular fifth-inning appearance on the Yankee radio broadcast. He merged himself with the Yankees in the national consciousness, and is still featured, with his old comb-over look, on the scoreboard screen during every game, leading cheers for a Yankee rally. On opening day in April, the presidential candidate also appeared in the Yankee radio and TV booth for full inning commentary, a sneer at the equal-time provisions of federal law.

In 2003, the Yankees paid a $75,000 fine to the state lobbying commission for not disclosing as a lobbying expense dozens of tickets given to public officials in 2002 and 2003. Even though Giuliani wasn't a public official anymore, his name appeared on a list entitled "Political Friends" that the Yankees turned over to the commission. He was one of the few with a special note by his name: "GMS list," referring to George Steinbrenner. He still had all 12 seats in the same section for playoff games, though he was listed as sharing them with Mayor Bloomberg on opening day. While a variety of credit cards or the word *invoice* is listed under the category of "method of payment" for many of the special seats, the space beside Giuliani's name is left blank. No explanation for those left blank was offered. Since the ring payments occurred as recently as 2004, the commission, too, may still have the jurisdiction to investigate whether the tickets were improper gifts granted to Giuliani while he was a lobbied public official.

While mayors in other cities may have tried to tie themselves to successful sports franchises like Giuliani, none, no matter how big a fan, has gotten a ring for his efforts. Team representatives, or mayoral representatives, in every city that's won a championship since 1995 tell the *Voice* that their mayor didn't get a ring. Not the Florida Marlins (winners in 1997 and 2003), Arizona Diamond-backs (2001), Anaheim (now Los Angeles) Angels (2002), Boston Red Sox (2004), Chicago White Sox (2005), or St. Louis Cardinals (2006). Team representatives also tell the *Voice* that rings are not for sale—to a mayor or anyone else. "The mayor didn't get a ring," says White Sox spokesman Lou Hernandez. "We did a World Series ring raffle and all the proceeds went to charity. So he could have won a ring. He's a ticket holder. But no public officials got gifts even if they helped." The Cardinals' DeWitt says: "We haven't allowed anyone to buy a ring, even some limited partners who wanted an extra. You can only have it given to you. We have a great mayor. He's been helpful for us. But we just felt like for us it was best to stick to employees and Hall of Famers." Asked if rings are ever given to public officials, DeWitt says: "I've never heard that politicians get them." Angels spokesman Tim Meade says rings are "absolutely not sold under any circumstances." In fact, the Angels fired an executive who put his ring up for sale, an action Steinbrenner is also said to have taken. "There were a couple of people from the city of Anaheim who got rings," acknowledges Meade. "They were people from the city manager's office who worked closely with the Angels."

Jerry McNeal, a World Series historian associated with the Baseball Hall of Fame, says that public officials don't usually get rings. "No, you have to be associated with the team in some way," says McNeal. "When the L.A. Dodgers won the world championship, Frank Sinatra was good friends with the manager, Tommy Lasorda, but he couldn't get a ring." Phyllis Merhige, senior vice president of the American League, says she isn't aware of rings going to public officials. "In a situation, I'm guessing, an official that was involved in the building of a new stadium or keeping a team in a city would be considered for a ring. But I couldn't tell you whether it's been done or not. There are no records." She says that congressional representatives are barred by law from receiving rings or other gifts from teams.

McNeal estimates that Giuliani's rings "would go for at least $50,000 apiece," adding that they "might even go for more than that." If Giuliani were elected president, he says, the rings "would skyrocket in value." Pete Siegel, the president of Gotta Have It Collectibles on East 57th Street, puts the value of Giuliani's four-ring set at a quarter of a million dollars. Siegel says that Giuliani has purchased sports items at his store and even came in once wearing a World Series ring. Having just sold two 1998 rings owned by a coach and front-office executive for $28,000 and $29,000, Siegel says that "Giuliani's rings would be on the same level as players' rings for all those years." He says he knows that Giuliani "definitely has a 1996 ring," though he is unsure if that was the ring the former mayor wore to his store.

Robert Lifson of Robert Edwards Auctions maintains that Giuliani's rings would be "more meaningful and valuable than some of the players'." Lifson's "gut" tells him the value could "go through the roof," estimating that they would sell for "north of $25,000 apiece." People would pay "a much bigger premium to have the ring of America's Mayor than an executive that nobody knows," says Lifson, who insists that "any modern Yankee ring" would sell for five figures even if it were the ring of an unknown. He says the rings are "works of art" that serve also as "a symbol of greatness in sports." Spencer Lader, a certified appraiser for the Yankees who has appeared on their TV network's memorabilia show, tells the *Voice* he puts the overall value of Giuliani's collection at about $200,000, adding, as did others, that the 1996 ring is "the most coveted."

But when did Giuliani get that 1996 ring? Did he, as the Yankee spokeswoman suggests, receive it only when he made a token payment for it in 2004, after he was no longer mayor?

Not according to the man who actually made the ring, William Sandoval.

Sandoval says he's made rings for 26 years. After attending a stone-setter school, he went to work for L. G. Balfour in Attleboro, Massachusetts, which manufactured sports and school rings at its plant there for 84 years. "I was a special maker, doing diamond settings and customer repair," the Guatemala-born jeweler, now with his own small business in Rhode Island, tells the *Voice*. "I did the Yankees, the Celtics, and the Baltimore Orioles. Balfour liked my work. I did every championship ring." He particularly recalls the 1996 ring he did for the Yankees. Fifty percent larger than any previous team ring, it featured the famous interlocking *NY* at the center that was made of 23 diamonds, one for each title, encircled by the words *World Champion*. With the Series trophy and *courage* and *heart* on one side, the ring also featured the Yankee Stadium facade, the Yankees top hat, and the word *tradition* on the other.

It was easy to remember because it was Sandoval's last championship ring. Balfour was acquired by a New York investment firm in 1996 and closed its Attleboro plant to move to Texas in late 1997, laying off hundreds of workers. Its successor firm, American Achievement, still does Yankee work.

Sandoval distinctly remembers that they made a ring for Giuliani because, he says, he crafted it himself. Asked if he was certain if the Giuliani ring was made at the same time as the rest, he says: "It has to be at the same time." Asked again if he "definitely" remembers making a ring for Rudy Giuliani, Sandoval replies: "Yes. Oh, yes." His memory is confirmed by a former Balfour vice president who oversaw sports sales and asked that his name not be used. "I honestly think that Giuliani did get a ring," he says. "The only people who could get rings had to have a letter signed by Steinbrenner on Yankee stationery." Attempts to get the current manufacturer to confirm that rings were made for Giuliani for the other three championships were unsuccessful; the sales representative for the firm referred all questions to the Yankees.

Two other sources who asked that they not be named recall the 1996 ring. A member of Giuliani's police detail remembers attending a barbecue at Gracie Mansion after the ticker tape parade for the Yankees on October 29, 1996. Giuliani was so involved in the Yankee celebration that he personally reviewed the guest lists for the barbecue and an earlier event at City Hall. A photo of him in Yankee pinstripes appeared on the passes for attendees. His two prime Democratic opponents for the 1997 campaign had to settle for seats in the crowd at City Hall, though both were borough presidents, one from the Bronx. "George and he went into the Green Room at one point," the ex-cop recalls, referring to a den where Giuliani frequently entertained friends and close associates. "They were gone for about 15 minutes. He came out and said to us, 'I'm getting a ring. George is giving me a ring.'" Though the cop can't recall seeing the ring after that, he says that another Giuliani aide told him that the mayor got it, as well as other rings.

That aide, who worked in City Hall throughout the Giuliani years, says the mayor got the ring sometime in 1997, around the time that the players got their rings in mid-May. "The ring was kept in the second or third drawer of Beth Petrone's cabinet in Rudy's outer office at City Hall," says the aide, referring to Giuliani's executive assistant, who is currently the office manager for Bracewell and Giuliani, the Texas-based law firm that Giuliani has joined. "He actually wore it about once a year. He may have worn it during the playoffs in 1997 as a lucky charm.

"The other three rings came collectively," the aide continues. "I saw them in wooden boxes with Plexiglas windows. They were either kept in the mayor's personal office on the main floor or his downstairs office. He didn't get the 1998 and 1999 rings as they were handed out. They were just given to him sometime in 2001 as a collection." The 2000 ring wasn't presented to players until late July 2001, so Giuliani's rings would've arrived sometime after that. Though gifts to mayors are routinely logged on a City Hall list, Giuliani listed only one Steinbrenner gift among his more than 8,500 gifts bequeathed to the city: a videotape and booklet from Joe DiMaggio Day.

This aide and other sources close to City Hall recall that Giuliani's name was misspelled on one of the rings, returned to the Yankees, and replaced. News accounts of the 1999 ring presentation in 2000 indicated that there were mistakes on six rings, but the only one specified in the stories was that Roger Clemens's uniform number was wrong. The sources say that Carmela Piazza, who ran Giuliani's correspondence office at City Hall, oversaw the return of the ring, another indication that it was given to Giuliani while he was still in office. Contacted by the *Voice*, Piazza, who is a current donor to his presidential campaign, said repeatedly that she couldn't remember anything about the incident. A Yankee official initially confirmed that there was a spelling problem with one of the Giuliani rings, but later said he could not definitely determine if it happened. Spokeswoman McGillion, who was receiving limited information from the Yankees, acknowledges that "another person" affiliated with the team "hinted this to us."

On December 31, 2001, First Deputy Mayor Joe Lhota was standing on the steps of City Hall, listening to the bagpipes playing in anticipation of Rudy Giuliani's farewell, when he was tapped on the shoulder and asked to sign a document. It was the last official act of the Giuliani administration: an amendment to the Yankee lease. Bills from Yankee lawyers that were reimbursed by the city indicate that the parties were busily negotiating the terms of the deal for at least five of Giuliani's final hours that day. Fourteen days later, Bill Thompson, the new city comptroller, would write the new mayor, Mike Bloomberg, to complain about the amendment Lhota signed, which allowed the Yankees to terminate their lease on 60 days' notice "anytime over the next nine years" if the team "reasonably determined" that the city was unlikely to proceed with the new stadium Giuliani had promised them. Previously, the Yankees had made a five-year commitment to remain in the Bronx if they stayed there through the 2002 season.

Bloomberg quickly moved to kill the lavishly subsidized term sheets that the Giuliani administration had signed to build new stadiums for the Yankees and the Mets. But he could do nothing about the $50 million in stadium planning costs that another last-minute lease amendment delivered to the teams. That amendment, signed by Giuliani in the closing moments, allowed each team to deduct from the rent they paid the city any costs they attributed to stadium planning—up to $5 million a year for five years.

A *Voice* story in 2006 revealed that the Yankees deducted the $203,055 they paid lobbyist Bill Powers, the former head of the state Republican party. They also deducted hundreds of thousands in other legal and lobbying fees retroactively, meaning that the city actually paid the Yankees' costs involved in negotiating, drafting, and pushing for the very lease amendment that allowed the deductions in the first place, an unprecedented circular giveaway. Though the amendment only permitted the Yankees to deduct for expenses from the beginning of 2001, the team submitted thousands in bills from the Regency Hotel as far back as 1999, a maneuver subsequently blocked by the comptroller. Remarkably, this was the Yankees' second dip into the city treasury to plan its own stadium. Giuliani's Economic Development Corporation had already reimbursed the Yankees $3 million for similar expenditures.

The ninth-inning amendments were just the latest in an orgy of favors that Giuliani granted the Yankees. When Thompson did an audit of the Yankees' payments to the city in 2004, it was only supposed to cover the period since 2002. But his office was so intrigued by the Yankees' meager payments to the city during the

Giuliani years that he extended its review back to 1997 and discovered that the Yankees had grossly shortchanged the city. The club is allowed to deduct from its rental obligation the revenue-sharing payments it makes to Major League Baseball. It had mysteriously overstated those payments by $34 million between 1997 and 2002, shortchanging the city by $2.7 million.

In fact, as astonishing as it may seem, the Mets, big-time losers for most of the Giuliani years, were assessed for twice as much in net rent to the city for a half-empty Shea as the Yankees were for their packed house, an average of $5.4 million a year versus $2.86 million. The Yankee lease has long allowed the team to do its own stadium maintenance and deduct its costs from the rent, while Shea is maintained by the Parks Department. The Yankees drove an armored truck through that loophole in the Giuliani years. Even though the loophole is still in effect under Bloomberg, the payment pattern has reversed itself, with the Yankees paying twice as much as the Mets for 2002–2004, an annual average of $4.93 million versus $2.58 million. The Yankees argue that Giuliani's final stadium proposal was a boon to both teams equally, though the 60-day escape clause and the quadrupling of luxury boxes were unique Yankee benefits. But Mets owner Fred Wilpon wasn't even seeking a new stadium until late 2000, asking for city help simply to renovate Shea. He joined the Giuliani feast only to keep pace with the hog in the Bronx. With *Daily News* editorials observing that the mayor "has created the impression that money is no object" in accommodating Steinbrenner, what else was Wilpon to do?

Of course, before Giuliani brokered his Bronx deal, he waged a three-year war to give the Yankees, not the Mets, a stadium on the West Side. He and Steinbrenner began that strong-arm campaign in 1996, just as the mayor was collecting his first ring. That's also when he amended the Yankee lease for the first of five times, quietly granting the Yankees permission to exclude much of cable and luxury-suite revenue from the calculus that determined the rent due the city. In fact, all the team paid the city to rent Yankee Stadium in a World Series year, when all deductions were made, was a measly $100,000. Giuliani was so committed to the West Side site that he created a phony charter commission to put manufactured amendments on the ballot in 1998, a legal maneuver that submarined a referendum opposing the stadium. When a steel beam at Yankee Stadium collapsed that year, he turned it into a campaign to virtually condemn the stadium, rejecting the findings of his own building commissioner that the stadium was sound. No fact could get in the way of what Steinbrenner wanted.

The goodies list seems endless. Giuliani spent $71 million on a stadium for the Staten Island Yankees, a low-level minor league team half owned by Steinbrenner's son. So few people go to games there that the team has yet to hit the minimal attendance threshold that triggers some rental payments to the city. Though the lease required the team to submit turnstile attendance numbers to the city, the stadium operated for years without turnstiles, and the comptroller has repeatedly found that it shortchanges the city. The city also helped the Yankees reconfigure Yankee Stadium in lucrative ways, including adding the very Legends seats in foul territory near the dugouts and home plate that Giuliani wound up occupying. On December 19, 2001, also just days before the end of Giuliani's term, Bob Harding signed a letter approving a million-dollar replacement of the playing field.

Those who know Giuliani well say that when he thinks he's in love, he waives all the rules of acceptable conduct. But the story of him and his team is not just a saga of disturbing infatuation and self-absorption. It is an object lesson in what kind of a president he would be, a window into his willingness to lend himself to a special interest, to blur all lines that ordinarily separate personal and public lives. It is not so much that he identified with the Yankees. It was himself that he was serving.

Knock on Every Door

Adam Fifield

THERE WERE TIMES during the year I spent with Wayne Barrett working on an in-depth biography of Rudy Giuliani when I thought much of our work was pointless.

In 1999 and the early months of 2000, Wayne dispatched me and my fellow research assistant, Jennifer Warren, on series after series of tedious and repetitive tasks: search probate records in Queens and on Long Island; go to the street where Giuliani's cousin once lived and knock on every single door—if no one answers, go back the next day; go to a courthouse on Staten Island and read every single scrap of paper on a lawsuit involving Giuliani's relatives.

It sometimes felt like Wayne was Mr. Miyagi and we were his karate students, and he was instructing us to "paint the fence" over and over and over again. "Are you tired? Don't care.... Bored? Too bad.... Want to cut out and stop working at 6:30? Not when you work for me."

So paint the fence we did. Again and again and again. This meant exhausting every paper trail we could think of. It meant leaving no stone unturned, no public record unperused, no door unknocked, no source uninterviewed.

This punishing persistence, as we soon learned, could pay off in a big way.

While searching through stacks of documents in a Staten Island courthouse, I came across a name I almost dismissed. It belonged to a friend of Rudy's late cousin. I remember thinking: if this guy is still alive, he probably doesn't know anything. Probably not worth it.

But when I mentioned him to Wayne in passing, his eyes immediately lit up. "Track him down," he told me. "See what he knows."

I can't remember how we found him, but once we did, I went to his place of employment. I was completely surprised when he agreed to talk to me. Standing in an alley behind the building where he worked, he told me astonishing things: Rudy's father, Harold, had been a violent and dangerous man and had worked as a leg breaker for Rudy's loan-shark uncle. Harold had even done time at Sing Sing prison for a mugging.

I was suspicious of these salacious tidbits. Maybe this guy was messing with us. But Wayne wanted to follow up. He sent Jennifer Warren to Sing Sing. At first, she couldn't find any records for Harold Giuliani. But after searching for an alternate spelling, "Guiliani," she located Harold's receiving papers. They contained an alias, "Joseph Starrett."

Under the alias, we dug up a trove of information on Harold Giuliani. We confirmed everything the source had shared and learned much more.

I soon realized that one of the key ingredients of our and Wayne's success was optimism. His dogged, disciplined sleuthing was rooted in an ironclad conviction that when you knock on every door, one will eventually lead you to valuable answers. If you keep knocking and keep asking the right questions, you will get the story. Working for Wayne, I began to believe there was no nut we couldn't crack, no secret we couldn't unearth.

Toward the end of our reporting on the Giuliani biography, Wayne asked me to write several chapters. I tried to refuse, but he pushed me to do it. And I'm glad he did. Seeing my name below his on the cover of the book was one of the greatest honors of my journalistic career.

Two decades after I last collaborated with him, Wayne Barrett's infectious optimism is still with me. I can still hear his gravelly voice urging me on, telling me to keep at it—telling me I'll get where I need to go.

Adam Fifield is the coauthor, with Barrett, of *Rudy! An Investigative Biography of Rudolph Giuliani* and the author of *A Mighty Purpose: How Jim Grant Sold the World on Saving Its Children.*

15

Rudy Giuliani's Five Big Lies About 9/11

July 31, 2007

With special research assistance by Alexandra Kahan

Barrett wrote a column days after 9/11 praising Rudy's handling of the crisis:

> Bonded in the rubble with the men and women in uniform whose sacrifices would instantly make them heroes, Rudy became one of them in our minds, a rescuer, a protector, selfless, steady and sure. Just as prostate cancer momentarily humanized him when he revealed it in April of 2000, his harrowing escape from a temporary command post, suddenly awash in the debris of death, seemed to make him whole....His recent public performance—on everything from divorce to "decency" to Dorismond—set so low a sneering standard that all he had to do was be clear and caring and the city would rejoice. He was better than that. At one informed and compassionate press conference after another, his ego appeared vaporized by a combination of term limits and terror. His face and tone took on a

243

244

gentleness we'd never seen....With no personal agenda or plausible political future, all he cared about was serving and calming us. With no need to invent or savage enemies, as he did with TWA when Flight 800 went down in 1996, he appeared finally at peace with the notion of a city that needed and believed in him. The moment and the man fit masterfully together, as if the catastrophe was so huge it humbled even him.

—"The Emperor's New Praise,"
September 18, 2001

By the following spring, Barrett was documenting the ways Rudy was turning the 9/11 attacks into personal financial gain. The following article is the result of years of reporting for *Grand Illusion: The Untold Story of Rudy Giuliani and 9/11*, coauthored with Dan Collins. —Ed.

NEARLY SIX YEARS AFTER 9/11, Rudy Giuliani is still walking through the canyons of lower Manhattan, covered in soot, pointing north, and leading the nation out of danger's way. The Republican frontrunner is campaigning for president by evoking that visual at every campaign stop, and he apparently believes it's a picture worth thousands of nights in the White House.

Giuliani has been leading the Republican pack for seven months, and predictions that the party's evangelicals would turn on him have so far proven hollow. The religious right appears as gripped by the Giuliani story as the rest of the country.

Giuliani isn't shy about reminding audiences of those heady days. In fact he hyperventilates about them on the stump, making his credentials in the so-called war on terror the centerpiece of his campaign. His claims, meanwhile, have been met with a media deference so total that he's taken to complimenting "the good job it is doing covering the campaign." Opponents, too, haven't dared to question his terror credentials, as if doing so would be an un-patriotic bow to Osama bin Laden.

Here, then, is a less deferential look at the illusory cloud ema-nating from the former mayor's campaign. . . .

Big Lie 1

"I think the thing that distinguishes me on terrorism is, I have more experience dealing with it."

This pillar of the Giuliani campaign—asserted by pundits as often as it is by the man himself—is based on the idea that Rudy uniquely understands the terror threat because of his background as a prosecutor and as New York's mayor. In a July appearance at a Maryland synagogue, Giuliani sketched out his counterterrorism biography, a résumé that happens to be rooted in falsehood.

"As United States Attorney, I investigated the Leon Klinghoffer murder by Yasir Arafat," he told the Jewish audience, referring to the infamous 1985 slaying of a wheelchair-bound, 69-year-old New York businessman aboard the *Achille Lauro*, an Italian ship hijacked off the coast of Egypt by Palestinian extremists. "It's honestly the reason why I knew so much about Arafat," says Giuliani. "I knew, in detail, the Americans he murdered. I went over their cases."

On the contrary, Victoria Toensing, the deputy assistant attorney general at the Justice Department in Washington who filed a criminal complaint in the *Lauro* investigation, says that no one in Giuliani's office "was involved at all." Jay Fischer, the Klinghoffer family attorney who spearheaded a 12-year lawsuit against the PLO, says he "never had any contact" with Giuliani or his office. "It would boggle my mind if anyone in 1985, 1986, 1987, or thereafter conducted an investigation of this case and didn't call me," he adds. Fischer says he did have a private dinner with Giuliani in 1992: "It was the first time we talked, and we didn't even talk about the Klinghoffer case then."

The dinner was arranged by Arnold Burns, a close friend of Fischer and Giuliani who also represented the Klinghoffer family. Burns, who was also the finance chair of Giuliani's mayoral campaign, was the deputy US attorney general in 1985 and oversaw the probe. "I know of nothing Rudy did in any shape or form on the Klinghoffer case," he says.

Though Giuliani told the Conservative Political Action Conference in March that he "prosecuted a lot of crime—a little bit of terrorism, but mostly organized crime," he actually worked only one major terrorism case as US attorney, indicting 10 arms dealers for selling $2.5 billion worth of antitank missiles, bombs, and fighter jets to Iran in 1986. The judge in the case ruled that a sale to Iran violated terrorist statutes because its government had been tied to 87 terrorist incidents. Giuliani has never mentioned the case, perhaps because he personally filed papers terminating it in his last month as US attorney: a critical witness had died, and a judge tossed out 46 of the 55 counts because of errors by Giuliani's office.

"Then, as mayor of New York," Giuliani's July speech continued, "I got elected right after the 1993 Islamic terrorist attack. . . .

I set up emergency plans for all the different possible attacks we could have. We had drills and exercises preparing us for sarin gas and anthrax, dirty bombs."

In fact, Giuliani was oblivious to the 1993 World Trade Center bombing throughout his mayoralty. A month after the attack, candidate Giuliani met for the first time with Bill Bratton, who would ultimately become his police commissioner. The lengthy taped meeting was one of several policy sessions he had with unofficial advisers. The bombing never came up; neither did terrorism. When Giuliani was elected a few months later, he immediately launched a search for a new police commissioner. Three members of the screening panel that Giuliani named to conduct the search, and four of the candidates interviewed for the job, said later that the bombing and terrorism were never mentioned—even when the new mayor got involved with the interviews himself. When Giuliani needed an emergency management director a couple of years later, two candidates for the job and the city official who spearheaded that search said that the bombing and future terrorist threats weren't on Giuliani's radar. The only time Giuliani invoked the 1993 bombing publicly was at his inauguration in 1994, when he referred to the way the building's occupants evacuated themselves as a metaphor for personal responsibility, ignoring the bombing itself as a terrorist harbinger.

US Attorney Mary Jo White and the four assistants who prosecuted the 1993 bombing said they were never asked to brief Giuliani about terrorism, though all of the assistants knew Giuliani personally and had actually been hired by him when he was the US attorney. White's office, located just a couple hundred yards from City Hall, indicted bin Laden three years before 9/11, but Giuliani recounted in his own book, *Leadership*, that "shortly after 9/11, Judith [Nathan] got me a copy of Yossef Bodansky's *Bin Laden: The Man Who Declared War on America*," which had warned of "spectacular terrorist strikes in Washington and/or New York" in 1999. As an example of how he "mastered a subject," Giuliani wrote that he soon "covered" Bodansky's prophetic work "in highlighter and notes."

The 1995 sarin-gas drill that Giuliani cited in his July speech was also prophetic, anticipating many of the breakdowns that hampered the city's 9/11 response. The drill was such a disaster that a follow-up exercise was canceled to avoid embarrassment. More than a hundred of the first responders rushed in so recklessly that they were "killed" by exposure to the gas. Radio communications were described in the city's own report as "abysmal," with police and fire "operating on different frequencies." The command posts were located much too close to the incident. All three failings would be identified years later in official reviews of the 9/11 response.

Giuliani went on, in this stump speech, to list other examples of his mayoral experience confronting terrorism. There was the time, he says, "we had what we thought was a sarin gas attack." And there were also the 50th anniversary commemoration of the United Nations and the 2000 millennium celebration to contend with, times, he said, "when we had a lot of warnings and had to do a tremendous amount to prepare." And let's not forget, he pointed out, the 1997 NYPD arrest of two terrorists who "were going to blow up a subway station." Giuliani used this thwarted attack as proof of the city's readiness: "A very, very alert young police officer saw those guys," he said. "They looked suspicious, [so he] reported them to the desk sergeant. The police department executed a warrant and shot one of the men as he was about to hit a toggle switch."

Each of the claims in Giuliani's self-serving account is inaccurate. The supposed "sarin attack" was simply the discovery of an empty canister marked "sarin" in the home of a harmless Queens recluse. It was sitting next to an identical container labeled "compressed air" with a smiley-face logo. Jerry Hauer, the city's emergency management director at the time, was in London, on the phone with Giuliani constantly. Hauer finds it ironic that Giuliani is still talking about the incident, since they both thought it was "comically" mishandled then. "The police went there without any suits on and touched all the containers without proper clothing. They turned it into a major crime scene, with a hundred cops lining the street. Rudy at one point said to me, 'Here we have the mayor, the fire commissioner, the chief of the police department, and one of my deputy mayors standing on the front lawn of this house. Shouldn't we be across the street in case this stuff ignites?'" This overhyped emergency led to a misdemeanor arrest subsequently dismissed by the district attorney.

Similarly, the security concerns during the 1995 UN anniversary focused on Cuba and China and didn't involve Arab terrorist threats. The millennium target, well established at subsequent trials, was the Los Angeles International Airport, not New York. While there's no doubt the Clinton administration did put the country and city on terrorist alert for Y2K and other reasons, it was an arrest on the Washington/Canadian border that busted up a West Coast plot.

The subway bombing, meanwhile, wasn't stymied by the NYPD. An Egyptian friend of the bomber—living with him in the apartment where the pipe bomb was being built—told two Long Island Rail Road police officers about it. When the NYPD subsequently raided the apartment, they shot two Palestinians who were there—one of whom, hit five times and gravely wounded, was later acquitted at trial. No one had tried to set off the bomb at the time of the arrest, though news stories reported that; the bomber had reached for an officer's gun, according to the trial testimony. The news stories also initially suggested a link to Hamas, though the lone bomber was actually an amateur fanatic with no money and no network. As conservative a source as Bill Gertz of the *Washington Times* wrote that FBI counterterrorism investigators were "concerned that the initial alarmist statements about the case made by Mayor Rudy Giuliani"—apparently a reference to leaks about Hamas and the toggle switch—"will prove embarrassing."

Giuliani's terrorism biography is bunk. As mayor, his laser-beam focus was street thugs, and as a prosecutor, it was the mob, Wall Street, and crooked politicians. He can't reach back to those years and rewrite such well-known chapters of his life.

Big Lie 2

"I don't think there was any place in the country, including the federal government, that was as well prepared for that attack as New York City was in 2001."

This assertion flies in the face of all three studies of the city's response—conducted by the 9/11 Commission, the National Institute of Standards and Technology (NIST), and McKinsey & Company, the consulting firm hired by the Bloomberg administration.

Actually, Giuliani didn't create the Office of Emergency Management until three years after the 1993 bombing, 27 months into his term. And he didn't open the OEM's new emergency command center until the end of 1999—nearly six years after he'd taken office. If he "assumed from the moment I came into office that NYC would be the subject of a terrorist attack," as he told *Time* when it made him "Person of the Year" in 2001, he sure took a long time to erect what he describes as the city's front line of defense.

The OEM was established so long after the bombing because, contrary to Giuliani's revisionism, the decision to create it had nothing to do with the bombing. Several memos, unearthed from the Giuliani archive and going on at great length, reveal that the initial rationale for the agency was "non–law enforcement events," particularly the handling of a Brooklyn water-main break shortly after he took office that the mayor thought had been botched. Before that, in December 1994, when an unemployed computer programmer carried a bomb onto a subway in an extortion plot against the Transit Authority, Giuliani was upset that he couldn't even get a count of patients from the responding services for his press conference.

Jerry Hauer, who was handpicked by Giuliani to head the OEM, testified before the 9/11 Commission that Giuliani was "unable to get the full story" at the firebombing and "heard about the huge street collapse" that followed the water-main break "on TV," adding: "That's what led the mayor to set up OEM." Hauer went through five interviews for the job, and the only time terrorism came up was when Giuliani briefly discussed the failed sarin-gas drill. He even met with Giuliani's wife, Donna Hanover; no one said a word about the 1993 bombing. Hauer's own memos at the time the OEM was launched in 1996 emphasize "the visibility of the mayor" during emergencies (rather than the police commissioner) as a major objective of the agency. The now-ballyhooed new office was, however, so underfunded from the start that Hauer could only hire staffers whose salaries would be paid for by other agencies like the NYPD. With that kind of history, it's hardly surprising that the OEM was anything but "invaluable" on 9/11. Sam Caspersen, one of the principal authors of the 9/11 Commission's chapter on the city's response, says that "nothing was happening at OEM" during the 102 minutes of the attack that had any direct impact on the city's "rescue/evacuation operation." A commission staff statement found that, even prior to the evacuation of the OEM command center at 7 World Trade an hour after the first plane hit, the agency "did not play an integral role" in the response. Despite Giuliani's claim today that he and the OEM were "constantly planning for different kinds" of attacks, none of the OEM exercises replicated the 1993 bombing. No drill occurred at the World Trade Center, and none involved the response to a high-rise fire anywhere. In fact, the OEM had no high-rise plan—its emergency-management trainers weren't even assigned to prepare for the one attack that had already occurred, and the one most likely to recur. Kevin Culley, a fire department captain who worked as a field responder at OEM, said the agency had "plans for minor emergencies," but he couldn't recall "anybody anticipating another attack like the '93 bombing."

Instead of being the best-prepared city, New York demonstrated a lack of unified command, as well as the breakdown of communications between the police and fire departments, that fell far short of the efforts at the Pentagon that day, as later established by the 9/11 Commission and NIST reports. When the 280,000-member International Association of Fire Fighters recently released a powerful video assailing Giuliani for sticking firefighters with the same radios that "we knew didn't work" in the 1993 attack, the presidential campaign attacked the union. "This is an organization that supported John Kerry for president in 2004," Giuliani aide Tony Carbonetti said. "So it's no shock that they're out there going after a credible Republican." While the

IAFF did endorse Kerry, the Uniformed Firefighters of Greater New York, whose president starred in the video, endorsed Bush. Its former president, Tom Von Essen—currently a member of Giuliani Partners—was the fire commissioner on 9/11 precisely because the union had played such a pivotal role in initially electing Giuliani.

The IAFF video reports that 121 firefighters in the north tower didn't get out because they didn't hear evacuation orders, rejecting Giuliani's claim before the 9/11 Commission that the firefighters heard the orders and heroically decided to "stand their ground" and rescue civilians. Having abandoned that 2004 contention, the Giuliani campaign is now trying to blame the deadly communications lapse on the repeaters, which were installed to boost radio signals in the towers. But the commission concluded that the "technical failure of FDNY radios" was "a contributing factor," though "not the primary cause," of the "many firefighter fatalities in the North Tower." The commission compared "the strength" of the NYPD and FDNY radios and said that the weaknesses of the FDNY radios "worked against successful communication."

The commission report also found that "it's impossible to know what difference it made that units in the North Tower weren't using the repeater channel," because no one knows if it "remained operational" after the collapse of the south tower, which fell on the trade-center facilities where the repeater and its console were located. The collapse also drove everyone out of the north tower lobby, leaving no one to operate the repeater console. In addition, the commission concluded that fire chiefs failed to turn on the repeater correctly that morning—another indication of the lack of training and drills at the WTC between the attacks. In the end, firefighters had to rely exclusively on their radios, and the inability of the Giuliani administration to find a replacement for the radios that malfunctioned in 1993 left them unable to talk to each other, even about getting out of a tower on the verge of collapse.

The mayor had also done nothing to make the radios inter-operable—which would have enabled the police and firefighters to communicate across departmental lines—despite having received a 1995 federal waiver granting the city the additional radio frequencies to make that possible. That meant the fire chiefs had no idea that police helicopters had anticipated the partial collapse of both towers long before they fell.

It's not just the radios and the OEM: Giuliani never forced the police and fire departments to abide by clear command-and-control protocols that squarely put one service in charge of the other during specified emergencies. Though he collected $250 million in tax surcharges on phone use to improve the 911 system, he diverted this emergency funding for other uses, and the 911 dispatchers were an utter disaster that day, telling victims to stay where they were long after the fire chiefs had ordered an evacuation, which potentially sealed the fates of hundreds. And, despite the transparent lessons of 1993, Giuliani never established any protocols for rooftop or elevator rescues in high-rises, or even a strategy for bringing the impaired and injured out—all costly failings on 9/11.

But perhaps the best evidence of the Giuliani administration's lack of readiness was that no one at its top levels had a top-secret security clearance on 9/11. Hauer, who had left the OEM in 2000 to become a top biochemical adviser at the US Department of Health and Human Services, was invited to Gracie Mansion within days of 9/11 for a strategy session with Giuliani and a half dozen of his top advisers, including Police Commissioner Bernie Kerik, Tom Von Essen, and Richie Sheirer, who succeeded Hauer at the OEM. Hauer, who had the highest-level clearance, says that "no one else in the room had one at all." He was told that the FBI "was trying to get them expedited clearances."

Hauer had previously taken Sheirer down to the White House to meet with top counterterrorism brass and learned on his way into the meeting that Sheirer hadn't "filled out the questionnaire." When Kerik's nomination as Homeland Security secretary blew up in 2004, news accounts also indicated that he'd never filled it out. Von Essen was so out of the loop that he said that prior to 9/11, he was told "nothing at all," and that he started hearing "talk of an organization called al Qaeda and a man named Osama bin Laden" a few hours after the attack. "It meant nothing to me," he wrote in his own book.

"I was reading the daily intelligence in Washington," Hauer recalled, "and I didn't feel comfortable talking about things that people weren't cleared for. Talking in general with Rudy one-on-one was one thing, but talking to Richie and Bernie and Tommy violated my security clearances." Though Giuliani's top team had failed to seek the clearances they needed prior to 9/11, Kerik and Giuliani attacked the FBI for not sharing information with local law enforcement officials when they testified a month after the attack at a House subcommittee hearing.

Big Lie 3

Don't blame me for 7 WTC, Rudy says.

In response to his critics' most damning sound bite, Giuliani is attempting to blame a once-valued aide for the decision to put his prized, $61 million emergency-command center in the World Trade Center, an obvious terrorist target. The 1997 decision had dire consequences on 9/11, when the city had to mobilize a response without any operational center.

"My director of emergency management recommended 7 WTC" as "the site that would make the most sense," Giuliani told Chris Wallace's Fox News Channel show in May, pinpointing Jerry Hauer as the culprit.

Wallace confronted Giuliani, however, with a 1996 Hauer memo recommending that the bunker be sited at MetroTech in Brooklyn, close to where the Bloomberg administration eventually built one. The mayor brushed the memo aside, continuing to insist that Hauer had picked it as "the prime site." The campaign then put out statements from a former deputy mayor who said that Hauer had supported the trade-center location at a high-level meeting with the mayor in 1997.

Hauer doesn't dispute that he eventually backed the 7 WTC location, but he clearly favored MetroTech. His memo said that MetroTech "could be available in six months," while it took four and a half more years to get the bunker up and running at 7 WTC. He said that MetroTech was secure and "not as visible a target as buildings in Lower Manhattan"—a prophetic comparison. Listing eight positives about MetroTech, the memo also mentioned negatives, but said they weren't insurmountable. "The real issue," Hauer concluded, "is whether or not the mayor wants to go across the river to manage an incident. If he is willing to do this, MetroTech is a good alternative." Notes from meetings indicate that Hauer continued to push MetroTech in the discussions with the mayor and his top deputy.

But Hauer says Denny Young, the mayor's alter ego, who has worked at his side for nearly three decades, eventually "made it very clear" that Giuliani wanted "to be able to walk to this facility quickly." That meant the bunker had to be in lower Manhattan. Since the City Hall area is below the floodplain, the command center—which was built with a hurricane-curtain wall—had to be above ground. The formal city document approving the site said that it "was selected due to its proximity to City Hall," a standard set by Giuliani and Giuliani alone.

The 7 WTC site was the brainchild of Bill Diamond, a prominent Manhattan Republican that Giuliani had installed at the city agency handling rentals. When Diamond held a similar post in the Reagan administration a few years earlier, his office had selected the same building to house nine federal agencies. Diamond's GOP-wired broker steered Hauer to the building, which was owned by a major Giuliani donor and fund-raiser. When Hauer signed on to it, he was locked in by the limitations Giuliani had imposed on the search and the sites Diamond offered him. The mayor was so personally focused on the siting and construction of the bunker that the city administrator who oversaw it testified in a subsequent lawsuit that "very senior officials," specifically including Giuliani, "were involved," which he said was a major difference between this and other projects. Giuliani's office had a humidor for cigars and mementos from City Hall, including a fire horn, police hats and fire hats, as well as monogrammed towels in his bathroom. His suite was bulletproofed and he visited it often, even on weekends, bringing his girlfriend Judi Nathan there long before the relationship surfaced. He had his own elevator. Great concern was expressed in writing that the platform in the press room had to be high enough to make sure his head was above the cameras. It's inconceivable that the hands-on mayor's fantasy command center was shaped—or sited—by anyone other than him.

Of course, the consequences of putting the center there were predictable. The terrorist who engineered the 1993 bombing told the FBI they were coming back to the trade center. Opposing the site at a meeting with the mayor, Police Commissioner Howard Safir called it "Ground Zero" because of the earlier attack. Lou Anemone, the highest-ranking uniformed officer in the NYPD, wrote memos slamming the site. "I've never seen in my life 'walking distance' as some kind of a standard for crisis management," Anemone said later. "But you don't want to confuse Giuliani with the facts." Anemone had done a detailed vulnerability study of the city for Giuliani, pinpointing terrorist targets. "In terms of targets, the WTC was number one," he says. "I guess you had to be there in 1993 to know how strongly we felt it was the wrong place."

Bizarrely, Giuliani even tried in the Wallace interview to deny that the early evacuation of the bunker left him searching for a new site, contrary to the account of that frantic morning he's given hundreds of times, often for honoraria reaching six figures. "The way you're interpreting it," he told Wallace, "it was as if that was the one fixed command center. It was not. There were backup command centers." To minimize the effect of the loss of the bunker, Giuliani said that, "within a half hour" of the shutdown of the bunker, "we were able to move immediately to another command center."

In fact, as Giuliani himself has told the dramatic tale, he and his entourage were briefly trapped in a Merrill Lynch office, "jimmied the lock" of a firehouse, and took over a deluxe hotel until they realized it was "sheathed in windows." They considered going to City Hall, but learned it was covered in debris. The only backup center that existed was the small one at police headquarters that had been put out of business when the WTC bunker opened; but Giuliani said its phones weren't working. "We're going to have to find someplace," Giuliani said, according to his *Time* account, which described it as a "long and harrowing" search.

"Our government no longer had a place to work," he wrote in *Leadership*.

They wound up at the police academy uptown and, according to the account Giuliani and company gave *Time*, "we are up and operating by 4 p.m."—seven hours, not a half hour, after the attack. But Giuliani told the 9/11 Commission that they quickly decided the academy "was too small" and "were able to establish a command center" at Pier 92 "within three days," virtually building it from scratch. Hauer said he'd asked for a backup command center years before 9/11, "but they told me there was no money for it." After Hauer left, and shortly before 9/11, the city announced plans to build a backup center near police headquarters—a site quickly jettisoned by the Bloomberg administration. Police officials told reporters that they were looking for space outside Manhattan and underground, citing the lessons of 9/11.

Big Lie 4

"Democrats do not understand the full nature and scope of the terrorist war against us."

Giuliani blames what he calls Bill Clinton's "decade of denial" for the mess we're in, and uses it to tarnish the rest of Clinton's party. "Don't react, kind of let things go, kind of act the way Clinton did in the '90s" is his favorite way of characterizing the Democratic response to the threat of terrorism. "We were attacked at Khobar Towers, Kenya, Tanzania, 17 of our sailors were killed on the USS *Cole*, and the United States government, under then-president Clinton, did not respond," Giuliani told the rabidly anti-Clinton audience at Pat Robertson's Regent University. "It was a big mistake to not recognize that the 1993 bombing was a terrorist act and an act of war," he added. "Bin Laden declared war on us. We didn't hear it. I thought it was pretty clear at the time, but a lot of people didn't see it, couldn't see it."

This is naked revisionism—and not just because of his own well-established, head-in-the-sand indifference to the 1993 bombing. It's as unambiguously partisan as his claim that on 9/11, he looked to the sky, saw the first fighter jets flying over the city well after the attack, and thanked God that George W. Bush was president. Bob Kerrey, the former Democratic senator who sat on the 9/11 Commission, put it fairly: "Prior to 9/11, no elected official did enough to reduce the threat of Al Qaeda. Neither political party covered itself in glory."

Giuliani's lifelong friend Louis Freeh, the former FBI head who has endorsed him for president, wrote in his 2005 autobiography that "the nation's fundamental approach to Osama bin Laden and his ilk was no different after the inauguration of January 21, 2001, than it had been before." As Bob Kerrey noted, the five Democrats and five Republicans on the 9/11 Commission said much the same thing. Freeh added that both administrations "were fighting criminals, not an enemy force" before 9/11, and Giuliani is now making precisely the same policy point, but limiting his critique to Clinton. Even the fiercely anti-Clinton Freeh credited the former president with "one exception," saying his administration did go after bin Laden "with a salvo of Tomahawk missiles in 1998 in retaliation for the embassy bombings in East Africa."

The best example of Giuliani's partisan twist is the USS *Cole*, which was attacked on October 12, 2000, three weeks before the 2000 election. The 9/11 Commission report found that in the final Clinton months, neither the FBI, then headed by Freeh, nor the CIA had a "definitive answer on the crucial question of outside direction of the attack," which Clinton said he needed to go to war against bin Laden or the Taliban. All Clinton got was a December 21 "preliminary judgment" from the CIA that Al Qaeda "supported the attack." A month later, when the Bush team took office, the CIA delivered the same "preliminary" findings to the new president. National Security Adviser Condoleezza Rice told the commission "there was never a formal, recorded decision not to retaliate for the *Cole*" by the Bush administration, just "a consensus that 'tit-for-tat' responses were likely to be counterproductive." Rice thought that was the case "with the cruise missile strikes of 1998," meaning that the new administration was deriding the one response that Freeh praised. Bush himself told the commission that he was concerned "lest an ineffective air strike just serve to give bin Laden a propaganda advantage." With all of this evidence of bipartisan paralysis, Giuliani has nonetheless limited his *Cole* attack to Clinton.

It is all part of a devoutly partisan exploitation of his 9/11 legend. Though Giuliani volunteered to execute bin Laden himself after 9/11, he's never criticized Bush for the administration's failure to capture him or the other two top culprits in the attack, Mullah Omar and Ayman al-Zawahiri, a silence more revealing than anything he actually says about terrorism. The old evidence that Bush relied on Afghan proxies to capture bin Laden at Tora Bora, and the new evidence that he outsourced him to Pakistani proxies in Waziristan, evokes no Giuliani bark. Imagine if a Democratic president had done that—or had said, as Bush did, that "I just don't spend that much time" on bin Laden.

At the Republican National Convention in 2004, Giuliani began his celebrated speech by fusing 9/11 and the Iraq War as only he could do, reminding everyone of Bush's bullhorn declaration at Ground Zero that the people who brought down these towers "will hear from us," and declaring that they "heard from us in Iraq"—a far more invidious connection on this question than Dick Cheney has ever made. Giuliani even went so far, in his 2004 testimony before the 9/11 Commission, to claim that if he'd been told about the presidential daily briefing headlined "Bin Laden Determined to Strike in the U.S.," which mentioned New York three times, "I can't honestly tell you we would have done anything differently." Pressed about whether the city would have benefited from knowing about a spike in warnings so vivid that the CIA director's "hair was on fire," Giuliani just shrugged. He'd seen many close friends buried after 9/11, but his answer had more to do with the November election than the September attack that took their lives.

"They don't see the threat," he derides the Democrats wherever he goes, ridiculing even their adjectives. "During the Democratic debates, I couldn't find one of them that ever mentioned the words 'Islamic terrorist'—none of them," he contends. "If you can't say the words 'Islamic terrorists,' then you have a hard time figuring out who is our biggest enemy in the world."

In fact, during the three Democratic debates, the candidates referred to "terrorism," "terrorists," or "terror" 24 times—only the modifier was missing, though John Edwards did warn in June that "radical Islam" could take over in Pakistan. By focusing on "radical Islam" as opposed to "Islamic terrorism," the Democrats may actually be avoiding any suggestion that America is engaged in a war against Islam—and even Giuliani would concede that Osama bin Laden is a perversion of Islam. Indeed, though Giuliani is claiming that he's been "studying" Islamic terrorism since 1975, a search of Giuliani news stories and databases reveals that the first time he was cited using the term was in his May 2004 testimony before the 9/11 Commission: he made a passing reference to the sarin-gas drill and said it simulated an "Islamic terrorist attack." If the use of this term is a measure of a leader's understanding of the threat, what does it say about Giuliani's own decade of denial that he never used it in the '90s, when he was the mayor of the only American city to have experienced one?

Big Lie 5

"Every effort was made by Mayor Giuliani and his staff to ensure the safety of all workers at Ground Zero."

So read a Giuliani campaign statement in June, responding to a chorus of questions about the mayor's responsibility for the respiratory plague that threatens the health of tens of thousands of workers at the World Trade Center site, apparently already having killed some.

The statement pointed a finger at then EPA Administrator Christine Todd Whitman, issuing a list of the many times that "Whitman assured New Yorkers the air was safe." Instead of also detailing the many times Giuliani echoed Whitman—for example, "the air is safe and acceptable," he said on September 28—the campaign cited several fire department "briefings" about "incident action plans" for the use of respirators, suggesting that the city had tried to get responders to protect themselves from the toxins at Ground Zero. The press release did not make a case that any of these "plans" had ever resulted in any real "action"; nor did it dispute the fact that as late as the end of October, only 29 percent of the workers at the site were wearing respirators. Of course, the workers might have noticed that the photo-op mayor never put one on himself. Instead, the other 9/11 visual we all remember is Giuliani leading at Ground Zero by macho example: the most in the way of protective gear he was ever seen wearing was a dust mask on his mouth.

When the cleanup effort was widely hailed as under budget and ahead of schedule, there was no doubt about who was in charge. "By Day 4," the *New York Times* reported in a salute to the "Quick Job" at Ground Zero, "Mr. Giuliani, the Department of Design and Construction (D.D.C.), the Office of Emergency Management, contractors and union officials decided it was time to bring order to the chaos." Giuliani controlled access to the site as if it were his backyard. Yet, when the scope of the health disaster was clear on the fifth anniversary in 2006, he told ABC: "Everybody's responsible." Throwing federal, state, and city agencies into the mix, he diffused the blame. On the *Today* show the same morning, however, he was more accusatory: "EPA put out statements, very, very prominent that you have on tape, that the air was safe, and kept repeating that and kept repeating that."

The city had its own test results, of course, and when 17 of 87 outdoor tests showed hazardous levels of asbestos up to seven blocks away, they decided not to make the results public. An EPA chief, Bruce Sprague, sent an October 5 letter to the city complaining about "very inconsistent compliance" with respiratory protection. Sprague, who wrote the letter only after unsuccessful conversations with Giuliani aides, likened the indifference in a subsequent court deposition to sticking one's head "over a barbecue grill for hours" and expecting no consequences. An internal legal memo to a deputy mayor estimated early in the cleanup that there could be 35,000 potential plaintiffs against the city, partly because rescue workers were "provided with faulty or no equipment (i.e. respirators)." Bechtel, the major construction firm retained by the city as its health and safety consultant, urged it to cut the exit-entry points from 20 to two so they could enforce the use of respirators and other precautions, just as was done at the Pentagon, but the recommendation was ignored.

A *Times* editorial concluded in May that the Giuliani administration "failed in its duty to protect the workers at Ground Zero," faulting its "emphasis on a speedy cleanup" and its unwillingness "to insist that all emergency personnel and construction workers wear respirators." John Odermatt, a former OEM director working at the campaign, couldn't tell the *Times* whether Giuliani had lobbied Congress on behalf of sick workers, nor could anyone at the campaign offer any evidence that Giuliani had ever, while earning millions at his new 9/11 consulting business in recent years, tried to secure federal funds for responders.

Should the current presidential frontrunners square off in 2008, Giuliani's culpability and subsequent indifference at Ground Zero will, no doubt, be sharply contrasted to Hillary Clinton's singular role in funding the Mount Sinai programs that have been aiding rescue workers for years. And the public price tag for the mismanagement at the pile (as the site was known among recovery and rescue workers) will run into the billions. Ken Feinberg, who ran the federally funded Victims Compensation Board, has already paid out $1 billion to the injured, concluding after individual hearings that hundreds "were diagnosed with demonstrable and documented respiratory injuries directly related to their rescue service." Anthony DePalma, whose extraordinary *Times* stories have lifted the lid on Giuliani's role, recently reported that the health-care costs for rescue workers could soar to as much as $712 million a year. And the city is administering a billion-dollar liability fund to satisfy the thousands of lawsuits.

Giuliani's fellow Republican and former EPA chief Christine Todd Whitman did tell WNBC a couple of months ago that there were "telephone calls, telephone meetings, and meetings in person with the city" every day, with the EPA repeating "the message" and emphasizing the "necessity of wearing the respirators." Whitman said she "would call my people at midnight after watching the 11 o'clock news and say, 'I'm still seeing them without the respirators.'" The EPA, she said, "was very frustrated." She also said "the better thing would've been to put out the fire sooner," certainly a function of the city's fire department, adding that it had "burned until January"—a continuous flame held to a smoking, toxic brew. Asked about the mayor himself, Whitman sputtered: "He was clearly in control and doing a good job. Everyone was applauding what was going on. EPA, we had some disagreements with things that were occurring on the pile, like not having people wear respirators—we wanted more emphasis on that. But overall, you know, it's hard. Those are emotional times."

The firefighters' union pointed out that the respiratory debacle was, like the malfunctioning radios and so many other things, another symbol of the city's failure to prepare for a major terrorist event. Fire department memos after the 1993 bombing had urged better protective gear, just as they'd screamed for better radios. The Uniformed Firefighter Association's leaders pointed out that the department had "ignored many issues related to respiratory protection" for years. The union's health-and-safety officer, Phil McArdle, likened the long-term effects of working at Ground Zero to Agent Orange in Vietnam. "We've done a good job of taking care of the dead," he said, referring to the hunt for remains, "but such a terrible job of taking care of the living."

PART IV
The Highest Bidder

"Many New Yorkers have an eerie feeling now that Mike's money is literally everywhere and that a city, said to be for sale in the era of the big-time bosses, has actually been bought by a mayor so much bigger than they ever boasted of being. The richest man in New York is also, for the first time, the mayor of the city and one of its grandest philanthropists, making it almost impossible for the rest of us to talk to him without wondering at some level of consciousness: 'Can I get a slice of this guy?' His personal and public outlays have flooded the city's bloodstream for years now, and few are so uninterested in a possible transfusion of their own that they will take him on."

—From "The Transformation of Mike Bloomberg," November 19, 2008

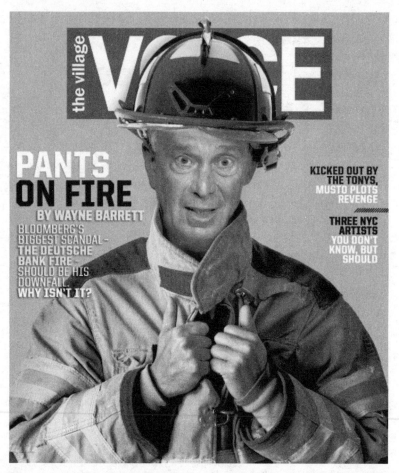

Barrett called Bloomberg both the best and worst of the five New York City mayors he covered. "Our billionaire mayor will never be tarnished by the traditional pay-to-play and influence-peddling schemes that compromise politicians with ordinary bank accounts. Instead, his defining debacle is a failure of leadership, accountability, and transparency," Barrett wrote in "Bloomberg's Biggest Scandal—the Deutsche Bank Fire—Should Be His Downfall. Why Isn't It?" (Courtesy of the *Village Voice*, photo illustration courtesy of Ivylise Simones)

The Price of Money

Jarrett Murphy

I N SOME WAYS, Michael Bloomberg was tailor-made to earn Wayne Barrett's admiration. Here was a mayor inoculated against the grubby give-and-take of campaign fund-raising, who had bypassed the ethical minefield of party apparatus and stood apart from the White-ethnic power base that Ed Koch and Rudy Giuliani had manipulated at the city's peril. Bloomberg and his aides must have sensed that Wayne was a potentially valuable ally, for in the early days of his tenure, the billionaire mayor regularly held an off-the-record dinner with Wayne and a select group of other journalists; no previous sitting mayor had thought to cultivate him so. And Wayne did admire much about Bloomberg's first years. In particular, he saw Bloomberg's taking control of the schools as a gutsy, over-due effort to shatter the ossified alliance between the Board of Ed bureaucracy and a teachers' union that Wayne had despised for decades.

Eventually, however, Wayne realized that Bloomberg's ability to transcend the pitfalls of typical politicians presented its own kind of danger. By casting himself above politics, Bloomberg escaped scrutiny from a press corps trained to scan only for the most venal sins. Bloomberg's tightly trained marketing team pumped a narrative of managerial competence as newsrooms cut the number of metro reporters who might sniff out the truth. Good-government groups allied themselves with the mayor, even though his massive election spending had turned the city's pioneering campaign-finance law on its head. Many Black and Latino leaders swung to his side despite Bloomberg having a remarkably White administration and amid swelling stop-and-frisk numbers. Nonprofits wrestled with how to criticize a mayor who, as one of the country's most active philanthropists, donated generously. Captains of industry and titans of wealth—who had for decades worked to wrest control of New York's unruly democracy from the masses—celebrated a City Hall instinctively aligned with their class.

After serving as an intern for Wayne in the spring of 1998, when I was witness to his weekly battle against Giuliani, I joined the *Voice* as a writer in late 2004, just in time for Bloomberg's first reelection campaign. It often felt as though the *Voice* newsroom on Cooper Square was the only one in town with the freedom and appetite to hold the mayor accountable. At first, Wayne did not throw an abundance of punches at Bloomberg, but the ones he launched were powerful. These included an article that etched out the many sexual harassment and gender discrimination complaints female employees brought against the mayor during his time as CEO of Bloomberg LP. I don't know that anyone before Wayne had dared brave the minefield of nondisclosure agreements cluttering that story.

Over Bloomberg's second term, Wayne's criticism mounted, especially after Bloomberg's cynical move to lift term limits. The article included here about the Deutsche Bank building fire, which killed two firefighters and nearly led to criminal charges against the city, is a superb counterpoint to the myth that Bloomberg was a peerless manager in City Hall. It also embodies the best of Wayne's reportage—muscled with fact, steered with exacting intellect, and driven by outrage at the price paid by those whom leaders fail.

Jarrett Murphy is the executive editor of *City Limits* and the cohost of Max & Murphy, a *Voice* staff writer from 2004 to 2007, he has written for *The Nation* and Huffington Post and teaches investigative reporting at the Craig Newmark Graduate School of Journalism at the City University of New York.

16

Bloomberg's Biggest Scandal—the Deutsche Bank Fire—Should Be His Downfall. Why Isn't It?

July 22, 2009

MIKE BLOOMBERG'S WORST scandal cost two firefighters their lives. If we lived in a media world in which facts and memories mattered, the nonchalance at the highest levels of the Bloomberg administration about the hazards and warnings at the Deutsche Bank building, where Robert Beddia and Joseph Graffagnino died on August 18, 2007, might cost him his reelection.

Our billionaire mayor will never be tarnished by the traditional pay-to-play and influence-peddling schemes that compromise politicians with ordinary bank accounts. Instead, his defining debacle is a failure of leadership, accountability, and transparency, revealed in one law enforcement report or news story after another, ever since Beddia and Graffagnino succumbed to smoke on the 14th floor of the city's most toxic building, just 118 feet from where 343 of their brothers perished six years earlier. Even Bloomberg's Department of Investigations (DOI) found last month, in a report barely noticed by the press, that it was a case of death by official dereliction.

By the time of the fire, city and state officials were so driven by their deal with J.P. Morgan Chase—which had agreed to begin building its new headquarters on the Deutsche site as soon as it was cleared—that they were pushing this unprecedented simultaneous decontamination and demolition project forward as quickly as possible. They did so without proper permits or oversight, determined to complete it before the opt-out 2008 deadlines written into the Morgan contract. Due to the extended delays that followed the fire, however, the deconstruction of the bank building remains unfinished, and Morgan has, for reasons more connected to the economic meltdown than to the Deutsche delays, walked away.

The original $45 million takedown price tag on the Deutsche building has grown by five times. Next year, finally, the blackened 40-story carcass is slated to be gone, nearly a full decade after a 15-floor gash was cut in its side by South Tower {of the World Trade Center} debris and it was filled with toxins and remains thrown into the bright morning air on the city's darkest day. Everything about this project and its fire has been bungled—by one city and three state administrations—yet yesterday's headlines have become today's haze, and the role of a mayor celebrated for his competence remains largely unexamined.

Deadly mismanagement cost one mayor his job. Yankel Rosenbaum's murder in a Crown Heights race riot mishandled by the NYPD finished David Dinkins in 1993, when the media refused to give a culpable administration a pass simply because its breakdowns were two-year-old news. But we are now in an era when media moguls get together to reverse two public referendums in an undisguised effort to keep one of their own in office, a time when the mayor may be the biggest new ad buyer in town. The question now is whether the press will hold accountable a mayor who has refused to hold any of his own appointees accountable for an avoidable disaster.

In the months before August 18, 2007, there were so many fires and accidents at the Deutsche Bank site that a high-powered consultant, URS, reported to state and city officials that the giant construction-management firm on the project, Bovis Lend Lease, could "no longer be trusted to ensure building safety," and that the project was "an accident waiting to happen." Fifteen days after that alarm, a cigarette butt discarded on the 17th floor sparked a fire that later consumed nine stories. So many firefighters rushed up steps and elevators that 115 were injured, 46 seriously enough to require medical leave.

The docket of pre-fire municipal malfeasance starts with the collapse of inspectional regimes at the fire and buildings departments, which combined to miss a 42-foot breach in the bank building's water-supplying standpipe for months, leaving firefighters without working hoses for more than an hour in what the Graffagnino family now calls a "death trap."

Though FDNY regulations require inspections of construction or demolition sites every 15 days, the department never inspected the bank building in the six months of work that preceded the fire. The Department of Buildings (DOB) granted the project a commonplace alteration permit, the kind that is only supposed to be approved when a project "does not change" a building's use—precisely the opposite of what was planned at the Deutsche site. According to one subsequent law enforcement report, this unusual choice of permit "allowed the building to undergo concurrent abatement and demolition," a rare and risky venture. Had a demolition permit been required instead, the building would have become the province of the DOB's demolition experts, literally called the B.E.S.T. team. Instead, "inexperienced inspectors who volunteered for the assignment and never traced the stand-pipe" were the ones regularly on site, with B.E.S.T. inspectors in a secondary role, the same investigative report concluded.

But the record of miscalculation is not limited to inspectional dysfunction. It extends into the upper reaches at City Hall, where the mayor's most trusted deputy, Dan Doctoroff, disregarded warnings from DOI commissioner Rose Gill Hearn in favor of the reckless predilections of Bovis, a company that had built the Lexington Avenue headquarters of Bloomberg's media company and prospered in the Bloomberg administration. Bovis insisted on making a mob-and-accident-scarred firm its prime demolition subcontractor at the Deutsche site, and Doctoroff bowed to the selection over the howls of Gill Hearn. Doctoroff later told the *Times* that he did it because he was satisfied that sufficient "safe-guards" had been put in place to make sure that the controversial subcontractor behaved itself.

The subcontractor, the John Galt Corporation,* is now under indictment for manslaughter in the case of Beddia and Graffagnino. Manhattan district attorney Robert Morgenthau found that a "behind-schedule" Galt "decided to shift the project's focus from cleaning pipes to removing them," sawing off "the hanging rods that supported the standpipe within inches of ceilings," causing "a large portion" of it to break free and crash to the ground. According to the district attorney, the Bovis site-safety manager and two top Galt supervisors—one of whom had been specifically objected to by Gill Hearn—"gathered at the foot of the broken standpipe" and decided to cut it up into sections, bagging and discarding it as asbestos-containing material. Though the building "was now defenseless against the threat of significant fire," Bovis

---

* The name is a reference to the character in Ayn Rand's *Atlas Shrugged*.

and Galt reported it to no one, said Morgenthau. When the fire hit, the water that Beddia, Graffagnino, and 100 other firefighters needed poured out of the wide-open standpipe into the basement.

In addition to the role of the building's safety manager in this alleged incident, Bovis replaced its site superintendent after he insisted, prior to the break in the standpipe, that it be pressure tested. Morgenthau said the new superintendent "proved to be less safety-conscious, and the standpipe was never tested again." Morgenthau concluded that Bovis prepared "fraudulent" daily checklists that failed to record not only the breach in the stand-pipe, but also "numerous fires and accidents" that occurred prior to August 2007.

Once the recipient of hundreds of millions of dollars in Bloomberg and Doctoroff largesse at nearly a half dozen city agencies, Bovis averted indictment only because it was too big an employer to fail, according to Morgenthau. An agreement ex-ecuted by Bovis and Morgenthau's office noted that the DA had "determined that it could institute a criminal prosecution" against the company on the same criminally negligent homicide and re-lated charges it brought against Galt.

Beyond these inspection and contracting mistakes, the cata-logue of fatal failings also includes the fire department's response the day of the fire, which offered chilling reminders of how little was learned from 9/11. Firefighters once again charged skyward in droves, though this time, there were no possible victims to rescue. A fire chief on the FDNY's executive staff had written a warning calling for a Deutsche Bank–specific response plan two years be-fore the demolition began, but he and the rest of the department brass failed to develop one tailored to this complex and dangerous site. Instead, the department, from the commissioner on down, behaved as if standard operating procedure were a sufficient response to any incident at the bank, even though, as Morgenthau put it, a project to concurrently clean and clear "a high-rise in a dense residential and commercial neighborhood had never been done before in New York City."

Bloomberg's tabloid-celebrated pretense at running a CEO-style government is belied by his response to these failings.

The only supposed culprits punished for the inspection breakdowns are people the mayor does not know or didn't appoint—line staff at the FDNY and the DOB—while the executives at these agencies, led by Fire Commissioner Nick Scoppetta, have yet to elicit so much as a critical word from him.

In fact, Bloomberg went out of his way to defend Scoppetta when Morgenthau pointed out, in a 32-page report, that the commissioner visited the firehouse next to the Deutsche building three months before the fire and never "inquired as to whether regular inspections were being conducted" at the bank building or "whether a special fire operations plan for this project was in place." Scoppetta was there that May because a 15-foot pipe fell from the Deutsche site through the roof of the firehouse and injured two firefighters, forcing the then 74-year-old commissioner to climb to the firehouse roof. Morgenthau added that "the failure to inspect"—which, he says, "contributed to the conditions that led to the deaths" of the firefighters—"implicates high-ranking FDNY officials" who "clearly recognized that buildings undergoing construction, demolition, and abatement were extremely dangerous for firefighting operations."

Bloomberg's lawyers, according to sources at Morgenthau's office, pushed unsuccessfully "to delete the Scoppetta language" from the report. The day after it was released, only seven months ago, Bloomberg said, "You just can't take it all the way to the top and always go fire the top guy." He insisted that whatever went wrong had occurred at another "level," consistent with Scoppetta's decision this June to discipline up to seven fire chiefs, none of whom were part of his inner circle. Scoppetta, who ran the Children's Services agency under Rudy Giuliani, is in his eighth year as Bloomberg's fire commissioner, the longest-tenured in half a century.

Even the DOI, while focusing favorably on the postfire reforms that Scoppetta introduced, quietly took him apart. Its June report, which drew only puny stories in two city dailies, noted that "after the fire," Scoppetta "became heavily involved with inspections," adding that what was missing "at each and every level within the chain of command" before Deutsche was an effort to "ensure" that "the rules" requiring inspections of construction and demolition projects every 15 days were "being followed." The report disparaged "the executive team"—including Scoppetta and his three top chiefs—finding that all four were "unaware of, or did not address noncompliance with, the 15-Day Rule," charging that "the importance" of the rule was not "reinforced to the lower ranks."

The DOI also blasted "a culture of widespread disregard of the 15-Day Rule," and said it was violated "in commands throughout the Department." That makes it impossible to contend, as Scoppetta and the mayor did, that the FDNY's borough, division, and lower-level chiefs overseeing the bank building did anything out of the ordinary. In fact, when Scoppetta finally issued reprimands against them a few days ago, the charges placed in their file made no reference to any specific failure to inspect the Deutsche building, instead faulting them for general inspection shortcomings.

The reprimands, which will be removed from the files of these chiefs in a year and are among the least punitive forms of administrative discipline, implicitly make the case against Scoppetta and his top brass. They could not press tougher charges against the chiefs, targeting failings at Deutsche, without exposing—at any ensuing administrative trial—their own failure to ever issue any orders or directives compelling compliance with the inspection rules. In fact, the DOI report had to rely repeatedly on the promotional exams that chiefs take as the only notice they ever had to the existence of the 15-Day Rule, a thin reed indeed, since exam preparation covers multiple volumes of department regulations. (Is lawyer Scoppetta responsible for recalling everything he learned for the bar exam?)

Frank Gribbon, the FDNY's spokesman, conceded in a *Voice* interview that Scoppetta and his top staff had said "nothing about the 15-Day Rule" in any of their regular department orders prior to the fire. He confirmed that William Siegel—the chief whose detailed 2005 memo urging a specific response plan and weekly surveillances for the Deutsche Bank site was used to justify some of the disciplinary actions—had actually been promoted to Scoppetta's cabinet by the time the demolition began in early 2007. Siegel did not, to Gribbon's knowledge, ever mention his own concerns about the site in Scoppetta's weekly executive sessions. That suggests that, at the highest levels in the department, even the two-star chief who'd written the book on the bank building was asleep at the switch. (Siegel, who has since retired, declined to answer questions when reached at his home.)

Gribbon added that the department was not going to investigate any managerial mistakes made during the fire response, and refused to answer questions about whether it believed any had occurred, despite critics inside and outside of the department who contend that so many firefighters were dispatched without water or purpose that it was fortunate only two were lost. He maintained that "the issue," when Scoppetta went to the firehouse next to the bank, was "protecting the firehouse," and that Scoppetta made Bovis "construct a platform" and "considered" pulling the firefighters out during the demolition, never focusing on inspecting the actual cause of the accident.

Asked if there was any indication, after the Morgenthau and DOI reports, that the mayor was contemplating any actions against Scoppetta or the rest of the executive team, Gribbon said simply, "No." Asked if the mayor was "considering any actions against executives" in the FDNY or DOB, Bloomberg press secretary Stu Loeser sent an email to the *Voice* recounting instead the disciplinary decisions those executives have taken against lower-level staff.

The buildings commissioner at the time of the Deutsche breakdowns was Patricia Lancaster, the first Bloomberg department head to be forced from office. Lancaster's departure in late April 2008, eight months after the fire, occurred the day after she testified at a city council hearing that the DOB had mistakenly issued permits for an East-side building where a crane collapsed, killing seven people and injuring 24 others. Her ouster was never said to have had anything to do with the fire-connected blunders of her department. Though the mayor acknowledged when Lancaster quit that he didn't "think anybody should be fully satisfied with the DOB's performance," he moved immediately to replace her with First Deputy Robert LiMandri.

Neither Morgenthau's nor the DOI's report indicate if either Lancaster or LiMandri was aware of any of the department mistakes in the lead-up to the fire—including the failure to ever do an inspection in the basement. Nor do the reports deal with the question of whether these top executives should have been directly involved in so high-profile a project, if they contended they weren't. A DOI spokeswoman told the *Voice* that it did not comment on the role of top DOB officials because that "would have been a judgment call," and all DOI was requested by the mayor's office to examine was whether city officials had violated or failed to enforce "any rules" in connection with the fire.

An email to the *Voice* from the DOB indicated that LiMandri "was aware of the decision" to issue alteration rather than demolition permits "and did not object," observing that, nonetheless, "no investigation has raised any questions about Commissioner LiMandri's role." In fact, without naming LiMandri or Lancaster, the DOI criticized the issuance of an alteration permit and concluded that "regardless of the type of permit issued to a contractor, the DOB should not permit projects to undergo demolition until the abatement process is fully completed," precisely what the DOB is now doing on the site. The FDNY's 176-page report on the fire similarly pointed out in the second paragraph of the first page that "no demolition permit was filed or issued," noting that, instead, the DOB issued alteration permits—a point the FDNY reiterated later in the assessment.

Loeser insists that "the issuance of alteration permits had no bearing on the level" of DOB oversight, a contention that is contrary to Morgenthau's finding that "inexperienced" inspectors, rather than B.E.S.T. inspectors, wound up in charge, as a direct consequence of the absence of a demolition permit. The DOB insists that it took "the unprecedented step of dedicating a permanent team of inspectors to the site," meaning it "received greater attention" than any other construction site in the city. That's a quantity-over-quality argument, since the DOI found that none of the DOB's inspectors assigned to the site "had any experience on site safety demolition projects," and one department supervisor is quoted as concluding that the inspectors examining the standpipe "really did not know what they are looking at."

LiMandri actually promoted Tom Connors, the Manhattan inspection manager, and named Chris Santulli, the Manhattan commissioner, to a citywide post—after both had been faulted by the DOI for "no follow-up to ensure that the B.E.S.T. Squad was training" the inspectors actually monitoring the site. Though Connors "never told" the inspectors "what to inspect at the site" or provided them "with any type of formal training," LiMandri elevated him around the first anniversary of the fire to executive director of construction site safety. Last October, LiMandri named Santulli the acting assistant commissioner of engineering and safety operations, and it was Santulli who appeared at a January 2009 city council hearing to offer assurances about how well the Deutsche project was currently proceeding.

Though Connors was a featured speaker at a DOB-sponsored forum for Construction Safety Week in April, and both Santulli and Connors appeared with LiMandri at a similar event hosted by the Building Trade Employers Association in November, they both finally got letters of reprimand placed in their file a couple of weeks ago. The reprimands (without demotions) were issued three weeks after the *Voice* began asking questions about whether they'd be disciplined at all. Connors has received a $15,052 raise since the fire, while Santulli is still at the same $138,403 level. (Both were included in the citywide managerial salary hikes released by the mayor the same day that the reprimand letters were placed in their files. The raises they received tallied a combined $19,944.)

Beyond the mild and late letters on Santulli and Connors, Robert Iulo, who took over the inspection unit at the Deutsche site shortly before the fire, is the only DOB employee to face formal departmental charges. Iulo is accused in the DOI report of killing a stop-work request from one of the inspectors, who observed a problem with the standpipe unassociated with the basement breach. The inspector testified that, two months before the fire, he reported this standpipe problem to Iulo, as well as to the same Bovis manager ultimately charged with participating in the cover-up of the breach. The inspector wanted the pipe tested immediately, but Iulo blocked a pressurized test and allegedly instructed the inspector not to include his concerns in his report. Of course, a stop-work order would have meant delays no one wanted, and the Bovis manager, if his indictment is accurate, knew that the pipe would fail a test, leading to a prolonged stoppage of the project.

Throughout this period, the DOB reported to Dan Doctoroff, the deputy mayor who also headed the eight-member city delegation on the 16-member board of the state's Lower Manhattan Development Corporation (LMDC), the entity that bought the bank building from Deutsche and hired Bovis to tear it down. None of the investigative reports examine Doctoroff's role, if any, in the DOB's alteration permit, which exempted LMDC from the requirement that abatement precede demolition, or the patchwork inspections, which fast-tracked the project. He was, however, the only city official with a heavy hand at both agencies. One source involved with the probe at Morgenthau's office said Doctoroff was "the guy pushing and pushing and pushing" to get the project "moving forward," and that he "didn't bother himself with the details."

Doctoroff attended the LMDC meetings in July and August of 2005, when the contracts with Bovis and a Galt-tied subcontractor named Safeway were approved. He was the mayor's representative to LMDC, but didn't actually join its board until a couple of months later. Though he didn't hesitate to raise objections to matters on the agenda before he became a board member, including at the August meeting, he said nothing about the two contracts for the Deutsche project. The Bloomberg administration had distanced itself from LMDC as part of a broader power-sharing arrangement with Governor Pataki, but just as the bank project got under way, it aggressively threw itself into the LMDC mix. The *Times* said the administration played a key role in determining "who was to do the work" at the Deutsche site. Doctoroff became so personally involved that he put two of his own aides on the board as well.

Even though Safeway was soon dropped—in part for violations it received that summer in connection with the collapse of a supermarket it was demolishing, injuring 10 people—Doctoroff has conceded that, in February 2006, after joining the board, he signed off on two Bovis deals with Galt, which the DOI branded "a reincarnation" of Safeway. He apparently found Bovis's pitch for Galt—which won a $58 million contract covering the abatement and demolition of the building—more persuasive than the DOI's 10-page January 2006 memo blasting the company. "Investigators felt that their warnings had been ignored," the *Times* later noted. The DOI told the *Voice* that it "made its objections well known," but the spokeswoman said she "would not comment" on the agency's interactions "with the mayor's office."

A second DOI letter to LMDC that April called Galt's hiring of ex-Safeway executives—specifying the person subsequently charged in the bagging of the broken standpipe—"shocking and disturbing." The letter branded one of Doctoroff's "safeguards," namely that the Galt/Safeway executives had to cooperate with investigators, "a disingenuous fig leaf intended to put the imprimatur of the DOI on your arrangement." Another Doctoroff "safeguard" supposedly made sure that Galt did not "funnel money back to Safeway," a charge that Morgenthau is investigating now. "Once Galt and Bovis" agreed to these "stipulations," Doctoroff said after the fire, he and the rest of the city members "voted to approve the contract amendment to Bovis" that okayed Galt.

The canard later invoked by the mayor himself—that "there was only one contractor willing to work on taking down the building"—is contradicted by the DOI's April letter. Robert Roach, chief of staff to the DOI commissioner, said that the agency had provided "the names of several demolition contractors" that the state and city had "previously used." LMDC told the DOI that it "found these alternative contractors too expensive," and Roach presciently replied, "New York City has a policy of hiring only the lowest responsible bidder, in part because non-responsible contractors, such as Safeway and its officers, frequently cost the City more in the long run by virtue of delays and mistakes."

This was hardly the only time Doctoroff sided with Bovis on the project. The company came back to the board four times for contract increases, and Doctoroff and the city team backed every boost. Indeed, the mayor's only known personal intervention in the five-year effort to take down the building occurred days after Eliot Spitzer became governor in January 2007. Bloomberg and Doctoroff hosted a cozy session at Gracie Mansion with Spitzer, attempting to add $38 million to the public bill due to Bovis, Galt, and others on the project. Though it was already known that a Galt director had been fingered at the trial of John Gotti Jr. as an "associate" of the Gambino crime family, a company executive sat confidently through the mansion meeting, having prompted it by pulling workers off the site. Doctoroff declared afterward, "I believe we have solved our problem."

A state official familiar with Doctoroff's disposition toward Bovis said he believed they had "a special relationship," adding that the Bloomberg administration "had a preference for them, was comfortable with them." Asked for an example of that, the official said that, up to the mansion negotiations, LMDC, with Doctoroff's support, "gave Bovis the increases they asked for" without conditions. The Spitzer team took the "We'll advance the money now and litigate later" position, with the understanding that LMDC might seek to recoup some of the payment. The state and the city made it clear that Bovis and Galt would be financially penalized if they failed to meet a year-end deadline, a commitment they made just months before the fire, feeding their recklessness. The negotiations with Morgan to do its linchpin downtown revival tower on the bank site, with Doctoroff at the helm, peaked in the same time frame.

Doctoroff now sits in the Bloomberg LP headquarters that Bovis built during the first few years of the mayor's administration. The mayor held his favorite deputy so accountable for the Deutsche Bank screw-ups that, five months after the fire, Doctoroff became president of the $5-billion-a-year company Bloomberg almost entirely owns. A Bloomberg LP spokeswoman says that the company did not select Bovis to build the headquarters (the developer did). But a tenant like Bloomberg LP, whose company occupies virtually all of the office space in the mixed-use tower and participated in every detail of the design, undoubtedly developed ties to Bovis during the project. Alan Gerson, the city council member from lower Manhattan who chairs the committee that monitors LMDC, says that "without question," he believes Bovis got "favored treatment" from the city, especially at the Deutsche site.

Though Bovis had a track record with the city before Bloomberg became mayor, it prospered even more once he took office. In 2003, the Doctoroff-run NYC Economic Development Corporation (EDC) picked Bovis as one of its three construction managers on projects, awarding it $75 million in jobs so far, and renewing the contract without bids three times. Similarly, the Department of Citywide Administrative Services (DCAS)—from where one official, who asked not to be identified, said that Bovis was seen as "a preferred contractor prior to the fire"—selected Bovis twice as the agency's construction manager for its work downtown, where most of the city-owned office buildings that the DCAS manages are located. Bovis is still performing many jobs awarded under the prior EDC and DCAS agreements that will produce millions more in revenue.

In the days immediately after the fire, the mayor said he wanted answers about the city's failings. "We will not stop until we get them," he promised. He repeated the vow to the Graffagnino family at the funeral: "We're going to get those answers, and those answers will be followed by actions." When he and Scoppetta announced nine days after the fire that three chiefs would be relieved of their commands, he said the actions were "strictly preliminary" and predicted they "could wind up being the least of the actions we will take." They actually turned out to be the city's toughest disciplinary decisions, as the recent reprimands of the same three chiefs, and four others, were a retreat from the 2007 threats.

Even as Bloomberg was making these public promises, his top lawyer, corporation counsel Michael Cardozo, was calling Morgenthau personally and telling him that "the mayor was taken aback" that the district attorney had told reporters he was investigating the fire. Cardozo's call, according to two sources familiar with it, came within hours of Morgenthau making his announcement. "Tell the mayor that I'm taken aback that he's taken aback," said the legendary DA, who then had to face what sources called many "contentious" dealings with attorneys in Cardozo's office. (One of the sources recalled Cardozo using a synonym for "taken aback.") Firefighters scheduled to appear at Morgenthau's office for questioning at 10 one morning were summoned to Cardozo's office at eight for a briefing, but refused to show.

Asked about this exchange, as well as the attempts by other attorneys representing the city to get Morgenthau's office to remove language from his report criticizing Scoppetta, Cardozo's spokeswoman said, "We will not comment on what specifically may have been discussed in conversations between the city and the district attorney's office." Loeser also refused to discuss the conversations, "other than to say that we defended the city's actions."

Bloomberg faced—at that moment, and for the next year and a half—a possible career-killing indictment. Morgenthau was openly considering an unprecedented indictment of the city for criminally negligent homicide. The exchanges with Morgenthau's office got so difficult that Bloomberg wound up hiring a respected criminal attorney, Gary Naftalis, to represent the city, and Cardozo's office paid Naftalis's firm $4.5 million in a single year. Cardozo is in the process even now of extending the contract and raising the price to $6 million, even though Morgenthau announced last December that he would not indict the city. Cardozo's office says that Naftalis is advising the city in its fight against the Beddia and Graffagnino families and in any other civil litigation.

When Morgenthau decided not to charge the Bloomberg administration, he made it clear that it wasn't for lack of evidence. He likened any attempt to charge the city to "tilting at windmills," citing its "sovereign immunity" as an insuperable legal obstacle.

Fortunately for Bloomberg, the trials of Galt and the three employees indicted for the deaths of the firefighters will not start until after the election, when defense attorneys plan to point the finger at the city in every way. Stu Loeser and Dan Doctoroff are refusing even now to answer any questions about the hiring of Galt, using Morgenthau's continuing investigation as their excuse. Loeser won't even say what the DOI warned city officials—including the mayor himself—about Galt, much less whether Bloomberg believes Doctoroff should have heeded the DOI and objected to its retention.

Cas Holloway, the top Bloomberg adviser on the Deutsche job and one of his current appointees to the LMDC board, appeared at a city council hearing weeks after Morgenthau closed the fire case, and joined Bovis in refusing to answer questions about it. "We're not prepared to speak to every finding" in Morgenthau's report, Holloway said, refusing, in fact, to address any of them. "What we really want to talk about is what is happening at the site now." Morgenthau told the *Voice* that his office "certainly didn't tell anyone" not to answer public questions about the Deutsche debacle. Gerson, the council member who chaired the hearing, called the city and Bovis's refusals "stonewalling."

The caged lion inside Bloomberg's administration, the DOI's Gill Hearn, wasn't asked by City Hall to look at Doctoroff's embrace of Bovis and Galt, but at the line staff at the fire and buildings departments. She couldn't resist pointing out in her press release five weeks ago that the city's "inspectional forces" were "no match for the contractors' cavalier disregard for public safety," noting in the final paragraph of the 35-page report that Galt "should never have had this project in the first place."

No one in the New York press printed that conclusion. Bloomberg's onetime closest aide, who now runs his company, approved a contractor under indictment for killing two firefighters; Bloomberg's own top investigator says categorically that the contract should never have been awarded; and not one news outlet in New York thinks it's a story. Similarly, although every city paper published penetrating stories in the aftermath of the fire, not one quoted the DOI's more recent searing language about Scoppetta's executive team or cited the issues that the DOI implicitly raised about the DOB's top management. It's as if a curtain has been drawn on the mayoral election, and the only show that will go on is the one Mike buys on the air.

17

Bloomberg Keeps His Billions Separate from His Mayoral Obligations? Yeah, Right!

September 1, 2009

"There is something so odd about Bloomberg. He saluted the women in his life in his victory speech last night but had none of them on the stage with him. No one from his coalition of supporters or his administration was up there either. He was a one-man show with multi-racial paid extras behind him. The Sheraton ballroom was flooded with glowing young professionals and students, well dressed and glass in hand, clapping indifferently for the Man with the Checkbook as if they were on the election-day tab. It's hard to imagine that so much money so recklessly spent could have its disadvantages. But one of them is that almost everyone around you expects to be paid, and few dare to tell you what they really think. Money trumps authenticity."

—From "Just How Strange and Pathetic Was Bloomberg's Victory," November 4, 2009

ECAUSE BLOOMBERG is not only the mayor but also the richest man in New York, he agreed to several conditions when he took office in 2002. In order to make sure that his decisions about the welfare of all New Yorkers would not be complicated by his personal business welfare, he was required by the city ethics board to sell his publicly traded stocks and his interest in a hedge fund. Much was made in the media of how well the billionaire, and the city he ran for a salary of a dollar a year, had been sealed off from his (potentially corrupting) billions.

After nearly two full terms, however, the walls between the mayor's money and his public office that once looked so strict have appeared more and more porous. In some cases, like with Time Warner, that may not have been Bloomberg's doing. And in others, it may not have even been what was on his mind.

But as he nears a third term, there's little doubt that Bloomberg's business interests have become increasingly intertwined with his government, a conflicted marriage unprecedented in the life of the city and unchecked by an independent overseer.

Everything Mike Bloomberg does—his three campaigns, his hundreds of millions a year in charity, even his public career—springs from his global company, Bloomberg LP, which has been called the Google of financial data. It does $6.2 billion of business a year and usually earns a 30 percent profit. He owns a hoggish 85 to 92 percent of it (depending on whom you believe).

Bloomberg planned his first mayoral campaign from his corporate offices. He began thinking about running as early as 1997, and eventually assigned the management of this uncertain enterprise to three of his aides at Bloomberg LP who would all eventually become deputy mayors: Patti Harris, Kevin Sheekey, and, to a lesser degree, Ed Skyler. This synergy was infectious: the company created a news division to cover the city at the same time that its owner started actively planning his first race.

Bloomberg's three executive assistants—Allison Jaffin, Irene Pistorino, and Karen Greene—came with him to city government from the company and the campaign. All of them now receive both a full-time public and part-time private salary in an unusual arrangement approved by city ethics officials, working for him on personal and corporate matters for up to 30 hours a week.

He converted the public hearing room at City Hall into a bullpen of wide-open offices that mirrored his corporate setting, installing a Bloomberg terminal on his own desk, with access to corporate email, and provided city agencies and his campaign with free access to the company's $1,590-a-month database.

Dan Doctoroff's move from deputy mayor to Bloomberg LP president last year reminded everyone of the seamless bond, if they even needed reminding: "I'm thrilled to remain part of the Bloomberg family," Doctoroff declared.

Bloomberg interviewed Doctoroff for his new job, presumably by moving their chairs together in the bullpen, where they sat only eight feet apart for six years. Ethics officials even allowed Doctoroff to temporarily take some of his key city business with him to his new bullpen at the company's elaborate Lexington Avenue headquarters. With Doctoroff's lateral move, all of the mayor's four most powerful city deputies have also worn Bloomberg LP hats, with the probability of more to come in a third term.

Joyce Purnick, the former *Times* reporter who has just written the first Bloomberg biography, concluded that "his identification with his company is so strong" that discussing it "animates him like no other" subject, adding that he cites "current facts and figures," though he theoretically left it eight years ago. In 2007, the *Times* reported that Bloomberg "talked regularly to senior executives at the firm," adding that the scope of the contacts was "at odds with the way the company and Mr. Bloomberg have frequently portrayed his role."

But over the past few years, that close role has repeatedly been illustrated:

- Insisting that he "did not get involved in the day-to-day stuff like personnel," Bloomberg wound up conceding that he'd actually recruited Bloomberg LP's communications director in a 2004 phone call. He talked to executives about the terminal sales, new markets, financial performance, and a gender discrimination suit charging that the company harassed, demoted, or fired more than 80 pregnant women who took leave.

- In 2005, when Bloomberg ran for reelection, Susan Calzone, a six-figure executive at the company with young twins, who had gone to a lawyer about filing a similar suit, ran Women for Bloomberg out of the campaign office for many months, but wasn't paid, at least not by the campaign (her first and only check appeared on the campaign filing after I wrote about her, and after Bloomberg won). Calzone was the first person Bloomberg hired in 2006 when he started his new Bloomberg Family Foundation. Spresa Sukalic, a City Hall staffer who accompanied the mayor to city events until she left to join Bloomberg LP, has been taking unsolicited grant applications for the foundation at the company headquarters, at least while the foundation's own offices are being built a block from the mayor's East 79th Street town house.

- Early this year, Judi DeMarco, a close confidante of Republican state senator Joe Bruno and other GOP senators, was hired by Bloomberg LP just as the mayor was assiduously seeking the GOP ballot line for the 2009 election. (A long-time aide in the state senate, DeMarco was hired by Andrew Cuomo on Bruno's recommendation when Cuomo became attorney general in 2007, and was given the job of lobbying Bruno. After Bruno resigned and was indicted, Cuomo laid DeMarco off.) Though she has a skimpy legal résumé in a recessionary market flooded with lawyers, she almost immediately got a job in Bloomberg's legal department. Just as immediately, she went on jury duty in the Astor case, where she has been for five months. (Stu Loeser, the mayor's press secretary, says Bloomberg had nothing to do with DeMarco's hiring at the company.)

- The Bloomberg campaign hired the son of the current state senate GOP leader, Dean Skelos, at about the same time that Bloomberg LP hired DeMarco, as well as Bruno's former top aide, Mike Avella. Jonathan Capehart, who moved from the 2001 campaign into a lucrative job at the company, later explained the lavish campaign expenditures subsidized by Bloomberg: "Basically, the culture of Bloomberg LP was transferred to the campaign."

- The global director of Bloomberg TV, Katherine Oliver, nicknamed "K.O." by Bloomberg, was appointed to head the city's Office of Film, Theatre and Broadcasting, and now oversees NYCTV.

- The construction company that built Bloomberg LP's headquarters, Bovis Lend Lease, became the government's favored builder, securing one hotly pursued job after another until its negligence contributed to firefighter deaths at the Deutsche Bank demolition and it became the target of an ongoing probe investigating its possible overbilling of the city.

- Bloomberg's designer, Jamie Drake, who decorated his homes in Manhattan, Bermuda, and London, also redid Gracie Mansion and the city's new marriage bureau.

- Structure Tone, a contractor that pled guilty to paying bribes, yet was hired by Bloomberg LP to build the office interiors at the headquarters, is now renovating the two buildings at 78th and Madison where the Family Foundation offices are under construction (with mayorally selected Italian marble bathrooms). Structure Tone recently bid on a job to renovate eight floors at the LP headquarters. The company has not sought any city work since its felony conviction. The delayed project is now set for completion, says a worker there, in November, just as Bloomberg plans to win a third term.

- Last year, Bloomberg LP's radio channel, WBBR, started supplying the news on WQXR, the classical music station owned by the *New York Times*, in what a *Times* spokeswoman described as a "barter" arrangement that allowed the *Times* to shut down its own news operation in a cost-cutting move. Bloomberg LP also cut a deal in 2004 to distribute the lifestyle features of WQXR, which the *Times* recently announced it is selling. In 2005, the mayor declared that four city agencies would use the *Times* station as a launching pad to announce cultural and other events in shows featuring city commissioners.

The city's rules sanitizing the management of the mayor's plentiful assets, variously estimated at between $16 billion and $20 billion, were approved by the only watchdog explicitly charged under the city charter with inspecting the crossed hairs in this thicket, the Conflict of Interests Board (COIB). Bloomberg appoints all five of its members. The agency described its own weaknesses in a March 2009 report, noting that New York "appears to be the only large municipality in the United States that has granted its ethics board the power to sanction violations, but not the power to investigate such violations." The same internal document points out that the COIB "regulates the very people who set its budget," meaning that "the Board invariably has before it matters involving high-level officials at the same time those officials are passing on the Board's budget, an unseemly situation."

If the board was viewed as toothless before Bloomberg's terms, its advisory opinions, when confronted with the myriad of cases involving this mayor, have raised questions about the health of its gums as well. When Bloomberg took office in 2002, the COIB, consisting of two holdover Rudy Giuliani appointees and a new chair installed by Bloomberg (a fourth member had to recuse himself because he was a lawyer for Bloomberg LP and the fifth seat was vacant), issued a comprehensive 16-page decision about the mayor's potential conflicts. It forced him to release a list of LP's 100 biggest clients, but the list was alphabetical instead of in ranked order, and the board concluded that the mere release of the names made "the risk" that he could use his position to benefit the customers "minimal."

The opinion—negotiated for months with city and Bloomberg LP lawyers—then picked a number out of a hat, saying that a customer would have "to constitute 10 percent or more of Bloomberg LP total sales" to trigger any conflict concerns and force the mayor "to seek further advice" from the COIB. Since this requirement remains in place today when revenues exceed $6 billion, a customer could do more than half a billion dollars' worth of business with Bloomberg LP and still walk into the mayor's office to get a land use or contract approval without tripping an alarm. Discussions with COIB staff turned up no rationales for the 10 percent threshold, and the opinion allows Bloomberg to police this vast and potentially troublesome terrain himself.

In 2002, Bloomberg told the COIB that the largest customer on the list accounted for less than 4 percent of total revenue, but no one knows how much that might have changed since then. (When the board got a fresher list of the top 100, still unranked, in December 2007, it says it mistakenly forgot to post it.) Bloomberg LP customers like Goldman Sachs, Bear Stearns, AIG, Citigroup, Credit Suisse, Deutsche Bank, HSBC Bank, J.P. Morgan Chase, Lehman Brothers, Bank of New York, Tullett & Tokyo, Morgan Stanley, GFI, State Street Bank, and Merrill Lynch have all hired lobbyists to lobby the Bloomberg administration, with several specifying the mayor's office. Of the 124 companies on one or both of the Bloomberg LP lists, 33 appear on the Campaign Finance Board's list of companies doing business with the city.

Citigroup, which was the only other office tenant in the Bloomberg LP headquarters building and is now subleasing its vacated space to Bloomberg LP, even lobbied City Hall—and Doctoroff, in particular—on behalf of the Alternative Investments Group, the very unit located in the Lexington Avenue tower. Goldman Sachs had so many issues before the administration that it took seven pages to list its lobbying activities in the city clerk system (it spent almost a million dollars). When the city and state approved $1.6 billion in low-cost, tax-exempt bonds for Goldman's new downtown headquarters in 2005, Doctoroff justified it by saying that Wall Street's top firm might otherwise leave the city. Last year, the *Daily News* editorialized that Bloomberg was "taken to the cleaners" in the Goldman deal. The city and state "are in line to forfeit a whopping $321 million to Goldman because the governor and mayor agreed to contract terms that were downright foolhardy." Because of the meager demands of the COIB opinion, no one knows how big a Bloomberg customer Goldman was when it won this largesse.

The botched and deadly demolition at the Deutsche Bank site had been rushed by Doctoroff to clear the way for a new head-quarters for another Bloomberg LP client: J.P. Morgan Chase. While the Goldman and Morgan projects are unquestionably projects any city administration would support, their worthiness is irrelevant to the conflict questions, which revolve around the appearance of impropriety at the highest levels of administration, the core question that the COIB routinely deals with aggressively when it fines lower-level city officials.

Although the COIB's 2002 opinion required Bloomberg to sell his publicly traded stocks and his interest in a hedge fund and, "for the remainder of his service as mayor," invest "only in large, professionally managed mutual funds," on the day after Christmas in 2007, the COIB gave the mayor a holiday present, a second opinion that widened the list of "investment vehicles" he could use. The mayor, whose reelection rationale is his sup-posed grasp of the economic forces battering the city, requested in 2007 that he be permitted to start dabbling in hedge funds, private equity funds, and derivatives (both currency and interest-rate derivatives). Hampered by the restraints of the first opinion, Bloomberg wanted to embark into riskier markets just as they were about to implode.

Though some news reports say that Bloomberg has been forced to put his assets in a blind trust, and though city charter language suggests that such a trust might be appropriate in Bloomberg's cir-cumstances, the 2007 decision explicitly exempts the mayor from any such requirement. Instead, at the request of his corporate and city attorneys, it permits Bloomberg to select an investment adviser (enter Steve Rattner, who also advises *Times* publisher Arthur Sulzberger Jr.) and empowers the mayor to "direct" those advisers "as to the allocation of funds among different categories of investments." He can also get reports from Rattner about how investments are performing by category. This opens the door wide enough that the mayor could conceivably have enough information to figure out if he has an interest in a company that comes before him in his official capacity.

Both COIB opinions barred the mayor "from all matters involving Merrill Lynch," his 20 percent partner in Bloomberg LP and a customer on the top 100. Noting that Bloomberg "is clearly 'associated' with Merrill within the meaning of the charter," the first opinion "prohibits his using his city position to benefit Merrill." The *Times* reported two years ago that Bloomberg called Merrill's CEO, Stanley O'Neal, "one or two times" to offer his help in keeping the company downtown when it was thinking of moving to Midtown, and then turned negotiations over to Doctoroff. Though the COIB has been aware for many months of Bloomberg's possible violation of this Merrill provision in connection with another development question—the investment bank's investment in the acquisition of Stuyvesant Town/Peter Cooper Village—it has not referred the matter to the Department of Investigation for review or taken any other action.

Bloomberg's handling of Stuy Town is significant not only because of what it suggests about his indifference to the letter of the law, but because of how he allowed a nest of his own intertwined relationships and hidden philosophical biases to damage a jewel of the city.

In the fall of 2006, amid a speculative frenzy that has since consumed world markets, the biggest real estate deal in history occurred on the East Side of Manhattan.

MetLife sold the 80-acre, 100-building, middle-income oasis called Stuy Town to a developer friend of the mayor's, Jerry Speyer, for $5.4 billion, a price tag at least three times the rent roll paid by the 25,000 people who lived in the 11,200-unit complex, the borough's largest. Anyone who could count knew the numbers would only work if Speyer could rapidly empty many of the 8,000 rent-regulated apartments and greatly increase prices, a result so predictable that tenants began filing lawsuits against Speyer as soon as he took over. Four appellate judges ruled unanimously this March in the tenants' favor in one key case, *Roberts v. Tishman Speyer*, which will be heard by the Court of Appeals in mid-September.

The mayor, mesmerized as ever by private deals involving 10 digits, called Speyer "a great landlord" and said, less than prophetically, "I think the tenants will be well-protected." Dan Garodnick, the understated city councilman who lives in and represents Stuy Town, said last week that Speyer has "moved against people in 1,500 apartments and been forced to drop half the cases."

At the time of the sale, Garodnick got every major Democrat in the city and state at the time—including Chuck Schumer, Hillary Clinton, Christine Quinn, and Bill Thompson—to raise alarms about the sale's inevitable detrimental impact on the city's affordable housing stock and even to join him in championing a $4.5 billion bid put together by tenant and union leaders.

Bloomberg appealed to fans of the free market. "MetLife owns it, and they have a right to sell it," he declared before the sale occurred. "When you have a lot of people wanting to live there, prices go up" was another Bloomberg presale explanation. "You always feel sorry for those who can't afford it," he mused on his radio show. "But those who can afford it say, 'Well, what about me?'" The *Daily News* called Bloomberg's comments an "endorsement" of the sale, and the *Times* later noted that "the Bloomberg administration supported Tishman Speyer's record-breaking purchase."

But Bloomberg wasn't just in favor of the sale. In fact, he and Doctoroff undercut efforts by others in the administration to come up with a proposal to save Stuy Town's affordable apartments. Emily Youssouf, the president of the city's Housing Development Corporation (HDC), said in August 2006, when MetLife formally put the project out to bid, that her organization could "use its reserves to make a loan to a buyer that would enable them, in turn, to offer the apartments to current residents at prices they could afford." Youssouf told the *Times* that MetLife "built the properties with the help of the city" and could "get the same price" from a city-assisted deal.

What she did not disclose was that her agency had already developed a plan involving a mix of affordable co-op conversions and market-rate apartments. Youssouf says now that she "spent a lot of time discussing it with Doctoroff," and is unsure if she ever discussed it with the mayor. She says he asked many "penetrating questions," and that "the price wasn't as high as the sellers wanted." To her knowledge, the proposal was never presented to MetLife.

When the tenants later put together their bid, HDC worked behind the scenes to try to help them shape it. While this "rogue" action, as one participant called it, went on, Housing Commissioner Shaun Donovan met with advocates of the tenants' plan and tried to figure out a way to make it work. Senator Schumer called the mayor and MetLife to push consideration of the tenant bid, according to his press spokesman. Quinn, as loyal an ally as Bloomberg has in city politics, told the *Voice* she believed that the tenant bid had "real potential and could be done," acknowledging that she raised it with the mayor "briefly" at the end of a private meeting. Thompson, who is now running against Bloomberg, but was then on excellent terms with him, proclaimed that he was willing to invest pension funds in support of the tenant bid, and contacted Doctoroff. The mayor's spokesman, Loeser, regurgitated the same numbers cited by Doctoroff at the time about how much more cost effective it was to use city subsidies to build new apartments than to safeguard Stuy Town's, a hotly disputed numbers game that does not address why the city offered no help at all and cheered MetLife and Speyer on as paragons of the market.

But Bloomberg had reportedly assured MetLife in a conversation that preceded the announcement of the bid process that he would not interfere with what he regarded as a "private transaction"—a meeting that Loeser acknowledges occurred, but he says "we don't recall" if Stuy Town came up, adding that, if it did, it would only have been "in passing." (He did not deny that Bloomberg made this premature assurance.) The advocates who were then pressing the mayor to act cited many instances when his administration saw a public purpose in helping to shape a deal between private parties. MetLife, alarmed by this public drumbeat, went back to City Hall to check the mayor's temperature, and Doctoroff calmed their jitters.

When Speyer beat the second-highest bidder—another real estate giant named the Apollo Group (the tenants came in third)—by less than $100 million, the *Times* reported that Apollo was "so incensed about losing the bid" that they went ahead with a planned victory party, convinced that Speyer had been given a "last look" at their bid so they could marginally exceed it. Doctoroff simultaneously agreed to only fine MetLife $5 million, rather than the $24 million penalty he could have imposed, for reneging on an unrelated tax-abatement deal with the city involving their headquarters building (Loeser says that this dispute was the focus of the earlier meeting between Bloomberg and the company).

Speyer has certainly always been a Bloomberg favorite. Rob Speyer, who spearheaded the Stuy Town negotiations for the family company, was appointed chair of the Mayor's Fund to Advance New York City by Bloomberg. Jerry Speyer, the patriarch at the firm that also owns Rockefeller Center, was the prime mover at the New York City Partnership, the elite business group that adopted Bloomberg as its pet mayor from the outset and would, in 2008, become the sledgehammer for a term-limits extension and another four years for Mike.

The only debate among Bloomberg insiders is whether his hands-off approach was more a favor for Speyer than it was an ideological market preference. With the Speyers dominating the headlines, no one paid attention to the fact that they had a partner in the purchase, or who their banks were. Merrill Lynch was involved at both ends. *New York* magazine later reported that Merrill was the second-biggest financier of the deal, putting up half a billion dollars. In the months leading up to the deal, Merrill also bought a 49.8 percent interest in Speyer's partner at Stuy Town, BlackRock, which matched Speyer and put up $125 million of equity in the deal.

The Merrill/BlackRock merger had been announced with great fanfare back in February 2006, but did not close until shortly before they and Speyer won the MetLife sweepstakes. So, at the very time that Mike Bloomberg was "endorsing" Speyer and stifling options like HDC's and the tenants', the mayor's only corporate partner since the inception of Bloomberg LP, Merrill Lynch, was becoming the top institutional investor in the company that, together with Speyer, would win the bid.

When Merrill began sinking into the mire that forced its collapse two years later, its interests in BlackRock and Bloomberg LP began appearing side-by-side in news story after news story. In a July 2008 search for new capital, Merrill was simultaneously shopping its stakes in both companies. Bloomberg LP wound up buying Merrill's 20 percent on Bloomberg's terms, with Merrill financing all but $110 million of the $4.4 billion purchase price with up to 15-year notes. Since Merrill was getting less than 3 percent of the value of its stake in cash, the business "association" between Bloomberg and Merrill referred to in the COIB decision, as well as the bar on Merrill dealings, continues (Merrill is, of course, now owned by Bank of America).

Conflicts of interest are not about motives. The charter prohibits a public servant from using "his city position for the private advantage of the public servant or of anyone associated with the public servant." It doesn't say that the city official taking the action does so with the intention of benefiting himself or his associate. If the result of the official action is to benefit his business associate—in this case, Merrill—a violation occurs. Presented with a series of written *Voice* questions about the mayor's knowledge of Merrill's role in Stuy Town and why he didn't see it as a reason for recusal, Loeser took a week and then declined to answer any of them, refusing as well to make available either of the city attorneys who have worked with LP's lawyer on these ethics questions.

As the *Voice* ran the question of Bloomberg's conflict past the public officials involved in the Stuy Town maneuvers—none of whom ever heard that he recused himself—most were unsure it was the driving force behind the posture he took. Some thought his ties with Speyer were more significant. Some attributed it to his presumed abhorrence of rent regulation, an issue he does everything to avoid discussing. While they conceded it might be some combination of these three, all of them agreed that the mayor's championing of the Speyer/BlackRock/Merrill combine did not end in 2006, when the deal closed.

In fact, when the Stuy Town tenants brought the *Roberts v. Tishman Speyer* case in January 2007, and when they won that unanimous Appellate Division decision this March, Bloomberg once again took a "neutral" nosedive, refusing to join other city officials on the side of the tenants. Since a city tax subsidy, J-51, is at the heart of the suit, the city's silence is deafening. The complaint alleges that Speyer et al. want to have their cake and eat it, too, seeking to retain millions in tax breaks linked by law to rent regulation, while, at the same time, deregulating thousands of apartments.

Manhattan borough president Scott Stringer, hardly a Bloomberg critic, filed amicus briefs in support of the 3,000 tenants covered by the *Roberts* complaint twice already and is planning a third. Quinn joined an overwhelming majority of the council in filing papers in support of the tenants last month, contending that Speyer and company "would unwork decades of commitment" by the council and, by extension, the government that implements the laws it passes, "to require that J-51 units be rent-stabilized."

Instead of joining them, Michael Cardozo, the mayor's corporation counsel, issued a statement in March indicating that the city "takes no position on the merits" of the case. Stringer says that the mayor should "absolutely" have joined him in siding with the tenants in court, adding that "anytime someone of that stature" takes a position on an issue like this, "it matters." Quinn says, "We wish that the city had been able to get involved"— both before the sale and in the court case. Garodnick, a Democrat who, like Quinn, is neutral in the mayoral race, says Bloomberg "was wrong in his assessment" of the tenant bid and the sale, and wrong about the ongoing litigation.

It is nothing short of astonishing that, in an election year, Bloomberg can not only sidestep this case, but also refuse to issue a single memo of support for any of the 10 rent-reform bills passed by the state assembly and still awaiting a senate vote this session. Even Giuliani, when he was running for reelection, pushed the legislature to back rent regulation, and tried to block vacancy decontrol (which allows landlords to exempt certain vacant apartments from rent laws), making Bloomberg the first mayor in modern times to abandon protections that affect a million New York homes.

His refusal to do so is a meshing—conscious or not—of his business and class interests.

PART V
Slouching Towards Bethlehem

And what rough beast, its hour come round at last,
Slouches towards Bethlehem to be born?
—W. B. Yeats,
"The Second Coming"

In the last year of Wayne Barrett's life, the man he'd done some of his earliest reporting on ran for president. Barrett had taken Trump seriously—not, like much of New York media, as a risible tabloid character, but as a symptom of a society with skewed priorities. He'd amassed a vast trove of information on the real estate con man, bulging files and stacks of lawsuits and a web of connections in his head and in yellow notepads. He began reporting on Donald when both men were in their 30s. Now he was 71. As Barrett grew sicker with the lung disease that killed him, reporters made pilgrimages to his house in Brooklyn to interview the dogged, dying reporter and to tap into his knowledge. As the Trump candidacy gathered pace, it seemed that facts no longer mattered, that lies had superior political power. Still, Barrett marshaled the facts he'd spent a lifetime accumulating. He was working a story when he went to the hospital and working the phones even there. —Ed.

Defiant Trespass

Andrea Bernstein

THE TIMING OF WAYNE'S passing was a short, sharp intake of breath, a surprise of history. That he would leave this world just hours before the inauguration of Donald Trump made me feel as if my own body were deprived of oxygen, my heart compressed.

Wayne's death wasn't a surprise. A few weeks earlier, I'd got to visit him in his book-filled living room in Windsor Terrace, Brooklyn. While depending on an oxygen tank to breathe, he was still working sources. He was still talking about crimes that Donald Trump might have committed, and the evidence he almost—almost—had, if he just could unlock the lips of one more ex-government official.

I'd met Wayne back in the 1990s, while a relatively low-level city official myself, subject to his questions, which were like no other journalist's questions. I can still remember devouring every word of *City for Sale*, the book Wayne and Jack Newfield wrote on the travails of the Koch era, and thinking: I want to do what Wayne does.

A few years later, I was doing that, with Wayne's encouragement. Though we worked for competing publications, Wayne always took my calls, always told me what hidden file to find to unlock the secret to the story I was working on. He answered his phone—landline, no answering machine—always with a sudden, "Yeah. Barrett."

In 1996, Wayne and I were arrested together at the Waldorf Astoria Hotel, trying to record who was at a $100,000-a-plate fundraiser, because we wanted to know who was trying to influence elected officials and we didn't want to wait until the campaign-finance reports came out, long after the legislative session was over. I didn't recognize many of the people, but I recognized one: Donald Trump.

Writing in the *New York Times* about the incident, Metro Matters columnist Joyce Purnick said: "There is no evidence that Mr. Barrett or Ms. Bernstein, though among the less placid of press practitioners, misbehaved." While we were waiting for a police officer to write up our pink Desk Appearance tickets, Wayne told me about the previous time he'd been arrested.

That was in Atlantic City, when Wayne was informed that he was "barred for life" from Trump events, arrested by off-duty cops working as Trump security guards at an event at the Trump Taj Mahal. Wayne was handcuffed for the night to a blood-stained cell. He liked to boast about his Atlantic City brush with the law: "I am a convicted, defiant trespasser." (Our Waldorf Astoria charges were dropped on a technicality.)

In June of 2019, while researching my book, *American Oligarchs: The Kushners, the Trumps, and the Marriage of Money and Power*, I spent a week with the Wayne Barrett papers at the Briscoe Center for American History at the University of Texas, Austin, digging through 40 years of papers about the history of New York City corruption, as collected by Wayne. One set of notes I found stopped me short.

Before he died, Wayne was on the trail of a story I would later report—in October 2017—as part of a collaboration between

WNYC, ProPublica, and the *New Yorker*. The story, "How Donald Jr. and Ivanka Trump Avoided a Criminal Indictment," documented how the president's adult children escaped possible felony fraud charges after a personal appeal to the Manhattan DA by a Trump attorney—who was one of the DA's largest donors.

I'd finished a story of Wayne's, without knowing it.

I've been documenting Trump's corruption and our nation's tilt toward oligarchy since the beginning of the Trump presidency. Almost every day, I curse the fact that I can't ask Wayne for advice or historical perspective, or just call him and exclaim at the sheer absurdity of some New York character's emergence at the center of the latest scandal.

I'm mad about that, and I miss him. I wish he were here. And I know, somehow, he still is.

Andrea Bernstein is the author of *American Oligarchs: The Kushners, the Trumps, and the Marriage of Money and Power* and cohost of the *Trump, Inc.* podcast from WNYC and ProPublica, which unravels the business conflicts that pervade every aspect of the Trump administration.

18

Donald Trump's Billionaire-Backed Super PAC Also Paying Rudy Giuliani's Law Firms

Daily Beast

November 5, 2016

In January 2011 Barrett was laid off from the *Village Voice*. He was too expensive, the paper's owners said. For the next several years he wrote for the *Daily Beast* and the New York *Daily News*, bringing the methods he honed in New York City to national politics. This piece, on his most familiar quarries and theme—the corrosive power of money in politics—appeared just days before the election. —Ed.

MAKE AMERICA NUMBER 1, the pro-Trump super PAC controlled by hedge-fund billionaire Robert Mercer and his daughter Rebekah, has paid law firms associated with Rudy Giuliani $563,003 in 2015 and 2016.

The PAC, originally called Keep the Promise 1, supported Ted Cruz before shifting to Donald Trump after he secured the Republican nomination this spring. It began paying Bracewell and

Giuliani for legal and compliance services in June of 2015, making $336,495 in payments until February 14, 2016. It stopped using Bracewell a couple of weeks after Giuliani left the firm in January.

Ted Cruz dropped out of the Republican presidential field on May 3. Sometime that month, Rebekah Mercer and Kellyanne Conway, who led the PAC when it was backing the Texas senator and is now Trump's campaign manager, had lunch with Ivanka Trump and Jared Kushner. There, the *Washington Post* reported,* "Ivanka and Rebekah bonded over parenting young children and being the daughters of hard-charging, successful fathers, according to people familiar with their conversation."

Also in May, on the 12th, the PAC retained Giuliani's new firm, Greenberg and Traurig, initially paying $99,470 for legal and compliance services. In June, the PAC changed its name and aligned itself squarely with Trump. On its website, the group described itself as "supporting conservative principles, upholding the rule of law, and opposing ethically challenged candidates.... It's [*sic*] first special project entitled, 'Defeat Crooked Hillary', will shed light on what the Clinton's [*sic*] want to keep in the dark."

On July 22, the PAC paid Greenberg $9,698 for "legal consulting services." That payment came the day after the Republican National Convention, which Giuliani spoke at and attended with his wife. If the payment had anything to do with covering the expenses of a convention speaker, that might well violate the federal guidelines—including operating independently of a

---

* Matea Gold, "The Rise of GOP Mega-Donor Rebekah Mercer," *Washington Post*, September 14, 2016, www.washingtonpost.com/politics/the-rise-of-gop-mega-donor-rebekah-mercer/2016/09/13/85ae3c32-79bf-11e6-beac-57a4a412e93a_story.html.

campaign—that Giuliani's firm was supposed to oversee as part of its compliance services.

Three payments in September and October tallied $118,340, also for "legal consulting services."

A call to Giuliani's aide at the Greenberg firm was not immediately returned. Hogan Gidley, the communications director for the PAC, said he could not answer the *Beast*'s questions but that he would try to get someone else at the PAC to respond.

After I reported in the New York *Daily News* in September that Greenberg and Traurig represents both Trump and Kushner Companies, the real estate firm headed by Trump's son-in-law, Jared, Giuliani took a leave of absence, saying he would return after the election. Kushner is one of Greenberg and Taurig's top development clients; Trump has used the firm himself for small Florida matters. Shortly after Giuliani joined Greenberg in January, Trump announced that the former mayor, who's become one of his most prominent surrogates, was acting as an informal adviser to the campaign.

Conway joined the Trump campaign on July 1 and was later promoted to campaign manager. She was briefly replaced at the PAC by David Bossie, the longtime head of Citizens United who has made a career of his war against the Clintons. Steve Bannon, who became chair and CEO of the Trump campaign on August 17, had previously been the executive chairman of Breitbart News, which counts the Mercers as major investors. After just weeks at the outside group, Bossie rejoined Conway as Trump's deputy campaign manager, and Rebekah Mercer herself then took charge of day-to-day control of the PAC.

While his firm has been on the PAC payroll, Giuliani has been fanning the flames of every Clinton controversy. But he has made it clear that he thinks the Clinton Foundation issues are the worst, saying on Fox this week: "This was the one I always thought was clearer." Invoking his history as a federal prosecutor, Giuliani said he could make a case against the Clintons on the foundation "in two months." The foundation has long been a fixation of the Mercers as well. They fund the Bannon-led nonprofit Government Accountability Institute, whose president, Peter Schweizer, is author of *Clinton Cash*, an innuendo-strewn book about the foundation that apparently became fodder for a probe initiated by FBI agents from the New York office earlier this year. Rebekah Mercer serves on the institute's board and coproduced, with Bossie, a documentary based on the book that was released just before the Democratic National Convention.

Giuliani confirmed in a Fox interview Friday what the *Beast* reported Thursday—namely, that he has been talking to agents about the Clinton cases. He didn't say if he'd told those agents that his firm represents a Trump super PAC run by one of Trump's biggest donors, the Mercers, who've given at least $15.5 million. Or that his firm's clients include Trump and the Kushners. Giuliani described his conversations with "outraged agents" as if they were one-sided exchanges, with agents complaining about FBI and Justice Department brass blocking legitimate probes for political reasons, and him just taking it in. "I did nothing to get it out," he said today, referring to the Comey letter renewing the email probe and subsequent leaks that have rocked the presidential campaign. Later that day, though, he said that he had spoken only to retired agents.

If Giuliani's firm had been charged with compliance oversight for the PAC, the results have been questionable, and not just because of the timely disbursement to his firm in July. The PAC has a substantial relationship with two companies that have been connected to Bannon and had shared the same Beverly Hills address as Breitbart, paying millions for video and data services from the production house Glittering Steel (which has worked with the Mercers' PAC in both its Cruz and Trump incarnations) and the political data firm Cambridge Analytica.

There may have been nothing questionable about that before August, but the two entities have been paid more than $4 million by Make America Number 1 since the Breitbart head—who said Friday that he intends to return there after the election—took over the Trump campaign. A film-industry source this week described Glittering Steel to the *Daily Beast* as little more than "a front for Bannon."

If the Federal Election Commission—presently deadlocked between its two Republican and two Democratic commissioners— actually looks at campaign violations, it might want to work out what interest, exactly, the CEO of Trump's campaign has in the two biggest vendors for a super PAC.

Avoiding legally prohibited coordination between campaigns and PACs, after all, is just the sort of conflict that they pay lawyers to ensure they're in compliance with.

Anna Lenzer contributed research to this report.

Never Give Up

Jennifer Gonnerman

I MET WAYNE BARRETT when I was assigned to work as one of his interns in January of 1994. I was in my last semester of college, hoping to become a reporter, and by the time the internship ended four months later, I realized I'd just gone to journalism school for free. He had three or four or five interns at a time assigned to work with him in his office: a cramped room on the third floor of the *Village Voice*, with three desks, three landline phones, and stacks of newspapers covering the floor. Wayne would usually work from home, and every morning about 10 a.m., the call would come in to the interns with a list of dozens of things we were supposed to get done before the day ended. A typical task involved trekking to a courthouse or a municipal building to try to get one document or another—which really meant trying to cajole some grumpy clerk into helping you, since you were still in college and had no idea what you were doing. And all the interns knew that if we didn't get all the tasks done by five p.m., Wayne would start screaming.

That's how I got started as a reporter, and though I did not end up covering politics like he did, the lessons I learned from him when I was twenty-two have fueled my entire career. There were lessons about how to sound authoritative on the phone when leaving a message with someone twice your age (leave your first and last names); how to follow the city's news (read every local news-paper every day); how to use New York's Freedom of Information Law to get documents from a government agency (send FOIL letters often—and follow up with frequent calls). Many years after I had finished my internship, I ended up interviewing Wayne. It was November 9, 2016—the morning after Donald Trump had won the presidential election—and, like every intern before and after me, I knew about Wayne's history with Trump.

That morning, reporters everywhere were trying to make sense of Trump's victory, and I found Wayne at home, in his bed at 10 a.m., propped up on pillows, a telephone beside him. Calls were coming in from journalists eager to hear his insights—the *Washington Post*, a radio station—and he was answering every call, despite being sick with lung disease and too weak to make it to the front door. Wayne's persistence and tenacity—his determina-tion to do whatever it took to get the story—had made him one of the greatest investigative reporters of his generation. And now, beside his bed, I saw two reporting pads. Though he was confined to his bed, he was still chasing stories: making calls, taking notes, reporting out every lead he got. He had just published two stories related to Trump, and, he said, he was working on two more. He was 71 and would live only two more months, and though I did not realize it at the time, that visit with him would leave me with perhaps the most important reporting lesson of all: never, ever give up.

Jennifer Gonnerman is a staff writer for the *New Yorker* magazine and the author of *Life on the Outside: The Prison Odyssey of Elaine Bartlett*. She was a Wayne Barrett intern in 1994.

PART VI
Armed with a Notebook

Records in the reporter's basement. It was all written down, organized on yellow legal pads and in manila folders. Wayne Barrett worked for four decades as a detective for the people of New York City. (Photo credit Marcus Barum)

19

Time for Something New

January 4, 2011

Eᴅ ᴋᴏᴄʜ ᴀɴᴅ I were inaugurated on the same day in 1978. He became mayor and I became his weekly tormentor.

I had written a few pieces for the *Voice* before I took over the Runnin' Scared column that January, going back as far as 1973.

But I was now inheriting a column that Mary Nichols, the *Voice*'s editor-in-chief, had made famous, and that had been written by greats like Jack Newfield, Ken Auletta, and Joe Conason. A country kid out of Lynchburg, Virginia, where I'd founded the Teenage Republicans, I was suddenly occupying the first two pages of New York's countercultural crier.

Since then, I have written, by my own inexact calculation, more column inches than anyone in the history of the *Voice*. These will be my last.

I am 65 and a half now, and it is time for something new.

If I didn't see that, others did.

The paper has always been more than an employer to me. I turned down other jobs that paid better three times to stay here. Though my mentor Newfield used to say we got our owners "from office temporaries," and though I worked for 14 different editors, the *Voice* was always a place where I could express *my* voice. And that meant more to me than larger circulations or greater influence or bigger paychecks.

It is called a writer's paper because we decide what we will write. That is not a license to spout and I never took it as such. Across all these years, I almost never wrote in the first person and, even when I did, the piece was still packed with reportage. In my extended family, I have become the go-to guy for eulogies and I report every one of them, learning more about my mother, for example, by interviewing her sisters than she ever told me when she was alive.

When I was asked in recent years to blog frequently, I wouldn't do it unless I had something new to tell a reader, not just a clever regurgitation of someone else's reporting.

My credo has always been that the only reason readers come back to you again and again over decades is because of what you unearth for them, and that the joy of our profession is discovery, not dissertation.

There is also no other job where you get paid to tell the truth. Other professionals do sometimes tell the truth, but it's ancillary to what they do, not the purpose of their job. I was asked years ago to address the elementary school that my son attended and tell them what a reporter did, and I went to the auditorium in a trench coat with the collar up and a notebook in a my pocket, baring it to announce that "we are detectives for the people."

When the *Voice* celebrated its 50th anniversary in 2005, I said, "We thought a deadline meant we had to kill somebody by closing time," and that, as a liberal Democratic paper, we were "better at goring one of our own." It never mattered to me what the party or ideology was of the subject of an investigative piece; the reporting was as nonpartisan as the wrongdoing itself. I never looked past the wrist of any hand in the public till. It was the grabbing that bothered me, and there was no Democratic or Republican way to pick up the loot.

The greatest prize I've ever won for the work I've done in these pages was when Al D'Amato called me a "viper" in his memoir. Chuck Schumer, who ended D'Amato's reign after 18 years, ascribed his victory in a 2007 memoir to a story I'd written a decade earlier that devastated the incumbent Republican. What Schumer didn't say was that as soon as Hank Morris, Schumer's media guru, went up with an ad based on my revelations about D'Amato, Arthur Finkelstein, who was running D'Amato's 1998 campaign, aired a commercial about Schumer's near-indictment and flashed my nearly two-decade-old clips breaking that scandal on the screen as well. I was the maestro of a commercial duel.

Even as my scandal stories skewered David Dinkins in the 1989 and 1993 mayoral campaigns, I chronicled the devolution of his nemesis, Rudy Giuliani, from hero prosecutor to used-9/11-memorabilia salesman.

As awkwardly as I felt about it, Carl Paladino's toughest shots at Andrew Cuomo this fall were garbled renditions of two 6,000-word exposés I'd done here about Cuomo's HUD record. For a week in the 2009 mayoral campaign, I couldn't turn on the TV without seeing a Bloomberg commercial drawn from my exposé of Bill Thompson's conflict-ridden home mortgage. But I'd delivered one cover-story blow after another throughout the cycle about everything from the mayor's culpability in the Deutsche Bank fire debacle to his own governmental incest with Bloomberg LP.

It was always the conduct that prodded me to write, not the person. And that is what I lived for, a chance to say something that revealed and mattered. To me, the story will always be the thing. It is all I can see.

I believe I have much left to learn, still armed with my notebook, and thus much left to tell you. It may be books or blogs or something in between. I hope to bring my trademark interns with me because they have, for more than 30 years, helped me think young, especially when it comes to the climate and water crises. The city and state beat are precious to me, but what is happening to our nation is also a frightening pull on me, so I don't know what I will wind up writing in this new life.

I have loved my bond with you and have never traded an inch of truth for a moment, or even a season, of access. I tell the young people still drawn to this duty that it is the most honorable one in America, and that I have never met a corrupt journalist. I even met one, Tom Robbins, so brave that when he heard I was leaving, he quit himself and didn't even tell me he was. "I'm going out with the guy who brought me to the dance," Robbins told me after he resigned, crafting a lede with the very fiber of his life.

"If a newspaper writes the story of its city without compromise or calculation," I wrote in that 50th-anniversary piece, "it is as breathtaking as a ballet, each detail another artful step. Put us together as bound volumes in the memory of this grandest of cities and the *Voice* reads like a classic, ever passionate and principled."

I will pray it always does.

My Old Man

Mac Barrett

Wayne's son, Mac Barrett, delivered the following eulogy for his father on January 27, 2017, at Our Lady of
the Presentation Church in Brownsville, Brooklyn. —Ed.

MY FATHER IS LISTENING, making a note, adding another to the cosmos of scribbles cover-
ing his calendar; he is answering the phone so abruptly you are
unprepared to speak, bringing the full brunt of his attention to
the world around him, belting out the Boss, Rod Stewart, Neil
Young, his voice reaching full gravel; I am a child and he is swing-
ing me around the dining room to "Born in the U.S.A.," pump-
ing a fist on a wedding dance-floor opposite the love of his life,
complaining, tailgating a tailgater, making the road just, late for
my mother's fund-raiser, changing the city alongside her, each
protector and adviser to the other, two inexorably entwined un-
stoppable forces.

He is shouting my mother's name to celebrate her return from
work, or mine, calling from his bed to lament the latest Knicks loss,
disgusted by the disregard of the league for its own players, mourning the death of Tom Hayden and Nat Hentoff, sharing a pastrami
lunch with his hero Jack Newfield, salivating over an FBI dossier,

bent over the keys, staring down a sentence, an alliterative phrase, as if to take his eyes off the keyboard would be to let something, or someone, escape; enormous, guileless pointer fingers in full flight, stabbing down at the truth as if to try to pin it to the desk, visiting with an intern from 36 years ago, putting her in touch with another intern from 28 years ago, passing a tip to a fellow reporter, meeting a source called X in the middle of the night on the shoulder of a highway, knocking on the door of a person he does not know, staking that person out when she does not answer, rifling through records of campaign donations on the beach, tanning toward the truth, being attacked, arrested, befriended, avoided.

He's taking me boogie-boarding in a hurricane, chasing down the 500th rebound of the day, passing it back so we can leave on a make; he's setting up one young intrepid journalist with another, smiling with delirious joy at the first intern baby; he's a mailman in a high school play dying an unscripted death as he crosses the stage to make a delivery, watching Fox News so we don't have to, getting furious at what MSNBC has not said, calling it a race game, plain and simple; he's a kid reporting on an event for Black farmers in Lynchburg, Virginia, watching his editor tear the piece to shreds with all the pride of his ignorance; he's being woken up in the middle of the night alongside my mother by an FBI raid, driving members of the Black Liberation Army to safety, hiding them in the backseat under mounds of *The People's Voice*, the publication he started right here in this neighborhood; he's calling out the landlords who mistreat their tenants, welcoming interns, friends, and virtual strangers to stay in our house.

He's not paying for parking; he's picking up my mother and taking her home safely, her lifelong designated driver; he's a St. Joe's college student pretending to know how to fix a car to get a woman to like him, delighted with himself, mailing her an engagement ring hidden in a giant box of foam nuts; he's making us mad, he's making us laugh, he's making us uncomfortable, questioning our focus, our dedication, criticizing our inability to answer our cell phones, but also that we have cell phones in the first place, pulling into Brooklyn Bridge traffic at the very last minute, flicking off the driver who dares not let him in, insisting that I not come home early to prepare him dinner, running across the Beesley's Point Bridge, Chris Christie's power plant fuming in the background, sitting breathless in the living room, sweating on the brick floor, calling out to my mother for "kisses."

Just a few weeks ago, he's eulogizing my mother's beloved brother Johnny, making palpable once again Johnny's presence; he's dedicating a book to her father, who hated him; he's eulogizing my grandmother, helping us to say good-bye to all those to whom we are not ready to say good-bye, surrounded by politicians and press at the 2017 Second Avenue Subway opening New Year's Eve party, more or less jokingly blaming the governor for making him sick with a so-called Sicilian kiss, being fired, difficult, refusing edits; he is explaining, yet again, that the struggle is its own reward; up to the very end, he is reporting from his bed, but to say that is to suggest he could somehow have stopped: to report was to breathe, to take in the world, the information around him, and exhale an analysis, a money trail, an indictment, the exposure of another power-abusing public official.

My mother is holding his long fingers on one of his final days, whispering to herself, and him, and me: "So many words."

I am writing this in the office at our house on Windsor Place where so many of those words were written, which I inherited as my own when he became too ill to climb the stairs. Ironically, it is here, where he chased down facts, that I come to make things up, to write fiction.

But over the course of the week since his death, I have been in here compulsively reading everything written about him, including 30-some beautiful odes and a Reddit thread that speculates he was murdered by the president. You might say I've been doing a bit of freelance fact-checking, even calling in corrections. He did not die of lung cancer, I told several major media outlets. He was a runner, not a smoker. He died of an illness you all have not heard of: interstitial lung disease. Yes, I can spell it. I stare in awe at words like *legend* and *icon*, so much more complicated to corroborate. The facts are important, though, even despite how they resist connection, and even though no pattern can be made of them. He was healthy and then he was sick and now he is gone, and he is still here, too, and no amount of dogged investigation can satisfactorily explain it.

I am unable to make distinct this, the deepest, most profound personal loss of my life, from the realities of this national and global political moment; my grief is inseparable from whatever inarticulate force, or longing or rage, finally motivated me and my girlfriend, Sheila Joon, to get in the car, less than 24 hours after he had passed, to make the sojourn down to D.C., to join hundreds of thousands in forming a massive, undeniable voice of resistance and dissent.

We stood for a long while, wearying, waiting for the march to begin, hearing a rumor that it may not, but when we did finally begin to inch forward, I closed my eyes and I felt him among us, with me. I had come to shout my disapproval, to add my voice to that of my people, but I fell quiet instead, let them do the shouting, and a deep solemnity came over me. To march was to mourn, and to mourn to march.

Sometimes I found myself frozen by the intensity of his attention, unable to do what it is I have in me to do, but I am enabled and emboldened by the warm glow of his memory, by his ongoing presence, and by all of you. It's now up to us, those who knew and loved him, as well as those who simply followed the countless miles of his copy, to embody his tenacity, his moral ruthlessness, his dogged heart, his restlessness for justice. Thank you all for coming. It means a lot to me, it means a lot to my mother, and it means a lot to my old man, the defiant trespasser, the viper, the legend.

Acknowledgments

THIS BOOK WAS BORN of the hope that by making our friend and mentor's work available, readers, voters, aspiring journalists, and seasoned reporters would catch some of his fire, benefit from his clarity, and learn from his method. This collection is a project of the Wayne Barrett Investigative Fund, an initiative established after Barrett's death to foster a new generation of investigative reporters. It was supported by Type Media Center and championed by Fran Barrett and Vincent McGee, who is indefatigable and a tremendous advocate. In addition to her own lifetime of advocating and strategizing to make the lives of poor people in New York more livable, Fran Barrett managed Wayne, made it possible for him to be single-minded, interpreted the world for him, and maintained relationships that threatened to fray. Her support for this project and my role in it makes me think I may have accomplished something after all. Mac Barrett is ever gracious with all the people who make claims on his father. He was a cheerleader for this book. I'm grateful he lets us in.

The advisory board of the Wayne Barrett Investigative Fund, particularly Tom Robbins, provided wise counsel, influence, expertise, and energy to make the book a reality. The world is better because of Tom Robbins's equanimity and groundedness. The advisory board is Marcus Baram, Neil Barsky, Bill Bastone,

Mohamad Bazzi, Andrea Bernstein, Eddie Borges, Gerson Borrero, Dan Collins, Joe Conason, Jim Dwyer, Jennifer Gonnerman, Errol Louis, Sheryl McCarthy, and Jarrett Murphy, who each fostered the growth of this project and lent their considerable abilities. I am grateful to Esther Kaplan for managing the complex negotiations necessary to make an idea a reality, to Hachette for approving an unorthodox project, to Type Media Center's Taya Kitman for believing in it, to Bold Type Books' Katy O'Donnell for shepherding it and me, and to Carl Bromley for insightful and clear-headed editing to get it over the finish line. I thank Kelley Blewster, Melissa Veronesi, and the production staff of Hachette Book Group for their attention, patience, creativity, and skill.

Bob Baker, artist, chief archivist, and senior editor of the *Village Voice*, was essential, welcoming me into the bare offices of the newspaper, opening the card catalogue and bound volumes of the physical paper to my perusal, and generously making digital files available for use, all while engaged in the monumental task of managing the digitization of the entire run of the landmark publication. He did this because he loved Barrett, knew how he matters and how much better off we'd be if he were still reporting. Thank you to Village Voice Media. Susan Perry Ferguson generously granted permission to reprint her iconic Ramon Velez photo. Getty Images shared the Fred McDarrah cover image. Thank you to David O'Keefe for the use of his illustration. A debt of gratitude is owed the Briscoe Center for American History at the University of Texas at Austin, and in particular the staff of the special collections for maintaining and making available the rich archive of Barrett's papers—and for making me welcome during a week of digging. A City University of New York, Lehman College faculty research grant paid for my travel to Texas. My colleagues in the Lehman College Department of Journalism and Media Studies, especially Jennifer MacKenzie, offered an ear. Madysen Luebke did excellent research assistance, running down hard-to-find microfilm at top speed.

I am indebted to the far-flung family of *Voice* alumni, including the administrators of the *Village Voice* Alumni Facebook page and Cynthia Carr, Tricia Romano, Richard Goldstein, and to the proud fraternity of Barrett interns for sharing memories, ideas, and contacts. Tracie McMillan, Mohamad Bazzi, and Ruth Ford offered bolstering support when the rabbit hole loomed too large.

Each of the essayists in this collection dug through their memories of a friend, colleague, and mentor to help the reader understand Barrett, his work, and journalism. They were generous with their thoughts and gracious about edits.

Dan Morrison's deep New York knowledge and ability to evoke a city that is receding, his store of NYC politics and newspapering memories, his keen intelligence and his tremendous affability provided instrumental help tackling the mighty task list accompanying this project. Dan dove into a database of more than 300 articles I'd assembled for potential inclusion, contributing hours of bonhomie, companionship, wit, and expertise as we sifted and evaluated, checked word counts, developed an organization system and work flow, and weighed which few of Barrett's articles would be included here. I leaned on his depth and willingness to grapple with loss, anger, and absurdity. David Gonzalez has been a good friend to me in a year when I thought more than usual about death, memory, and what lingers.

Tom Shea and Jack Flynn introduced me to the *Village Voice* when I was a teenager and made being a reporter look fun and honorable. Ray Schroth, S.J., wrote the recommendation letter that got me a Barrett internship. When Jarrett Murphy and I interned for Barrett in 1997 and 1998, we had already been together for a few years, but Barrett liked to claim credit for our relationship. Maybe he just wanted to remind us how damned lucky we are. My greatest gratitude, love, and respect go to Murphy for being patient and kind as I worked on this, but really for being an excellent man always. From wide-eyed kids in the city to something like experts, there is no better companion with whom to uncover the story. We will go on comforting the afflicted and telling the truth for a very long time.

—Eileen Markey, The Bronx, July 2020

Index

WAYNE BARRETT (1945–2017) was a celebrated investigative journalist. He spent most of his 40-year reporting career at the *Village Voice*, where he became, in the words of the *Washington Post*, "dreaded if not loathed" by public officials for his relentless scrutiny of such major political figures as Ed Koch, Rudy Giuliani, and Donald Trump. After his departure from the *Village Voice*, he became a fellow at Type Media Center, then known as the Nation Institute. He is the author or coauthor of four books, including *Trump: The Greatest Show on Earth* (1992) and *Grand Illusion: The Untold Story of Rudy Giuliani and 9/11*, with Dan Collins (2006).

EILEEN MARKEY is an assistant professor of journalism and media studies at CUNY's Lehman College, and the author of *A Radical Faith: The Assassination of Sr. Maura*, also from Bold Type Books. Her work has appeared in the *New York Times*, the *Daily News*, the *Wall Street Journal*, *Daily Beast*, the *New Republic*, the *Voice*, and on WNYC: New York Public Radio, among others. She was a Barrett intern in the summer and fall of 1997.